Managing a Diverse
Work Force

Managing a Diverse Work Force

Regaining the Competitive Edge

John P. Fernandez

Lexington Books

D.C. Heath and Company · Lexington, Massachusetts · Toronto

Library of Congress Cataloging-in-Publication Data

Fernandez, John P., 1941–
Managing a diverse work force : regaining the competitive edge /
by John P. Fernandez.
p.   cm.
ISBN 0-669-26903-4
1. Manpower planning. 2. Minorities—Employment.   3. Women—
Employment.   4. Pluralism (Social sciences)   I. Title.
HF5549.5.M3F467   1991
658.3—dc20   90-23171

Published simultaneously in Canada
Printed in the United States of America
International Standard Book Number: 0-669-26903-4
Library of Congress Catalog Card Number: 90-23171

The paper used in this publication meets
the minimum requirements of American National Standard
for Information Sciences—Permanence of Paper
for Printed Library Materials, ANSI Z39.48-1984.

Year and number of this printing:

91 92 93 94   8 7 6 5 4 3 2 1

This book is dedicated to my wife, Maureen.
She is a wonderful human being who accepts,
appreciates, and respects the diversity in America.
With much love, John.

Contents

Preface

The main thesis of this book is that the key to the United States' successful competition in the new global marketplace will be the diversity of its people. Its long history of attempting, no matter how ineptly, to absorb and treat equitably people from many cultures and backgrounds gives the United States a significant advantage over Japan and the European Community.

Regardless of which competitive theory one proposes, the success of the theory depends on the people who must carry it out. If the same employees with the same mentalities are responsible for establishing the new structures, few differences will result in the effectiveness of the company.

People are the most important bottom-line cost for most corporations. To be competitive, companies must seriously concentrate, in both the short term and the long term, on developing value systems and human resource practices that take into account and respect diversity. In addition, they must develop a balance between individual and corporate needs.

Naisbitt and Aburdene sum up well the essential premise of this book:

> The corporation's competitive edge is people—an educated, skilled work force that is eager to develop its human potential while contributing to the organization's growth.[1]

We believe that the United States has the correct philosophy, the correct laws, and a valuable diversity in its population to gain the competitive edge over Japan and Europe in the 1990s and beyond if it will just take the final step of dealing fairly with, appreciating, and utilizing the talents of the many different people who make up the nation.

Acknowledgments

My deepest appreciation goes to my new wife, Maureen. Even though I worked four to five hours each day on our honeymoon, she was extremely patient and understanding. After the honeymoon, she not only attended school full-time but also spent numerous early mornings and late nights assisting me with the book. She is wonderful.

My good friend, John Salzer, took time from his busy schedule to write the appendix, which is about his experience with managing diversity. I thank him for his effort.

Kathy Pennisi has been very supportive in all phases of the book. Her three-year-old daughter Anna was also supportive in behaving so well at the office. I thank both of them.

My daughter, Eleni, my mother-in-law, Mary Heaney, my sister-in-law, Pat Phillips, and my close friend, Kelly Burke, all made significant contributions.

1

The U.S. Workplace

How It Looks Now and How It Will Change

In this book, we present data to illustrate the demographic trends that will greatly affect U.S. competitiveness in the global marketplace during the next decade. A great deal of the material we present focuses on data from major surveys that we conducted in 1971–72, 1976–78, 1986, and 1988–89. In total, over 50,000 lower-level, middle-level, and upper-level managers as well as occupational workers participated in these surveys. In all of them, participants were given the opportunity to provide written comments about a variety of issues, and their verbatim comments will add life and flavor to the data. The comments are selected to give a clear idea of the topic to which they pertain and to present representative views from respondents of both genders and various work levels and ethnic groups.[1]

Another important source of our information is seminars on diversity and managerial issues conducted by our company, ARMC (Advanced Research Management Consultants), from 1988 to 1990, in which more than 5,000 employees participated.

With these data we can describe the problems of managing a diverse work force that will arise in corporate America in the coming years and also propose solutions to these problems. The problems arising from diversity are caused not by the changing composition of the work force itself but by the inability of companies to integrate and utilize a truly heterogeneous work force at all levels. Companies that are willing to accommodate diversity will reap rewards in dollars-and-cents terms because they will fully utilize their most valuable resource: people. We predict that those companies that are unwilling to take into account their employees' differences will be unable to attract a sufficient number of workers to fill their needs, because workers will gravitate by preference to organizations where they are fully appreciated.

Demographic and Economic Changes in the United States

In this section, we present key demographic and economic facts about the United States.[2] We also briefly discuss their implications and potential impact on the U.S. workplace.

Facts: Job Growth and Education

In the next ten years, given moderate economic growth, there will be a total of 21 million new jobs in the United States, mostly in the service sector. More jobs will require problem-solving and communication skills in addition to basic skills, yet many labor force entrants will lack these skills. In the same period, there will be a "baby bust": about 25 percent fewer workers aged eighteen to twenty-four years will be available than during the "baby boom" years. A shortfall of 23 million qualified workers is expected in the 1990s.

Jobs requiring college degrees will increase from 22 percent to 30 percent by the year 2000. About half of U.S. workers have not attended college or lack the skills for jobs in the next century. Fewer than 60 percent of high school graduates aged twenty-one to twenty-five years, and only 80 percent of college graduates, read at an eleventh-grade level. If one defines literacy as the ability to write, think systematically and logically, and speak with clarity and precision, 30 percent of all U.S. adults are illiterate.

The National Science Foundation estimates that only 7 percent of high school seniors have the necessary background to major in engineering. A national survey of 8,200 high school students found that fewer than one-third understood that increasing investment was a way to stimulate economic growth, and two out of five understood the role of the market in our economy. U.S. students scored lowest on a geography test to locate sixteen spots in the world. The U.S. score was 6.9, compared with 8.2 for Mexican students and 11.9 for Swedish students.

Approximately 30 percent of minority workers are either unskilled or semiskilled. Hispanic Americans, the fastest-growing group of new entrants into the U.S. labor force, have a drop-out rate three times the national average.

In a study to determine how many foreign-born students with degrees in particular areas remain in the United States, 90 percent of undergraduate engineering majors in U.S. schools were found to be U.S. citizens, but 60 percent of engineering Ph.D. degrees went to foreign-born candidates. Of employed scientists and engineers in 1986, 23,600 were Native Americans, 93,400 were Hispanic Americans, 114,900 were African Americans, and 240,000 were Asian Americans.

Implications

With the anticipated labor shortage and the need for workers with better education and more complex skills, corporate America will find it increasingly difficult to attract enough qualified workers to fill jobs. This problem will be aggravated because the population will be made up increasingly of African and Hispanic Americans, whose education, in general, is not what it should be. Overall, children in the United States are not receiving a good education. U.S. companies will have to become more closely involved in the educational process from preschool through graduate school. In addition, they will have to develop new ways to train their workers to keep skills current.

Facts: Women and Family

All analyses show that 65 percent of the new jobs created during the 1990s will be filled by women. By the year 2000, nearly one-half of civilian workers will be women. In 1988, women held about 40 percent of office executive, administrative, and management jobs, nearly double the percentage in 1972. One-third of computer scientists are women, and more than one-half of officers, managers, and professionals in the fifty largest commercial banks are women. Fifty-two percent of college graduates are women. They are earning 13 percent of engineering degrees, 33 percent of medical degrees, 34 percent of business degrees, and 41 percent of law degrees.

By the year 2000, 62 percent of all women will work full-time, compared to 75 percent of all men. More than one-half of women with children under one year of age now work outside the home, compared to about one-quarter in 1970. In 1990, two-earner families composed as high as 90 percent of the working married population. The rise in dual-income families is one of the most important socioeconomic developments of the past two decades. At the same time, as people live longer, more middle-aged workers (the "sandwich generation") will have the double burden of child care and elder care.

Sixty percent of African American children, 29 percent of Hispanic American children, and 20 percent of white children live with a single parent.

The number of single-person households has increased from 7 million in 1960 to more than 21 million in 1986. The percentage of the adult population living alone is expected to double over the 1980 percentage by the year 2000.

Implications

Corporate America must recognize that women with many different family structures and family responsibilities will become an increasingly important part of the available labor pool and of the work force. Unless companies begin to seriously address the issues of family care and discrimination against women in the workplace, they will not be able to attract and retain these valuable workers. They will lose out to competitors who are more progressive and supportive of women workers.

Facts: Race, Ethnicity, and Immigration

The United States is ethnically a very diverse nation. The population includes 14 percent of Anglo-Saxon ancestry, 13 percent of Germanic ancestry, 12 percent of African ancestry, 10 percent of

Hispanic ancestry, and 2 percent of Asian ancestry. By the year 2050, one-half of the U.S. population will be African American, Hispanic American, Native American, and Asian American.

About 500,000 immigrants arrive in the United States legally every year, and about 1.5 million arrive illegally; the majority of legal and illegal immigrants in the past two decades were born in Third World countries. The United States, which has only 5 percent of the world's population, takes in almost 50 percent of the world's migrants (excluding refugees). One should keep in mind when reviewing statistics about immigrant and minority groups that many representatives of these groups are not counted, either because they cannot complete census forms or because they avoid officialdom, having entered the U.S. illegally. However, they are certainly part of the economy.

In 1990, minority workers accounted for more than 20 percent of New York City's resident labor force. More than one-third of African and Hispanic Americans are considered middle-class. About 30 percent of black Americans, 40 percent of Hispanic Americans, and 60 percent of white Americans have annual incomes of at least $25,000. But about one-third of minority people live in poverty.

Asians constitute 7 percent of the California population but nearly 30 percent of students at the University of California at Berkeley. In addition, one out of five students at Harvard, Stanford, Yale, M.I.T., and Brown, which are among the top U.S. colleges, is of Asian ancestry. In 1989, among students receiving Ph.D. degrees in the natural sciences and engineering were 37 Native Americans, 133 African Americans, 186 Hispanic Americans, and 427 Asian Americans.

By the year 2000, 40 percent of children under eighteen years of age will be of African, Hispanic, or Asian ancestry. Currently, at least one-half of public school children in the twenty-five largest metropolitan areas are people of color.

Implications

The work force and the markets will be increasingly made up of native-born people of color and immigrants who come from Third World countries. Their potential as workers and consumers must be fully utilized by companies to survive and prosper in the coming decades. Not only will ethnicity and gender issues continue to need resolution but also cultural and language issues will become increasingly complex. U.S. companies must appreciate and deal with a diverse work force. They must develop short-term and long-term plans to manage this new work force effectively; if not, they will lose out to competitors.

Finally, as U.S. companies enter the global marketplace, they will have to integrate foreign employees into their organizations, not only on foreign territory but also in the United States. This will add to the diversity of the work force.

Facts: Age

The median age of the U.S. population is projected to rise from the current 32 years to 36 years by the year 2000 and to 39 years by the year 2010.

The number of elderly people in the United States is increasing at a faster rate than at any other time in U.S. history. In 1987, "young old" groups—those aged 65–74 years and those aged 75–84 years—were eight and twelve times larger, respectively, than they had been in 1900. The "old old" group—those aged 85 years and older—was 23 times larger.

In 1900, only 4 percent of the U.S. population was 65 years or older; by the year 2000, 17 percent will be in this category. By the year 2030, one-third of the population will be 55 years or older, compared to one-fifth in this category now.

Between 1980 and 1990, the number of prime mid-management candidates increased by 10.4 million, but there were fewer than 2 million job openings in this category.

Implications

Corporate America must change its practice of forcing older, higher-paid workers out of their companies. As the "baby bust" and skills issues become more prominent, the skills and knowledge of the older workers assume increasing value. Companies will have to develop creative ways for these employees to stay in the work force longer, to offer part-time or flexible schedules, and to retrain them to upgrade their skills. In addition, companies will have to address more seriously the issue of elder care.

In sum, the forthcoming demographic and economic change could present either great opportunities or great problems. For example, if companies (and private donors and the government) started investing in education, we could have a literate country and a labor pool of qualified candidates. If we ignore the statistics about work force composition and education, we will have a severe shortage of qualified workers and a country with large pockets of disadvantaged people. The ultimate outcome of large pockets of disadvantaged populations will be significant, violent social unrest.

What Are the Issues?

In order to get a grasp of the multitudinous conflicts that exist in U.S. society and the U.S. workplace because of changing demographics, we will review some employees' comments from our studies and seminars about people who are different from themselves. In order to show the complexity of the issues, we present some comments from participants who have multiple prejudices.

I fear blacks. I think of women as mothers and home-bodies. I don't understand Asian culture. (White, middle-level, man)

I have a hard time listening to Asians with heavy accents. I distrust white males in groups. I am sometimes slow recognizing technical abilities in women. I feel Asians are not assertive enough. I do not like "Uncle Tom" minorities who say things like "there is no discrimination" or who try to neutralize the instructor to please the white men in power. (Hispanic, lower-level, woman)

I have a short temper when trying to understand persons who can't speak fluent English. I fear situations where I am in the minority. (White, lower-level, man)

Sometimes, I stereotype people, thinking that Orientals are smart, Southerners are slow, and so on. Often I feel that minority groups may have gotten help getting a job because of their race, not their abilities. . . . For instance, if one woman gets a job because of her sex, it makes the entire female work force less valid in my eyes. (White, lower-level, woman)

If there is a strong accent that inhibits understanding, I tend to avoid working with the person. I am trying to become more comfortable with women socially. (Hispanic, lower-level, man)

I have lower expectations for blacks in general. I have learned to compensate for this. I have been unable or unwilling to change. I know this is my biggest obstacle in dealing with blacks. I don't like to deal with women. I think they are unwilling to compromise. (White, lower-level, man)

I need to break some stereotypes . . . for instance, white men are good at presentation but poor at technical stuff. (Asian, lower-level, man)

I feel that many blacks have a chip on their shoulder that makes them too sensitive to comments and interactions with whites. It affects working relationships negatively and has the opposite effect of what affirmative action is trying to achieve. I have a need for women to prove their intelligence and common sense before I accept them. I have a sensitive nose, and I can't deal with people who smell bad. Many Asians smell bad, and I have to learn to deal with it. (White, upper-level, man)

I try to keep my personal opinions to myself. I despise group or female "cattiness." Personal opinions should be kept out of the boss's office. (White, lower-level, woman)

I'm very intolerant of the traditional Hispanic male attitude of superiority over women, the cultural ideas of a number of Middle Eastern societies, and loud and insensitive people. (Hispanic, occupational, woman)

I am concerned about the skill level of someone from a predominantly black American college, and I question women's technical skills. (Asian, middle-level, man)

I have lower tolerance to extremes in life-styles, dress, personal hygiene, and religion. (White, middle-level, man)

Problems: Having patience with people who use English as a second language. Dealing with someone who has a special diet at a luncheon or business trip. Some ethnic men exhibit sexist behavior. White men have it good in this company. Don't like it when women have organized "networks" instead of the informal fun that men have together. (White, occupational, woman)

I have problems dealing with peers who come from Asian countries and who speak with heavy accents. I tend to view such people as less competent if they have communication problems, and I tend to view women as less aggressive and, all other things being equal, as slightly less competent than a male counterpart. I tend to view blacks in the same way as women. (White, upper-level, man)

Those biases are so deep and hiding from myself that I am un-aware of them, yet they affect my behavior toward others white and Asian. (Black, middle-level, man)

I like having a wife at home, mother at home, and I see women in these roles. Brought up in the South, I must constantly battle stereotypes of blacks as lazy, inferior, and so on. Have difficulty accepting persons with strong accents or poor English as equals. (White, occupational, man)

I believe that a woman who wants to get married and have chil-dren should be at home and not providing a second income. Being raised a racist, I do have racist feelings, but I know this is wrong. I try to control them and not put them on my children. . . . Feelings are hard to control when I see blacks, not all blacks, blame their failures on racism when it is because they have not given it their best effort yet. (White, occupational, man)

I have prejudices against homosexuals. I cannot tolerate them. I have some prejudice against Jews. I think they are selfish and do not share. I believe they are a closed group, looking for power and controlling the world. (Hispanic, lower-level, man)

I stereotype people who do not catch on technically as fast as I think they should and have a problem with white women. (Black, middle-level, woman)

My preconceived classification of people? In general: Orientals are hard workers; blacks often have complexes and act accordingly; women are more emotional. (Asian, lower-level, man)

These comments demonstrate that no matter what a person's race, ethnicity, gender, or work level, most are not free from a variety of prejudices about groups other than their own. It seems clear that these potential conflicts in a diverse work force must be resolved, at least in the workplace, if U.S. companies want to be competitive.

Issues Other than Diversity

There are some value conflicts other than those discussed in the last section that also must be resolved by companies wanting to compete successfully. These value conflicts are based more on the givens of the human personality than on cultural background.

Few people in U.S. society have escaped the effects of the radical social changes of the past three decades. The new values have affected increasing numbers of employees' needs both inside and outside the workplace.

Many employees are no longer willing to subordinate their needs totally to corporate dictates. They say, "We appreciate the opportunity to work in this corporation, and we recognize and try to fulfill the corporation's needs and goals." However, they also say the following:

> While we recognize the corporation's needs and goals, the corporation must recognize our goals, needs, and contributions. We want interesting, challenging, fulfilling jobs that we control. We want to be treated fairly and equally. We want a say in the evaluation of our performance and potential. We want to play an active role in determining our career plans and our training and development needs. We want to be recognized for our individuality and uniqueness. We want to have both a work life and a personal life. Finally, our personal lives ... should be of no concern to the corporation unless they affect our job performance.[3]

In other words, the new breed of employees wants to be heard. They are no longer likely to accept corporate decisions, policies, and practices without questioning the whys, whens, and hows. They believe in individualism and oppose conformity. They do not believe in one right style of management; they believe in many different styles of management as long as that style is based on openness, honesty, respect and humaneness. They also expect their individual life-styles to be accepted as long as these do not interfere with actual job performance.

Not surprisingly, these new values have created increasing conflict, particularly in corporations that have been run like military organizations, in which orders were given and followed without question, where the organization came first and the individual was second (or last), and in which the tried and proven way of doing things was greatly favored over taking risks and moving in new directions. Lou O'Leary, former vice president of AT&T, writes,

> The pluralism of values is significant for us as managers. My management generation was more of a piece. Even where we had very obvious individual differences, there still was an agreed-upon model of values and beliefs, an ideal person—employee and manager—who exemplified them. Norman Rockwell could have painted such an ideal; in fact, he did—a number of times. Today, we are faced with burgeoning pluralism. Our people are coming from a lot of different places. We simply can't manage everyone the way we were managed, and expect it, and them, to work. Observers predict this will hold true well into the future. This, then, seems to us . . . to be our central problem. In a company metamorphosing in the '80s and '90s, many of us are managing people who grew up in the '60s and '70s, and we are managing them with the management style and techniques we learned in the '50s. To the extent that the style of those techniques is based on eternal verities of the human condition, fine. To the extent that they are based on values that have changed and are changing, we are in trouble.[4]

Thus far we have two major changes occurring in corporate America simultaneously: (1) the increasing diversity of the work force in terms of race, gender, ethnicity and so on and (2) the changing values of many employees as they relate to work and family. There are two other factors that will make the problems of dealing with a diverse work force more difficult than most managers recognize: the basic characteristics of bureaucracies, and the fact that we as human beings are basically to varying degrees neurotic.

The conflict between the needs and aspirations of individuals and the goals and requirements of organizations has always been present. In the past, the outcome was that the organization socialized the person into accepting its goals. This usually stifled creativity and suppressed individuality. Today, in large part, because of the increasing diversity of the work force, many employees are trying to make the organization more human. They are gaining an increased sense of identity and power that reduces the odds against them and against possible change. They are beginning to recognize that although bureaucracies have brought about some efficiency in the production of goods and services, they are insensitive structures. Bureaucracies employ people in the service of their own needs. They are inherently unfair. Despite their claim to equitably reward all those who are deserving, bureaucracies have too few advancement opportunities, limited resources, and out-of-date and inflexible reward systems to keep this promise to all employees. This problem of rewarding employees will increase greatly in the next two decades as millions of "baby boomers" compete for limited opportunities and the work force becomes increasingly diverse.

Despite the conviction that we are, on the whole, objective, rational, healthy people, we must acknowledge that human beings as a species are not objective, rational, or wholly healthy. On the contrary, the operative question is to which degree, as individuals and groups, we are unhealthy. People who recognize their neuroses and work on them are healthier than the majority who have never taken a hard look at themselves. People who recognize their neuroses and work on them are much more likely to operate effectively in a diverse work force than those who do not. In short, corporate America is in large part an inherently unfair organization made up of many unhealthy people.

Despite these facts, we teach our children that if they work hard, get an education, and don't rock the boat, the world will be their oyster. This is a myth that our so-called meritocracy feeds us. The reality is that even if bureaucracies were fair, and even if we were totally healthy, bureaucracies would still be inherently hierarchical. At each successive step up the corporate ladder, increasing numbers of people slip into "failure." Such failures are increasing, as we just noted, because growing numbers of educated "baby boomers" are competing for fewer managerial and professional jobs, especially at the middle and upper levels of management. Most of these employees, taught to believe that American society is a meritocracy, are shocked when their careers seem to end prematurely. And, in a diverse work environment, they begin to take out their frustrations and anger at the lack of opportunities on those people who are most obviously different from themselves.

The inherent nature of bureaucracies, together with the neurotic nature of human beings who have been brought up in a society professing but not having unlimited opportunities, has led to many of the conflicts detailed by employees in the surveys we have conducted in the past twenty years. These problems are compounded and exaggerated by the inability of companies to equitably employ an increasingly diverse work force. This inability will have a tremendously negative impact on the corporate bottom line.

In short, all these conflicts create a negative picture of corporate America for many of its employees. Overall, they believe it is unimaginative, authoritarian, has untrustworthy leadership, is a debilitating environment not conducive to risk taking, has a plethora of politicking, insufficient opportunities, lacks for proper recognition and rewards, and discriminates on the basis of race, gender, age, and so on. The biggest conundrum for corporate America is how to determine what is the real problem. Is it a people's prejudices? Is it their changed values? Is it the person(s) her/him self? Is it the nature of bureaucracies?

The following comments from employees expressing dissatisfaction with the workplace come from both genders and from all races and work levels. They were made in response to open-ended, neutral statements such as, "Please make any additional comments you wish to make about yourself and your career."

The following responses primarily concern corporate leadership.

I know that sales and customer service keep our company running, but there are sales tactics our business office uses to satisfy quotas that only cause resentment and distrust among our customers. Can we afford to jeopardize our company's reputation?
(White, occupational, woman)

It's pretty difficult when your middle-level supervisor lies to you and afterward admits that he lied in order to advance his own objectives. It would be a lot less aggravating if he were honest in his approach; after all, he is middle management and has the final word. Being pluralistic, I believe, is necessary in order to compete; however, being honest in one's approach is most important. (Hispanic, occupational, woman)

My second-level manager is not second-level material. He causes friction, mistrust, and cannot control his temper. He only listens when he wants to, and to what he wants to. My first- and third-level managers are very good. We need more of them. (Hispanic, occupational, woman)

I feel this is a good job and a good company to work for, but there seem to be a lot of things that could be done more efficiently. We seem very unorganized, and our policies and procedures are not very clear. (White, occupational, woman)

Getting access to information generated in other departments is a problem. I am constantly duplicating information that has been done by others because "proprietary" seems to mean department, not company. (Native American, lower-level, woman)

The company or management only wants to hear good things. Doesn't want to know of a problem. (Asian, occupational, woman)

Communications from the top down nonexistent. Responsibility to perform, but no authority to make decisions. (White, lower-level, woman)

My boss is too involved in my daily work—won't let me do my job. (Hispanic, middle-level, woman)

Some managers treat occupationals like children and draw a definite line between managers and occupationals. (Native American, occupational, woman)

There is very little feedback concerning what is considered when promoting, giving raises or bonuses. Our department head and his high-level staff do not fight for the staff, and the staff is aware of this. (Black, upper-level, man)

I really like the challenge of my job, but things would go much smoother if I had a middle-level manager who appreciated my knowledge and job expertise. Instead, decisions are always second-guessed because he manages by the "shut up and do it because I am the boss" style of management. (White, occupational, man)

As an employee with a college degree, I feel my contributions would be better recognized in another company where creativity, risk ambition, and marketing are recognized as key components for success. (Black, lower-level, woman)

I feel strained without support, goals, paths, or challenges. I feel underemployed as compared to my positions in the past. I want a chance to succeed but cannot find a way. I want to use the knowledge and skills I've obtained. (White, lower-level, woman)

A closed-minded, tunnel-vision attitude of accomplishing tasks, by our second-level managers. (Hispanic, occupational, man)

Jealousy and distrust of co-workers—their below-standard work is accepted by supervisors, and they are protected.
(White, lower-level, woman)

Everybody here works nine-to-ten-hour days and usually some part of the weekend, and still can't get caught up. People are beginning to dread coming to work. (White, lower-level, woman)

The next series of responses demonstrates the pervasiveness of politics, particularly with regard to promotions, as perceived by employees in the corporate bureaucracy.

Generally, I believe promotions are too often given to those who have "showcased" or otherwise exercised political means to get recognition. Often the results are not evaluated but the window dressing is rewarded. In our efforts to encourage a pluralistic mix, I hope we will not continue this propensity toward promoting the "flashers." Among all groups of employees there are those who deserve promotion and don't necessarily "grab the microphone" at every opportunity. (White, upper-level, woman)

I wish playing good-old-boy politics was not a prerequisite for any type of promotion. It makes me feel bad.
(Native American, occupational, woman)

I truly feel that most women who advanced got there for favors rendered or for knowing the right person. Management is a buddy system that promotes friends and partners. Rarely does someone who really deserves it get promoted to management. (Black, occupational, woman)

It is always back to the supervisors' pets who get upgrades or promotions. There are certain people who take tests and don't pass and still get upgrades. For instance, the test for a technical assistant is a joke. Whether you pass a test or not does not mean you can't do the work. If you have experience and knowledge, that's enough. (Black, occupational, woman)

Even the constant management changes in my area always have to "reinvent the wheel." Nepotism is too often the factor for who gets the attention. (White, occupational, man)

I have finally come to grips with what is possible in this company and what isn't—that is, unless you're willing to sell your soul and give up who you are, you won't advance. I now work for quality in my life and what I have control of and I have quit worrying about what I don't. (White, lower-level, woman)

Although there is much rhetoric about excellence, we seem to be managing the same old way. The company still seems to place more weight on political acceptability than on honest, dedicated performance. My last appraisal was based 100 percent on perceptions of personality, not on performance. (White, lower-level, man)

I know what I want for a career, but the company's way of determining qualifications is not fair. Just because a person has not performed a certain job for ten years does not mean he/she is no longer experienced; siblings, friends, and relatives should be judged by the same standards as all employees, including executive officers. (Black, occupational, man)

Too much jockeying for power and not enough communication and leadership in top management. (White, upper-level, man)

A tremendous problem in corporate America is the general denial of the importance of politics by the majority of leaders. In addition, many of those who complain about corporate politics play it but deny they do. Wherever there are people, there is influence, power, and competition. Add to these personality clashes, differing leadership and cultural styles, different races, genders, religions, and sexual preferences, conflicting goals, limited budgets, and rapid change, and you have corporate politics. In addition to criticizing their companies' leadership and the politicking necessary to achieve promotion, employees sometimes feel simply that they are not recognized for their contributions and good qualities, that they are not valued and rewarded.

I am a hard-working, conscientious, devoted employee. I should be treated as a valued employee who earns his money and then some—instead of the same or not as good as the flunky who doesn't earn his pay and gets promoted.
(Hispanic, occupational, man)

My experience has been that informal rewards are seldom received. "No news is good news" holds true here. You are told only about the mistakes, and no one says, "That was a good job." This is a shame because often a lack of informal rewards leads to frustration. (White, lower-level, woman)

I feel that many employees with talent and ability are routinely overlooked and unappreciated regardless or race, sex, or cultural background. The company does not discriminate against any particular group nearly as much as it discriminates against individuals who show signs of intelligent, independent thought.
(White, occupational, woman)

The company should also recognize employees who take the initiative to train and develop and reward them accordingly.
(Asian, occupational, woman)

I have extensive book production background which has qualified me for a special program. However, management has no apparent interest in utilizing me to my capacity: frustration has ensued.
(White, lower-level, woman)

My supervisor does not care about anyone but himself!!!
(Asian, occupational, man)

I believe it's mostly up to me. However, I think the company should communicate to the employees that the opportunity exists to move up and that the machinery is in place to do so. For certain elite persons, this is probably done. (Black, occupational, woman)

Don't receive credit or any recognition for work well done. Lazy people are praised for getting something finally done. (Asian, occupational, woman)

It is clear that the issues of diversity are complex and very strongly related to other corporate issues. One cannot be solved without solving the others. For example, rigid corporate structures that don't accept and respect divergent views about basic corporate operations will have a very difficult time accepting people of different races, genders, cultural backgrounds, and so on. Also, employees working for a company with poor, rigid, out-of-date employment practices and poor supervision qualities could have many employees believing that they are being treated unfairly because of personal characteristics when in reality most employees are treated that way because the corporate structure is poor.

Thus, corporate America is faced with a number of problems that must be resolved in order to manage the work force of the 1990s: bureaucratic structures, human neuroses, changing value systems with regard to work, and the myriad conflicts between different cultural groups. Companies can relieve some of the stress by implementing more objective, systematic employment practices in place of current policies that might be idiosyncratic, subjective, and nonsystematic, or developed for a mythical, rational, homogeneous meritocracy with unlimited opportunities and rewards. Current policies allow employees to blame work problems on others' discrimination rather than on their own shortcomings and economic and psychological realities.

If the conflicts discussed in this chapter are not dealt with honestly and effectively, the results will be decreased organizational effectiveness, absenteeism, high turnover, and decreased levels of productivity. Serious stress-related symptoms such as headaches, asthma, uncontrolled use of drugs, and depression stem from unresolved conflicts in the workplace. They all contribute to occupational burnout, corporate ineffectiveness, and increased health-care costs.[5]

Bureaucracies and Human Nature

As we have noted, in order to understand the problems of managing a diverse work force, it is necessary to understand the true character of bureaucracies and human nature. This is because many times people perceive a problem as arising out of racism, sexism, ageism or another form of a negative ism when in reality it is due to the nature of bureaucracies or to people's own neuroses. Despite the fact that we discuss these issues from an American perspective and the quoted comments are from employees in U.S. corporations, we believe the issues are the same for bureaucracies in Japan, Europe, and most other parts of the world. In addition, the views of the American employees are very similar to what we have heard from employees in various parts of the world who have participated in our seminars, in particular, China, India, Japan, and South Africa. Finally, many of the Asian employees and some Hispanic employees quoted from our studies are recent arrivals in the United States, mostly in the past ten years, and so could be expected to reflect the views of both their native and adopted societies.

The Ideal versus the Real Bureaucracy

Max Weber, one of the founders of sociology, believed that bureaucracies, primarily because of their technical efficiency, are indispensable in meeting the production needs of modern society. According to Weber, bureaucracies ideally are rationally organized structures bound by specific rules. They are characterized by a hierarchical division of labor among bureaucratic members, each with sufficient competence and authority to carry out designated tasks. The authority is inherent in the position and not in the person. Individual officials should be appointed on the basis of technical qualifications rather than chosen by an electorate, because only knowledge gives power and control. The bureaucratic structure as Weber envisioned it pays a fixed salary according to level or responsibilities. Promotions follow achievement or seniority, based on the superior's judgment, which is, of course, objective. In addition, Weber described bureaucracies as ensuring the right to employment security. Only under certain (fair) circumstances should employment be terminated. On a personal level, individuals are free to be and to act. On an organizational level, they are under the authority of the bureaucracy only with respect "to the impersonal official obligations." Despite the formal hierarchical nature of bureaucracies, Weber felt, employees should have the right to appeal decisions and enter grievances from lower to higher levels. In addition, relationships, according to Weber, are clearly defined and formal, based on social rituals reserved for various office levels.

Weber wrote that bureaucracies tend to develop a rational, unemotional set of interactions:

> The following are the principal more general social consequences of bureaucracies:
>
> 1. The tendency to "leveling" in the interest of the broadest possible basis of recruitment in terms of technical competence . . .
> 2. The dominance of a spirit of formalistic impersonality . . . without hatred or passion, and hence without affection or enthusiasm.
> 3. The dominant norms are concepts of straightforward duty without regard to personal considerations. Everyone is subject to formal equality of treatment. . . . This is the spirit in which the ideal official conducts his office.[1]

These views are still held on an intuitive or intellectual level by many corporate executives, professors, consultants, and parents, who maintain that the corporate world is basically an objective, rational, efficient, and fair meritocracy. Others, however, have disagreed, this includes many of the participants in our studies and seminars. It is clear from some of their comments that they do not perceive their companies as operating as efficiently, harmoniously, and fairly as Weber described.

Many employees express concern about the political, militaristic, intimidating, less-than-open atmosphere and unfair treatment in their companies. Most of these issues, except the last one, are not perceived very differently by different ethnic or gender groups, but they are by work level.

There is corporate direction from the top officers, but the implementation of this direction breaks down somewhere at the middle because of turf issues, basic philosophical differences among the entities, and sluggish acceptance of the benefits of pluralism. (Black, lower-level, man)

The amount of energy and time spent on politics and turf issues is ridiculous. If the same amount were spent on productive activities, the results would be staggering. (White, lower-level, woman)

There may be corporate direction, but it seems like each company is still doing their own pet projects. Then much money and time is spent selling the pet projects to different niches while someone else is simultaneously selling an opposing project to another niche. Who's controlling the organization? (White, middle-level, woman)

The company is very militarily regimented and politically oriented in its working system on most levels. Since this is the way it works, there's no sense in changing it on any level to be pluralistic, even if it does help the company function better.
(Black, occupational, man)

The company is a great group of people, but has spent years creating cliques and lots of in-fighting, has never really had to focus on competition. Doesn't have the team spirit yet.
(White, upper-level, man)

My managers are very political. They base all decisions on the political outcome instead of on what's good for our customers and company. (Black, lower-level, woman)

Too much throat-cutting and back-stabbing going on. This is suicidal competition within the company.
(Native American, occupational, man)

Some cannot be trusted because they're "brown-nosers" and the supervisor's buddies. (Asian, occupational, woman)

Things won't change until craft and management work together instead of old-thinking. (Hispanic, occupational, woman)

My goals and advancement are benefits for myself and whoever wants to use my knowledge, capabilities, and dedication. It is an "old boy" system, bend—no backbone to get what you want—the corporate game. I exhausted myself trying to impress people with my work at this company; I don't bend for no one.
(Hispanic, occupational, man)

These comments reflect some of the tension and problems that exist in the corporation. If Weber read or heard the comments of modern-day employees and saw the failure of many modern bureaucracies to be objective, rational, and efficient, would he question some of these theories?

The key to global competition is to try to reach the Weber ideal through the increasingly diverse work force. Let's look at some of Weber's major points and analyze them within the context of what really happens in bureaucracies rather than what should ideally happen.

The glaring flaw of Weber's theory and of executives who have internalized it is the omission of the human element. One cannot separate the human beings from the social process. Bureaucracies as perceived by the employees in our studies do *not* operate rationally, objectively, or efficiently.

We agree with Karl Mannheim and others who have recognized that bureaucracies are arenas in which individuals compete and struggle for limited commodities such as authority, power, status, money, promotion, and recognition. Mannheim also wrote that a fundamental characteristic of bureaucratic thought is that it treats problems as administrative rather than as political. He argued, however, that behind all the laws and rules of bureaucracies are "socially fashioned" interests of specific social groups. Order, therefore, is based not on reason but on socially conflicting, irrational forces that become reconciled in the "rational" order—in short, a very political process.[2]

Ferguson supports Mannheim's views of the true political nature of bureaucracies. She writes,

> A bureaucracy is not just a structure but also a *process* that orders human interactions. In order to remain viable, the bureaucracy searches for and suppresses opposition. Because it is both structure and process, a bureaucracy can be understood only in its social context . . . a context in which social relations between classes, races, and sexes are fundamentally unequal.[3]

As noted earlier, Weber believed that formal sets of rules help bureaucracies secure specific behaviors and eliminate friction, thus increasing efficiency. Notwithstanding the assumptions of Weber and the modern corporation that rules are necessary to ensure the predictable, rational, efficient functioning of bureaucracies, such rules, as Merton noted, do not always prevail. Rules and regulations can be transformed into absolutes and become ends in themselves. When this occurs, bureaucracies have great difficulty in adapting to special conditions and new situations not envisaged by the rule makers. (The changing demographics and the increasingly diverse work force are examples of this.) Merton concludes, "The very elements that are supposed to produce efficiency instead produce inefficiency in specific instances."[4]

In addition, rigid rules and regulations stifle creativity and innovation in most areas. To be effective in a rapidly changing environment, corporations need flexibility, not rigidity. There are not sufficient rules and regulations to cover all possible contingencies. This is especially true in industries where high levels of skill adaptability are necessary and technology is changing so rapidly that product life cycles are not five years but six months. One could also argue that as the work force becomes more diverse, new ways of thinking and accomplishing tasks will become common. If bureaucracies do not learn how to utilize these differences, their competitiveness will suffer greatly.

Another widely accepted Weberian notion, used as a double-edged sword in today's business world, is that of technical competence. No one can argue that technical skills aren't necessary.

However, as Merton warns, training that is too specific can bring about a failure to recognize new conditions that require new procedures and strategies. In other words, overtraining and experience in an area could become incapacitating.[5] Also, as we have mentioned, jobs are increasingly requiring people to think, to be analytical, and to be able to communicate well with people who come from many different cultures and value systems.

Additional problems are created in bureaucracies by their hierarchical nature, which dictates that few people reach the top while most believe that they should reach the top. This phenomenon, together with the fact that the higher one goes in the corporation, the more one is likely to be "elected" rather than "selected," creates a stressful, hostile, uncooperative, competitive environment. Furthermore, this hierarchical structure emphasizes special privileges for higher-level managers relative to lower-level managers and occupational workers. Such special privileges do not encourage cooperation, teamwork, and open communications; they foster divisiveness, selfishness, and poor communications.

The division of labor, which is supposed to enhance efficiency, also leads to inefficiency. The hierarchical nature of bureaucracies, coupled with individual competitiveness, creates divisiveness, and in some cases alienation, among people in various functions and departments as they compete for scarce resources.

A most perceptive statement about bureaucracies was made by Ferguson. She argues that the main purpose of the rules, regulations, and cultural values of bureaucracies is to eliminate uncertainty and to ensure control. She believes that political situations depersonalize social relationships, mystify communications, and disguise dominance, and that the claims of efficiency and effectiveness are secondary and frequently irrelevant. In her words, "They are justifications, rather than explanations, of bureaucracy." She believes that fragmented work, work isolation, strict adherence to rules and procedures, formal relationships, and the "illusion of upward mobility" that promises opportunities for the masses of employees are all strategies to control employees and make them dependent on the higher levels of management. All these factors create anger, frustration, and alienation, and cause physical and emotional problems, which ultimately result in lower productivity. These, in turn, affect the economic health of the corporation.[6]

Considering the nature of bureaucracies, it is not surprising that an unpublished survey (Fernandez) of over 10,000 employees in several high-tech firms found that only a small percentage of employees believed their company was not too bureaucratic. Many of the employees—especially managers (64 percent) and, to a lesser extent, craftspeople (47 percent)—rated their companies as poor or very poor on having successfully minimized bureaucratic characteristics. Less than 18 percent, regardless of occupational level, rated their organizations good or very good in this respect.

When employees in our 1988 survey were asked to respond to questions about their companies' effectiveness, 83 percent stated there were a lot of internal "turf" issues, 77 percent believed there was little understanding about the integration among various business activities, 68 percent did not believe there were timely communications among parts of the organization, 59 percent believed various parts of the organization worked at cross-purposes, 57 percent did not believe there was a great deal of trust among parts of the organization, and 57 percent believed there were a lot of conflicting value systems.

The top leadership in the companies did not get high marks in some crucial characteristics. The following percentages of employees described the leadership in the following terms: market-driven 64 percent, decisive 60 percent, team-focused 55 percent, creative 50 percent, long-term focused 49 percent, approachable 44 percent, risk takers 42 percent, flexible 39 percent, participative 38 percent, and proactive 28 percent. In the same survey, only 44 percent of the employees believed they were performing their jobs as effectively as they could.

One should not rush to assume that Weber's conceptualization of bureaucracies is totally invalid; it still holds in many cases. The problem is that Weber described an ideal bureaucracy; he failed to take into account the impact of human nature on bureaucracies. In addition, he did not imagine the effect of a heterogeneous work force on bureaucratic success. The vagaries of human psychology play a crucial role in determining the bureaucratic process, especially in diverse societies that have not learned to accept, appreciate, respect, and value differences.

Some Basic Concepts about Human Nature

Most corporate executives and consultants argue that a manager cannot be a psychologist. Nonetheless, to survive, a manager must understand some basic concepts about human nature and how people interact in bureaucratic social systems. As the work force becomes more diverse, understanding people will become more complex but more crucial. As many of the employees' comments suggest, management is greatly lacking in these skills. Levinson writes,

> Managers must know and understand . . . psychology [and] . . . motivation with the same degree of proficiency as . . . marketing, manufacturing, economics, sales, engineering, and so on. Not every manager must be a master of all these, but each must have a basic knowledge and understanding of people or he will be unable to meet the demands inside and outside of the organization that are inevitably to come.[7]

There will always be conflict between an organization's goals and employees' aspirations, needs, and desires. As more minorities, women, immigrants, disabled, and older people make up the corporate work force the aspirations, needs, and wants will vary greatly and will create additional conflicts. Selznick notes that although bureaucracies attempt to mobilize human and technical resources as means of producing goods or services,

> . . . the individuals within the system tend to resist being treated as means. They interact as wholes, bring to bear their own special problems and purposes; moreover, the organization is imbedded in an institutional matrix and is, therefore, subject to pressures upon it from its environment, to which some general adjustment must be made. As a result, the organization may be significantly viewed as an adaptive social structure, facing problems that arise simply because it exists.[8]

Levinson expands on this concept by stating that bureaucracies are social instruments that people use to meet their own basic needs. Since people influence bureaucracies, and vice versa, it is of crucial importance to understand both.[9]

The basic observations about people introduced here will be expanded and reiterated throughout this book. The concepts about individual subjectivity and neuroses may be unpopular; however, managing in the 1990s requires the understanding of and acknowledgment of these points. Many of the prejudices that people possess are based on their neuroses, and no program of managing diversity or differences can be successful if the program is not formulated with this factor in mind.

Several employees' comments from our studies reflect the introspection and honesty needed to improve the effective interaction of a work force.

I have doubts about my own desire/efforts to achieve "color blindness" (or gender blindness). I doubt that I am as aware of my prejudices as I would like to believe. (White, middle-level, man)

I believe I do not have shared experiences, interests, etc. with blacks, Asians, . . . My aggressive mannerisms versus some less aggressive Asian women's mannerisms . . . .
(White, occupational, man)

Inability to accept that I am not who I think I am or who I want myself to be with regard to other people. (Others do not always perceive me as I intend to be perceived. My behavior evidently does not always reflect my conscious intentions.) Criticism sometimes makes me defensive. I tend to be confrontational—raise uncomfortable issues—ask direct questions. May make others uncomfortable with this style. (White, lower-level, woman)

Admitting the fact that I am racist and sexist. It's easier to believe that each of us is perfect in our own minds. It's hard to see yourself as having this large imperfection. It comes out in my impatience in dealing with people, particularly if I feel superior due to education or experience. Also denying others the "better" opportunities for exposure to outside customers or internal upper management, believing I am more qualified.
(Black, middle-level, man)

In my dealings with others, I have noticed sexism, racism, and intolerance of foreign accents in my reactions. When I notice these reactions, I try to eliminate or overcome my own one-on-one. I tend to be opinionated and domineering. Therefore, I don't always give others the chance to express their opinions, or don't give their opinions the chance they deserve. (White, middle-level, man)

Prezzolini makes some astute observations about human nature:

People seldom believe what seems reasonable, nor do they always willingly accept what is expressed clearly, because logic and clarity have a weaker hold than imagination and mystery. Propositions that run counter to common morality do not create a desire for discussion or even contradiction but rather an urge to sidestep, ignore, or misinterpret. Life, which is full of such blindness to the most clearly expressed ideas, is ruled not by intellect but by desire and pride. People want to live, not to understand; and they want to live in their own way. If an idea seems to contradict what they want to believe, they refuse to accept it. If they understand it, they either suppress it or avert their gaze in order not to see it.[10]

In describing the value of psychoanalytic theory, White notes that "the constant play of impulse beneath and through the rational, conscious, goal-directed activities of everyday life" discussed by Freud shows that "beneath the surface of awareness lies a zone of teeming emotion, urge, fantasy, from which spring the effective driving forces as well as various disrupting agents in our behaviors."[11]

The employees in our studies describe personal interactions and people in some very unflattering ways. However, one must ask what part of these views is based on objective observations and what part on the individual's own neuroses. Is it a combination? Finally, one must ask to what extent the speakers behave in the same manner as those they are describing, and to what extent they recognize their own behavior for what it really is?

It seems to me that different ones are interested only in glorifying themselves, which invalidates the team concept.
(Black, occupational, woman)

There is always one in the group who is a backstabber, who always talks behind your back and not to your face.
(Black, occupational, man)

The people of color are placed in a group, and if you are respondent to white ideas, actions, or roles, you are in for a short while, until you disagree with them. (Hispanic, occupational, man)

All of the clerks are so distrusting, because the company has the "I don't care" attitude. (White, occupational, woman)

It's dog eat dog. People look out for themselves. I don't know whether that's good or bad. It's just a matter of opinion. (White, occupational, man)

Trust is difficult. Generally, at work, don't say anything you don't want repeated. (White, lower-level, man)

Good ol' boys' club is strong and well in our district. (White, middle-level, woman)

I dislike those who are nonaggressive. I set high standards for myself and at times expect others to measure up to them. The people I have the most problem with are those who are given advantages which I did not have and then fail due to not putting in enough work. I can accept others for what they are, but once I see them as failures I rarely give them a second chance. (White, middle-level, man)

I hate abusive people. There are a couple in our group that are always offensive when they talk to you. They are minorities and make me feel like I have done something to piss them off. (White, lower-level, man)

We have too many old-age thinkers/traditionalists at the top that are too concerned about their own empire and turf. I would like to contribute more. (Hispanic, lower-level, man)

The company wants paper pushers and smiling people who always agree with their bosses and who can stab their co-workers in the back without blinking an eye. (Hispanic, lower-level, man)

As we noted earlier, the question is not whether we are mentally healthy but the extent to which we are unhealthy. Levinson, who has written numerous books on managerial psychology, would agree, but his definition of mental illness allows for ups and downs in human nature. All of us have days when we are on an even keel and other days when we are not. When we are in emotional distress, we can be considered to be temporarily mentally ill. Given the inherent inequality, stress, conflicts, and contradictions of bureaucracies, it is clear that some employees in corporations are in a constant state of stress and are therefore mentally ill.

The degree of mental illness or mental health we possess has a great deal to do with our natural temperament. One can look at children at birth and recognize that some are quiet and some are not, that some are easy-going and others are not. Levinson notes, "Each person from birth differs both in his particular combination of natural endowments and in the degree to which these permit him to contend with various aspects of life."[12] These tendencies are either encouraged or discouraged by cultural conditioning, by parents, teachers, and other agents of socialization.

Keniston notes that as adults we lose touch with our spontaneity; growing up means leaving "a world of directness, immediacy, diversity, wholeness, integral fantasy," in favor of "abstractions, distance, specialization, dissociated fantasy, and conformity."[13]

White maintains that studies of culture and psychoanalysis have a great deal in common; namely, the belief that personality is more than the sum total of conscious, rational self-direction and also includes irrational urges, anxieties, and overworked protective devices. Similarly, our customs, beliefs, and cultures exercise a tyranny of unconsciousness through socialization.[14]

We contend that our psychological problems are compounded because these socialization processes do not always send either clear or objectively healthy signals about our worth, who we are, and what we are. Many of us have not taken the time to understand ourselves, and so have no real understanding of our own neuroses.

We use such coping strategies as sublimation, repression, rationalization, projection, displacement, substitution, and denial. Levinson delineates four basic ways that people cope: (1) channeling their energies into problem-solving or environment-mastering activities; (2) displacing energies onto substitute targets; (3) containing or holding onto energies by repression; and (4) turning energies against themselves, which leads to self-defeating behavior and accidents. Most of us use all of these modes to varying degrees at various times.[15] The employees' comments throughout this book show that all of these coping mechanisms are used.

Probably the most serious conflict in corporations occurs over the lack of sufficient resources to fulfill the pledge that people will be rewarded on the basis of their skills and ability. This conflict is inherent in hierarchical bureaucracy because of the limited opportunities and resources in a society that tells everyone they need only to work hard, keep their noses clean, and the world is theirs—a society that prides itself on being a meritocracy but is a far cry from it.

As Levinson writes, while much is said about organizations as instruments for individual achievement, and about motivational practices as being rewarding rather than punishing, the fact is that bureaucratic organizations are essentially geared for defeat. For every person who is promoted, a vast number are left behind.

The above fact, tied in with some factors about socialization and human nature concisely stated by Machiavelli, leads to tremendous conflicts. Machiavelli said,

> "For it may be said of men in general that they are ungrateful, voluble, dissembling, anxious to avoid danger, and covetous of gain. As long as you benefit them, they are entirely yours; they offer you their blood, their goods, their life, and their children, as I have said before, when the necessity is remote; but when it approaches, they revolt. In prosperity men are insolent, and in adversity abject and humble. How blind men are to things in which they sin, and what sharp persecutors they are of the vices they do not have."[16]

Machiavelli made other comments about the human inability to be satisfied:

> Nature has made men able to crave everything but unable to attain everything.[17]

> Men are never contented but, having got one thing, they are not satisfied with it and want a second.[18]

Men [are] wont to get annoyed with adversity and fed up with prosperity.[19]

At an early age, we learn that the United States is the land of opportunity and that success will be ours if we really want it, if we work hard, and if we stay out of trouble. In fact, opportunities in corporate America are severely limited and shrinking. The factors that determine success are far more complex and subjective than sheer determination and hard work. But because, as Machiavelli tells us, human beings always want more than we can get, and think we deserve it, we are lured by the myth of infinite opportunity, much as gamblers are lured by the jackpot or the million-dollar sweepstakes. We ignore the odds, pin our hopes on winning, and walk away in anger and resentment when we lose. Machiavelli put it this way:

> Certainly anybody wise enough to understand the times and the types of affairs and adapt himself to them would always have good fortune, or he would protect himself always from bad, and it would come to be true that the wise man would rule the stars and the Fates. But because there never are such wise men, since men in the first place are short-sighted, and in the second cannot command their natures, it follows that Fortune varies and commands men, and holds them under her yoke.[20]

The bureaucratic structure not only condemns practically everyone to achieve less than they wanted; it also does something to those who succeed. Merton accurately cites the constant pressure on corporate managers to be "methodical, prudent, disciplined" as a means of ensuring that they will be predictable and conforming.[21] Employees who want to be promoted will behave as the corporations want them to. These arms of the corporate leviathan reach out to control the lives, actions, and thoughts of employees who are upward-oriented, influencing them in direct proportion to the extent of their ambitions.

Conclusions

Weber defined the ideal bureaucracy as a hierarchical structure with a rational division of labor or activities, all governed or ruled by a set of general policies and procedures, administered by objectively evaluated, recruited, and promoted people who are loyal to the organization and who have a clear understanding of their limited and specific role, its values, and its culture. He believed that bureaucratic authority resides in the office, not the person, and that a strict separation should exist between professional and personal life. This supposedly leads to the smooth functioning of the organization.

This chapter presented data that contradict many aspects of Weber's theory. Weber's equation did not include a most important element, human beings. He also developed his theory for bureaucracies whose work forces were basically homogeneous rather than for modern-day bureaucracies, which have diverse work forces.

What we have in corporate America is a structure that pits people against one another competitively and eventually condemns all but a few to achieve less than they had wanted to. This structure discourages cooperation and risk taking and nurtures empire building, self-centeredness, inertia, conformity, and employer control. It breeds fear, distrust, dishonesty, and intolerance of diversity. It allows people to point fingers at others for problems they in reality create, and it does not create an atmosphere where real problems are dealt with effectively.

We propose that the popular misconceptions of the true nature of bureaucracies and of human nature, along with prejudices of all kinds, create the conflicts to which corporate employees have alluded. The denial of these problems creates an atmosphere that has led to the inefficient utilization of large numbers of employees, especially those who are different in terms of race, gender, age, religion, and life-style, and therefore to the inefficient functioning of the corporation, with a resulting negative impact on the corporate bottom line.

In the next chapter, we explore how neurotic human beings, which we all are to some extent, develop racist, sexist, and ethnocentric attitudes and behaviors. These mental illnesses are a main impediment to any society that wants to be competitive in the new global village.

3

Racism, Sexism, and Ethnocentrism

Before we examine in detail the problems confronting minorities and women in the workplace, it is important to understand what we mean by racism, sexism, and ethnocentrism, three of the most powerful forces affecting the ability of societies to have efficient, competitive economies.

Most people are socialized by the societies in which they grow up to have some degree of discomfort with people who are different than they are. Such feelings touch all facets of people's lives and cause presumably rational, objective people to harbor a large supply of stereotypes about people who are different. Women and minority workers have a particularly difficult time in trying to become full and equal members of business organizations no matter where they are located. White men, for instance, suffer discrimination in Japanese companies, and non-Europeans in European companies.

The negative effects of such exclusion are evident throughout the ensuing chapters, which discuss discrimination in Japan, Europe, and the United States. The most prominent cultural difference distinguishing ethnic groups is language. It has created tremendous conflicts in Western and Eastern Europe, the United States, Canada, and other countries. In U.S. companies where large numbers of employees speak English as a second language, language conflicts take their place right next to racial and gender conflicts.

Definitions of Racism, Sexism, and Ethnocentrism

We define racism, sexism, and extreme ethnocentrism as cultural ideologies that characterize the dominant race (for instance, white people), men, and specific ethnic groups as being inherently superior to minority races, women, and other ethnic groups solely because of their race or skin color, gender, or ethnic origins. People of the majority groups, through societal institutions, develop, nurture, spread, impose, and enforce the myths and stereotypes that are basic foundations of these views in the minds not only of the oppressors but also of the oppressed. These myths and stereotypes are used to maintain and justify the oppressors' dominant social, economic, and political position.

These isms are rooted deeply in the structure and fabric of societies. They are not solely a matter of personal attitudes and beliefs. Indeed, it can be argued that these negative isms are accessory expressions of institutionalized patterns of the majority's power and social control.

Underlying these isms are power struggles between the dominant groups, who seek to maintain their privileged positions in society, and the out-of-power groups, who are determined to change the status quo. Even while they control society's major institutions, the oppressors have great fear of losing their hegemony. This drives them, consciously or unconsciously, to nurture myths and stereotypes about the oppressed in order to preserve the status quo.

We suggest that racism, sexism, and extreme ethnocentrism are defensive adjustment mechanisms used by the dominant groups to deal with psychological insecurities and anxieties. While we have argued that all human beings are mentally unhealthy in varying degrees, we believe that racism, sexism, and extreme ethnocentrism reveal severe mental disorders that more often afflict those with the most interest in preserving the system than those interested in tearing it down.

A *Time* article entitled "An Outbreak of Bigotry" noted that there is an epidemic of ethnic hatred sweeping the world: "These violent acts are dismaying and perplexing fair-minded people who are at a loss to explain it." The article uses the word *bigotry* "to describe the whole sickening phenomenon" of hatred and violence among racial, religious, and ethnic groups.[1] Official, legally sanctioned discrimination is minimal in the United States (that is its strength) though not in the institutions of many other countries. But covert discrimination exists all over the world. It is this covert form of prejudice that is wreaking havoc in U.S. corporations.

As discriminatory treatment of minorities and women has been outlawed in the United States and some other parts of the world, many people have not come to terms with their prejudices but just modified their external image and actions to be more palatable to others and, to some extent, to themselves. The covert forms of discrimination are just as harmful as the overt forms.

An example of covert racism and sexism is the lack of mobility beyond middle levels of management of more than a few minority and female managers in U.S. companies. We believe racism and sexism are the key factors in this lack of mobility, despite the contention of the white male–dominated bureaucracy that the causes are lack of experience, bad timing, poor image, or lack of political skills. Also, confident and ambitious minority people and women are seen as being too confident, too ambitious, and aggressive, while white men exhibiting the same characteristics are viewed favorably. Identical behavior is often construed differently, depending on who is doing the behaving.

An example of ethnocentrism in Japanese-owned companies is the exclusion of non-Japanese managers from "inner circle" meetings of top management.

Institutional Racism, Sexism, and Ethnocentrism

As we have noted, resistance to change tends to characterize bureaucracies. The rate of change of bureaucracies is naturally slower than those of the individuals who compose the organizations. Bureaucracies tend to capture these groups and use them in a way that defies individual influence, that is, the bureaucracies become systems or entities separate from the people whom they employ. Institutional racism, sexism, and ethnocentrism are based on these systems.

Institutional isms are bureaucratic rules, regulations, policies, and practices that in and of themselves exclude people who are different. They were established in times past, when discrimination was more acceptable. Even though they were not established to discriminate, they do in fact do so. A good example of institutional racism and sexism is seen in the "old-boy" network, an informal system that, among other things, helps its members to find higher-level jobs in public and private institutions. In the United States, the network is composed of white men; therefore, if the network serves as the primary recommendation agent, the candidates selected for these jobs will be white men.

Women's moving into nontraditional jobs is still another example highlighting institutional sexism. The system had promulgated the belief that some jobs could not be done by women, that some of the equipment and tools used in "men's work" could not be handled by women because of their weaker physique. However, most equipment and tools could be modified, if necessary, for use by women. Determined women have demonstrated that if selected, and if not prevented by their work groups, they can perform these jobs as well as men (or better).

A final example of institutional ethnocentrism is the controversial issue of whether U.S. schools should teach non-English-speaking immigrant children only in English or in bilingual programs. In the past, the U.S. educational system, without apologies, expected immigrant children to learn and study in the dominant language of their adopted country. But the current preference for taking account of diversity suggests to many people that this policy leaves many children behind their peers in learning and should be changed.

Development of Racist, Sexist, and Ethnocentric Attitudes and Behavior

A discussion of how people develop racist and sexist attitudes can be instructive with regard to how these issues should be resolved. Racism, sexism, and ethnocentrism are nurtured by all the societal institutions controlled by the dominant group. Babies begin their lives with a sense of kinship to all human beings regardless of skin color or other physical features. Most infants and very young children are open, loving, and comfortable with people who show them love, attention, and caring. However, children learn racist, sexist, and ethnocentric attitudes and behaviors at an early age. Families, schools, churches, government, the media, and other institutions socialize them by communicating what is "good" behavior and what is bad. They teach children what to expect of themselves, their friends, their families, and "outsiders." As a result of their socialization, children learn how to be bona fide members of their groups and how to get along with—or hate—other groups.

Many studies over the past fifty years have explored the development of racist attitudes in white children at very early ages. One study of children in the United States done in the 1950s and repeated in the 1980s found that very young American children preferred the color white over black and that their lack of preference for black was transferred to their perception of black people.[2] This finding applied to both black and white children who lived in the United States.

Thus, despite the messages "Black Is Beautiful," "Brown Is Beautiful," or "Red, Green, or Purple Are Beautiful," few of the society's members will believe them unless most of the society's institutions support these propositions.

That there is self-dislike among many minorities can be demonstrated by the fact that an increasing number of black Americans are having plastic surgery to make their features more like "white" people's. Patti LaBelle and Michael Jackson are among famous African Americans who have had such surgery.[3] In addition, there are many in the Hispanic community who classify themselves as "white" even if they are very dark in skin color.

With regard to gender socialization, boys become aware of gender roles as early as age two, according to Lewis. She observes that they seem compelled to show that they are different from their mothers and to renounce all characteristics that may be considered unmanly. She wrote, "No wonder they have more trouble with the gender identity than little girls. And no wonder men are more prone than women to obsessional neurosis and schizophrenia."[4]

Experimenting with the roles of the opposite gender is much more acceptable for girls than for boys. Girls learn early that male roles are to be envied and imitated. They are free to dress in boy's clothes, but the reverse is certainly not the case. Parents who are amused to see their daughter become a "tomboy" are distressed if their son becomes a "sissy."[5]

In our 1986 study, we asked the following two questions about employees' children: How frequently do you encourage girls to do activities other than those which have been considered to be only for girls? and How frequently do you encourage boys to do activities other than those which have been considered to be only for boys? We found that 35 percent of African American men, 39 percent of white men, and 50 percent of other minority men never or infrequently encouraged girls to do activities not normally for girls. Between 24 percent and 29 percent of the female employees never or infrequently encouraged girls to do activities normally for boys. Between 58 percent and 64 percent of the male employees never or very infrequently encouraged boys to do activities not normally considered masculine. The women's responses ranged from 32 percent to 36 percent.

These findings indicate that we as a society still interpret male and female roles fairly rigidly and restrictively. In addition, the data show that it is more acceptable, especially to men, to encourage girls to do boys' things than vice versa. Certainly, the attitudes of the Japanese and Europeans would be at least similar.

Through role models, women's need to achieve is sublimated into a need to nurture and serve: "She is discouraged and protected from taking risks by her parents. At the same time she is subjected to peer pressure to fit the mold. 'If you take chemistry, you won't have time to date'; 'If you really swim, your hair will look a fright and your muscles will bulge'; 'If you get good grades, you're a drag'; 'If you always win at tennis, no one will want to play with you.' "[6] The result of all of this is that a girl follows tradition: "She doesn't plan for the long range and doesn't recognize choice points but begins to back into or avoid decision making. She becomes more dependent on others because it is easy and comfortable. She ceases her formal education, takes a job, finds a man, and becomes the role model."[7]

It is not surprising that when women enter the corporate world, where men are the role models for success, they begin to adopt male styles of management, dress, behavior, and language.

While many people acknowledge these socialization patterns

on an intellectual level, many also believe that somehow they have escaped or dealt with their racism, sexism, and extreme ethnocentrism. It is always "the other person" who is racist, sexist, or ethnocentric.

Pettigrew, a psychologist specializing in racial prejudices, makes some relevant comments: "The emotions of racism are formed in childhood, while the beliefs that are used to justify them come later. Later in life, you may want to change . . . but it is far easier to change your intellectual beliefs than your deep feelings." An example of what Pettigrew is saying is that many white people can change their intellectual beliefs that African Americans are not inferior to white people, and they perceive them as equals; however, they would react between violently to slightly uncomfortable if their child were to marry an African American person.

An example related to sexism is when men say they believe women should be treated fairly in their companies, but they have strong to mildly negative reactions when they have a woman boss.

An example of ethnocentrism is when Japanese companies open a factory in the U.S. with sufficient knowledge that the Japanese style of management will not work well, over the long term, with U.S. workers. When the workers begin to rebel, some Japanese become slightly irritated and others begin to feel angry that these Americans are not behaving well.

Finally, we would like to point out what our research over the years has shown. While there is less racism, sexism, and ethnocentrism among younger educated people there is still a great deal. In fact, there has been a dramatic increase in racist, sexist, homophobic, and antisemitic behavior on college campuses. Gibbs writes that compromises are faced with hateful behaviors, which sometimes border on the barbarous. She cites the example in Mississippi where white fraternity members wrote "KKK" and "WE HATE NIGGERS" on the bodies of two white pledges.[8]

The main point one should draw from this example is that to manage differences effectively we must teach our children to tolerate, respect, appreciate, and value differences at a very early age. We must make certain that our societal institutions also send the correct message. Corporate competitiveness will not be significantly enhanced if new recruits are full of hate toward people who are different than they are. Changing attitudes at such a late date is considerably more difficult than earlier in life.

Language and Language Conflicts

A great deal of ethnocentrism is centered around language. Language issues are becoming a considerable source of conflict and inefficiency in the increasingly diverse work force throughout the world. According to H. Ferguson, language makes culture possible. Language lies at the very heart of culture. It makes possible the abstractions that govern people's behavior and their beliefs, values, and attitudes, ". . . and this makes business possible within culture. To go global means to be able to find common understanding of what those abstractions mean in other languages and other cultures."

Continuing, he writes,

> The way executives use language acts as either the grease that slides this adaptation into place or the grit that keeps it from fitting. The global executive is, if anything at all, a global communicator, using spoken language, written language, and nonverbal communications to the advantage of his or her business.[9]

As corporate America becomes part of a global network, and as our work force is composed of more people who use English as a second language, the issue of accepting and understanding languages other than English becomes critical to corporate success. Despite this fact, one of the most striking examples of antipluralistic thinking is the strong movement toward declaring English the official language of the United States. Between 1985 and 1990, eighteen states, including Florida, Arizona, and Colorado, passed resolutions making English their official language. Some twenty other states are considering similar measures to limit public discourse to English. Recently, Senators Richard Shelby and Howell Heflin from Alabama introduced a bill to make English the official language. Some have labeled this type of law government-sponsored racism.

Specifically, from our research, Figure 3–1 shows that only 33 percent of the employees surveyed in 1988 are not at all both-

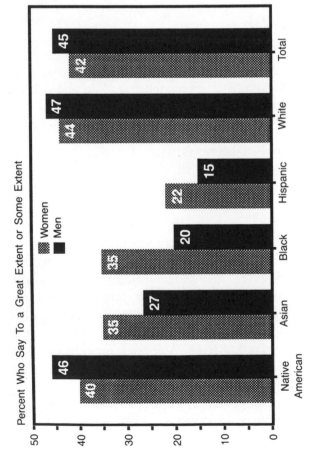

To what extent does it bother you to hear employees at your company speak a language you do not understand?

To a great extent	19%
To some extent	24%
A little	24%
Not at all	33%

Percent Who Say To a Great Extent or Some Extent

Women
Men

	Native American	Asian	Black	Hispanic	White	Total
Women	40	35	35	22	44	42
Men	46	27	20	15	47	45

FIGURE 3–1

Who Is Bothered by Hearing Different Languages?

*Total number of respondents for all figures are between 25,000 and 26,000.

ered when they hear other employees speak in a language they do not understand. In particular, white men (47 percent) and Native American men (46 percent) are most likely to be bothered to a great extent or to some extent, and Hispanic men (15 percent) are bothered the least.

In our seminars with over 5,000 employees in the past three years, the most frequent problem indicated was with language and cultural areas. The following comments reflect a range of reactions, from hostility toward people who speak foreign languages to legitimate concerns about how to work effectively with people who speak English as a second language. We should note that 70 percent of the employees in our studies who speak English as a second language are from Asian countries. We believe this fact leads to the significant negative reactions from non-Asian Americans. We have noticed that many Americans like a French accent; they think it is beautiful. They like an English accent; they think it is aristocratic. They like a German accent; they think it is elegant. However, many of these same people complain that Spanish accents do not have nice tones and Asian accents are too complex, harsh, and hard to understand. As a white female lower-level manager said, "I have problems tolerating foreign accents or even foreign-language-speaking persons. I tend to enjoy an English accent but dislike Spanish (Hispanics') accents." Some other comments follow.

> I don't feel that I should have to deal with accents that are so bad that certain people have to talk in their native tongue to be understood. An accent is okay if it is just an accent and not a few jumbled words. (White, middle-level, man)

> The language barrier is a major problem for me. In my job, I represent a service where a variety of people interface with me to get speaker support material. A growing number have English as a second language and speak in extreme accents. Coupled with the fact that each person is bringing their own technical jargon to the discussion, the meeting can often become strained for both sides. (Black, lower-level, woman)

> I have a low tolerance to deep foreign accents or the inability to speak English at all. It makes my job harder and sometimes impossible. (White, occupational, woman)

People with foreign accents can be very hard to deal with. Because of this, I avoid having to deal with them. (White, lower-level, man)

I have problems with the language barriers. Try to learn the main language of the country you have chosen to live in.
(White, occupational, woman)

I am tolerant of foreign accents, but I am not tolerant of people speaking foreign languages in this country. If you're here, speak English, except for tourists. (White, occupational, man)

It's not tolerance of foreign accents, it's being able to understand what they're saying. I get upset when I can't understand what they're talking about. And I wish they would speak more clearly so I and others can understand them. (White, occupational, man)

I have a difficult time dealing with people who cannot speak the English language; I cannot understand them. If they live in this country, [they should] try to speak the language. . . . I have enough trouble with English (my only language) so that I have problems with others whose understanding and speaking skills are weak. (Black, middle-level, man)

I need to have patience with more foreign-speaking people. They are not easy to deal with on the phone and hard to understand, which makes communication difficult . . . .
(Hispanic, lower-level, woman)

I feel awkward to have someone who has trouble with English constantly repeat themselves because I don't understand.
(Black, occupational, man)

This is an English-speaking country. If a person wants to advance in an English-speaking country, he should learn the language and learn it well. (White, lower-level, man)

Conversational fluency and clear enunciation should be the reasonable expectation of all employees in customer contact or supervisory roles. An accent is okay, but you've got to be able to speak "mainstream" adequately, no excuses. (Asian, middle-level, man)

People of color with foreign accents are often treated as less intelligent. It takes too long a time to prove yourself (as compared to others) among peers. (Asian, middle-level, man)

Since we live in America, I believe all employees should speak English and speak it well, if they want a job. Customers do not like to deal with those they cannot understand.
(White, middle-level, man)

No corporation can be competitive if co-workers avoid, don't listen to, perceive as incompetent, or are intolerant of employees who have problems with the language. In addition, these attitudes could be carried over into their interactions with customers who speak English as a second language, resulting in disastrous effects on customer relations and, thus, the corporate bottom line.

Language is an important form of communication and source of unity. Therefore, when in a common situation, it is important for two persons to be able to converse. In the United States, the vast majority of the population speaks English fluently or at least has some working knowledge of the language. In the interest of basic practicality, immigrants and other residents use English when imparting most public information. However, there are large segments of some states, and especially some cities, in which using a foreign language is the normal way to conduct business and personal affairs. No one would argue that we should use language other than English as the primary mode of communication in the United States. We would argue, however, that important signs should be printed in several languages to make their messages clear to everyone. Also, private discussions (even if they take place in public) should not be subject to legislation. We believe that, in certain situations and communities, speaking in a foreign language is more productive for business purposes than speaking in English. For example, many Hispanics who are new arrivals would respond better if advertisements and salespeople used Spanish. Similarly, business between prospective Japanese clients and U.S. business leaders might be much more productive if discussed in Japanese.

H. Ferguson recognizes how one could make a blunder even when speaking to someone who speaks the "same" language:

Even English-speaking countries don't speak American. One American banker was asked to be after-dinner speaker in Australia. He blundered in his first sentence, when he said he was "full." When he heard the nervous laughter, he changed that to say he was "stuffed." In Australia, *full* means "drunk" and *stuffed* means being on the receiving end, so to speak, of sexual intercourse.[10]

The new statutes seeking to limit all public discourse to English have nothing to do with the mere practicality of English use; they have more to do with U.S. fear of "foreigners" taking over the country. Many forget that it was not long ago that their ancestors arrived speaking their native tongues. Visitors to the United States are expected to enter the country equipped with a full knowledge of English. Interestingly, many Americans expect to visit other countries and hear and speak nothing but English. Most don't bother learning how to speak Spanish when they visit Mexico, for example. This extreme ethnocentrism is dangerous, given the emerging global marketplace. With rapid modes of transportation and business deals to be cut, Americans will increasingly find themselves in other countries and will find foreigners in their country. They must not only get used to hearing languages other than English but must actually learn them in order to maintain a competitive edge.

Many U.S. students cannot speak, read, or write any language correctly. This deficiency is deplorable, as is the mind-set that assumes competence in one language to be incompatible with the command of another. On the contrary, a student fluent in Spanish can more easily acquire good English than a student who is incompetent in either tongue.

In short, to be successful in the global village, one should adopt this dictum: "The language of business is your customer's language, whatever it is."[11] Several employees in our studies support the previous statement, but they are a small minority.

Of the three major economic forces that will be competing in the 1990s, the United States, Japan, and Europe, the last two have a great language advantage over the United States because most school-age children study English and other languages early in their school years. They also study languages for more than just one or two years. What can balance these differences and make the playing field more level is that the United States has by far the largest number of first- and second-generation immigrants fluent in both their native tongues and in English. The problem we must overcome is corporate America's not fully accepting and utilizing these foreign-language speakers, primarily those from Third World countries. Even with this large immigrant population, to be competitive, business, government, and educational institutions must begin to require all schoolchildren to become fluent in a foreign language. For those already in U.S. companies, programs must be developed to teach a second language to key personnel. In addition, companies must begin to institute accent reduction and accent listening courses. It is not just a matter of English speakers developing better listening skills but also those with accents striving to minimize their accents.

Different Cultures

As we have noted, language is the basis of culture; thus when one discusses a truly diverse work force, there are numerous cultural issues that must be raised. Accepting diversity means much more than being able to look at another employee whose skin is a different color and feeling comfortable with that employee. It can mean accepting speech in a different or accented language; it can also mean accepting people who dress differently and eat differently.

Perhaps more difficult ways to accept diversity include learning about, accepting, respecting, and valuing different values, morals, and styles. For example, we must become astute students of body language. What signals are we getting when someone from a different culture moves their arms, hands, or head? What are the acceptable spatial distances in each culture? What does it mean if someone stands too close to you? What is meant by the tone of the voice?[12] In short, we must be able to understand and appreciate different cultures and recognize competence in new packages. We must recognize that a culture may have a more laid-back style, but that doesn't necessarily mean that members of that culture are lazy. Their approach may be even more appropriate than ours in a crisis.

As we have noted, immigration made up 28 percent of U.S. population growth during the 1980–85 period, representing an almost 50 percent increase from 1975 to 1979. Most demographers project that the immigration percentage of U.S. population growth will increase to 35 percent through the 1990s. The recent immigration law that President Bush signed could increase this estimate by 5 to 10 percent. Considering these facts in light of the globalization of U.S. business, the inevitable increase in foreign nationals, and their becoming an integral part of day-to-day U.S. business, it is clear that unless the diverse work force is managed properly, the different cultures will clash and U.S. corporate competitiveness will suffer.

Although employees in our studies were never asked specifically about foreign cultures, their responses paint a picture of conflict and intolerance in such areas as hygiene, dress, food, religious holidays, praise, eye contact, modesty, and aggressiveness.

> I think [pluralism workshops] should be mandatory, but you have people who are angered by this because they feel they have been violated. Why can't they understand that violating others' rights hurts also. It's okay because we are a different color.
> (Hispanic, occupational, man)

> My biggest issue is dealing with people from other countries and cultures where communication (spoken language, writing skills, and the way in which a person thinks) is difficult.
> (White, middle-level, man)

> Lack of understanding and involvement in other cultures is a problem. I need to participate in activities that will help me to understand other cultures. (Black, occupational, woman)

> We tend to see our own faults in others, but overlook them in ourselves. (White, middle-level, man)

> Work standards are different for ethnic minorities. No one acknowledges my presence when I walk into someone's office and they are in a conversation. Key word is "acknowledge."
> (Asian, occupational, man)

> Have been brought up in a macho environment. Hence, tend to relate to the more aggressive males in a group, sometimes ignore the more timid people. (Hispanic, occupational, man)

I tend to presume how someone of a particular background will react to me before allowing them to react on their own. (White, middle-level, woman)

I don't like to be around anyone with personal hygiene problems. Unfortunately, this seems to apply to Orientals, Asians (although not all). And of course, if this was a white with the same problem, I wouldn't like it either. (White, lower-level, woman)

I don't seem to have problems working with "Americans" of any race or creed. I do have trouble working with people from other countries [non-English-speaking countries]. (White, occupational, woman)

Fear of groups of minorities—feeling intimidated when surrounded by nonwhite people. (White, lower-level, man)

I have an inherent bias to prefer someone who looks and acts like me, without consciously relating it. (White, upper-level, man)

Asians are usually quiet in the meetings. I did not speak enough in the meeting, and other people think I am stupid and cannot participate. (Asian, middle-level, man)

Not only do Americans have problems dealing with other cultures but also the cultures of immigrants and foreigners who come to the United States to work and live clash with Americans' culture. When they come to the United States, their socialization creates problems. For instance, many U.S. colleges and universities are experiencing difficulties with the treatment received by women and minorities by foreign faculty members. "Anecdotal evidence suggests that women and minority students may suffer more discrimination and harassment from foreign-born faculty than from American faculty,"[13] explains Elinor G. Barber, assistant provost of Columbia University.

Conclusion

In this chapter, we defined racism, sexism, and ethnocentrism. The fact that everyone in all societies is socialized from birth into holding certain prejudices becomes evident from our definition. The extent to which adults remain racist, sexist, and ethnocentric depends on their sense of person, that is, to what extent they have dealt with their own personal neuroses and sorted through who they are and how secure they are. Those who have gone through this process and feel secure about themselves, and like themselves, are least likely to be racist, sexist, or extremely ethnocentric.

This chapter also discusses the fact that an important basis of ethnocentrism is language. It is the basis of culture and how people define themselves. Many Americans are bothered by people who speak with foreign accents, and this creates problems in the workplace.

Americans must become more tolerant and better listeners. Those who speak English as a second language must work to reduce their accents. They must also work on their cultural backgrounds if these are racist, sexist and ethnocentric. They must recognize that behavior toward outsiders that may be acceptable in their country is not acceptable in the United States.

In the global village, people must become multilingual and learn to respect, appreciate, and understand different races, ethnic groups, genders, cultures, and languages. In concluding, it is important to remember that while there are many cultural differences among us, we also have cultural similarities: we are all part of the human race.

4

Japan

In our opinion, during the next decade, Japan will not be as economically competitive in the global marketplace as will the United States, not because of factors like technology and finance, but because of Japan's inability to change rapidly its racist, sexist, ethnocentric, and xenophobic culture. Japan's isolationist history and limited exposure to different cultures until the late nineteenth century allowed the Japanese to develop a sense of superiority that still encourages negative feelings toward foreigners.

In the first part of the twentieth century, the Japanese had more frequent contact with the outside world, but only through imperialistic wars. As a result of its defeat in World War II, Japan had a large number of foreigners living in the country as occupation forces. Yet most Japanese remained isolated from the outside world and outside influences. Ordinary Japanese citizens were not exposed to any significant outside influences until modern technology like satellite networks penetrated their island fortress. In addition, the tremendous wealth of the Japanese in the 1980s has for the first time allowed large numbers of Japanese to travel abroad and see how other cultures live.

Despite these increasing outside influences, however, internal information sources like the news media and educational institutions try to maintain the ancient Japanese culture, traditions, and images of superiority. The messages that Japanese citizens receive from these institutions are controlled by government and big business. This alliance allows certain superficial, but no substantive, changes to occur in Japanese culture. The changes that must occur in Japan's social and cultural structures to allow it to remain competitive in the global marketplace go beyond the love of the Japanese people for American fast food, American baseball, American music, and American clothes. Some of the changes that must occur are to allow women to be equal to men at work and at home; to allow more foreign people to live and work in Japan and to be treated more equitably; and to allow foreign employees to become full and equal members at all levels of Japanese-owned companies located throughout the world.

There are some indications that the Japanese élite is losing control of the Japanese people. That Japan's successes have created wealth for some in Japan and not for the majority of the population has caused resentment among some Japanese toward other Japanese. There is also some evidence that Japanese are beginning to question whether the communal "one for all, all for one" mentality really exists. Women in Japan are becoming more vocal in demanding equality; so are the more than 2 million Japanese who are considered to be of the outcast class and the 600,000 Koreans who live in Japan.

Not only is Japan faced with rising discontent at home, but many people from other nations are increasingly expressing anti-Japanese sentiments. One reason for this hostility toward Japan is Japan's economic success and another is Japan's racist, sexist, and ethnocentric attitudes.

Although Japan's homogeneity may have served it well in the past, there is evidence that it may now pose one of its most severe problems. In their book *The Third Century*, Kotkin and Kishimoto note,

> As racism has colored European responses to Japan, the extreme ethnocentrism of the Japanese has prevented them from developing political, cultural, and social skills appropriate to their great economic power. Even with its global financial and industrial reach, Japan today remains . . . a "nation village," a country that functions with the strong but narrow kinship loyalties characteristic of a small hamlet.[1]

Japanese Culture

Japan has been praised for its communal orientation, which is based on living patterns of Japanese over the centuries. Early in its history, Japan had minimal contact with its Asian neighbors but on occasion would borrow from their cultures. The ethos of Japan has been built around its sense of racial superiority and uniqueness. In the early nineteenth century, in order to keep out Western influences, which they believed had made the Chinese Empire a semicolonized possession of Europe, the Japanese Meiji dynasty and its successors reinforced at every occasion the feeling among Japanese that they were superior to others. In the early twentieth century, Japan's successes in Asia reinforced the Japanese feeling of superiority. Japan's superiority complex is still alive and well, but it will be the major obstacle to the success of Japan in the coming decades.

There is a general misconception about Japanese culture that says it is "one for all, all for one," in contrast to the United States culture, based primarily on individualism. Despite Japanese scholars writing that Japan is not a class-conscious society, in reality it is. These scholars argue that Japan is not horizontally stratified by class or caste, but it is vertically stratified by institution or groups of institutions. Nakane wrote,

> Even if social classes like those in Europe can be detected in Japan, and even if something vaguely resembling those classes that are illustrated in the textbooks of Western sociology can also be found in Japan, the point is that in actual society this stratification is unlikely to function and that it does not really reflect Japan's social structure. In Japanese society it is really not a matter of workers struggling against capitalists or managers but of company A ranked against company B.[2]

Sugimoto and Moyer take strong issue with this argument, and so do we. They note that the vertical relationships within groups of institutions are maintained by the power of the ruling class: "Nakane ignores the power of big business and others who have enough concentrated power to control or to co-opt other members in society. . . . Power is more centralized in Japan than in other industrial countries, and Japanese managers seem to enjoy more rights vis-à-vis the worker than do managers in other countries." [3]

That Sugimoto and Moyer are correct in their analysis is demonstrated by the fact that the economic miracle in Japan has not benefited a considerable segment of Japanese society. The Japanese élite convinced ordinary Japanese citizens to sacrifice for the nation, work hard, and help Japan be successful. As a result, more and more Japanese who are left out are questioning the common tenet of Japanese culture that the individual should sacrifice for the group. They are asking, "Why sacrifice for the group when only the élite are benefiting from Japan's dominant economic power?"

The extreme stratification of Japanese society and the questioning of the communal concept can also be attributed in part to the fact that 10 million Japanese traveled abroad in 1989. They have seen that in some ways in the "degenerate" societies of the West, many more people benefit more equitably from the economy than do Japanese in Japan. They are beginning to understand that they are paying prohibitively high prices for goods because of extremely restrictive trade tariffs, because of a distribution system that is archaic, and because of price rigging that adds tremendous cost to goods. For example, a Japanese camera selling in New York City for about $380 would cost $550 in Japan. Japanese beer costs more than 40 percent more in Japan than in the United States. The Japanese must pay five times higher prices for the basic staple in their diet, rice, than they would have to pay if Japan would allow the importation of rice. Poor policies are also responsible for the land shortage, which along with the rapid increase in home prices has left many "have-nots" unable to buy homes. In Tokyo, a square inch of land costs $160; 88 square inches of land cost $14,080.

Even for Japanese who own homes, there are serious problems. Silva and Jögren observe that because of Japan's emphasis on producing goods for the outside world and its mission to buy into other nations' economies, many internal Japanese infrastructure needs are going unmet. They note that more than half of Japanese households remain unconnected to a municipal sewage system. In addition, Japan has the lowest percentage of paved roads of any industrialized nation.[4]

In short, the Japanese "have-not" class has become increasingly aware of the class structure and that 90 percent of them are not middle-class, as the Japanese press likes to claim. They recognize that only a small minority has really prospered because of the Japanese economic miracle and that the welfare of the common folks has been sacrificed in order to support business and the élite of Japanese society.

A *Business Week* article that surveyed 10,000 Japanese found the following percentages of respondents agreeing:[5]

- Japan should review its economic structure (47 percent).
- Japan should open up its markets (47 percent).
- Changes in these two areas would improve their quality of life (57 percent).
- Japan should open its doors to foreign rice (60 percent).

As more Japanese travel and work abroad, they will become more conscious of the disparities in their society and no doubt fuel a consumer revolt.

Japanese Workers Are Changing

Japan is not a classless society in the Japanese workplace, either. The workers of Japan have for years been praised for their hard work, dedication, and loyalty. Employers have been praised for offering lifetime employment, good benefits, and a family-type work environment. Akio Morita, chairman of SONY Corporation, put forth the general philosophy that Japanese managers are supposed to follow.

There is no secret ingredient or hidden formula responsible for the success of the best Japanese companies. No theory or plan or government policy will make a business a success; that can only be done by people. The most important mission for a Japanese manager is to develop a healthy relationship with his employees, to create a family-like feeling within the corporation, a feeling that employees and managers share the same fate. . . . The emphasis on people must be genuine and sometimes very bold and daring, and it can even be quite risky. But in the long run—and I emphasize this—no matter how good or successful you are or how clever or crafty, your business and its future are in the hands of the people you hire.[6]

Books like Ezra Vogel's *Japan as Number One* and Bill Ouchi's *Theory Z* have also suggested that for U.S. companies to survive they must adopt the Japanese management style, which in theory takes a holistic approach and makes working in a large organization enjoyable.

The comments from these writers apply more to the top-tier companies like SONY and Toyota than to second-tier companies. In addition, there are signs that, according to Japanese workers, things are not as rosy in corporate Japan as Japan would like us to believe. M. Cetron and co-authors write,

> Remember, Japan has a two-tier business hierarchy, and there's a world of difference between the first and second layers. In any first-tier firm—SONY, Toyota, etc.—the pay and benefits are top-notch, working conditions good, lifetime employment the rule, and pension programs certainly adequate. However, in the bottom-tier companies, where 76 percent of the Japanese work, most likely out of necessity rather than choice, wages and benefits are one-third to one-half of top-tier minimums, working conditions can be unbelievably miserable, job security is nonexistent, and retirement programs are inadequate and uncertain.[7]

Seven years ago, the *Japan Economic Journal* warned its readers that increasing numbers of blue-collar workers were losing the group orientation, flexibility, and diligence that brought about Japan's economic miracle. These workers are finding more reasons for being outside of work, the *Journal* said. They are not hesitant in expressing their individuality. The *Journal* urged Japanese corporations to begin to recognize and develop systems to bring the blue-collar workers back into the fold.

A more recent example of how the myth of the loyal, hardworking, "company is first" Japanese worker is falling apart was cited in a 1990 survey of Japanese workers. The survey noted that in top-tier companies, two out of three new male recruits thought they would be with the company until they retired;

however, after two months, almost one-third were contemplating quitting because things were not what they had expected. In addition, two out of three men and three out of five women said they would not work overtime if they had a date.[8] Joe Coates, a futurist, noted that, in a recent survey, only 38 percent of Japanese workers aged 20–39 gave priority to work over family. In addition, 86 percent would switch jobs if they could.[9]

One must point out, however, that some Japanese workers, especially older ones, do have a strong work ethic and loyalty to their companies. In fact, a recent report suggested that some Japanese died from working too hard. As a result, the Japanese Health and Welfare Ministry put out a book, *A Study on How to Take Proper Rest and Recuperation*, which encourages Japanese workers to take vacations and enjoy them.

Kotkin and Kishimoto believe that the real life of the Japanese manager is "anything but enjoyable." They cite extreme fear of failure, institutional rigidity, murderous competition, lack of opportunities, extremely long hours, little rest and recreation, and a truncated family life as some of the factors that lead to Japanese employees' dissatisfaction with their work.[10] Many of these problems are typical problems found in bureaucracies, regardless of the country in which they are located. In 1988, we conducted a seminar for top executives from China on human resource issues and problems in the United States as compared to China. It was evident at the end of the seminar that despite the different cultures, languages, and so on, the problems the Chinese saw in their firms were similar to the ones occurring in U.S. companies. Thus, it is not surprising, when one looks at how Japanese employees really feel versus how they are supposed to feel, that there are problems to be dealt with. Two recent books, *Working for the Japanese: Inside Mazda's American Auto Plant* by Fucini and Fucini and *Jump Start: Japan Comes to the Heartland* by D. Gelsanliter, point out the difficulties Japanese companies are having in trying to impose a company-first work ethic on U.S. workers. In the Mazda plant, dissatisfied employees were producing cars one-third of which had quality problems. A recent *New York Times* article discussed the rapid rise in lawsuits against Japanese companies in the United States. Some lawyers believe that many suits result from clashes between the Japanese and American cultures.

Japanese Racism and Ethnocentrism

Not only does Japan have a class-oriented society, both socially and economically, but it also is a caste society on the Asian Indian model. In India, there are "untouchables," and numerous castes; in Japan, there are the *burakamin*. They were originally assigned an outcast status very similar to African American slaves in the 19th century. They were forced to live in ghettos, they had to wear distinct clothes, and they were not allowed to marry outside their caste. They killed and butchered animals, tanned hides, and made leather products. They also performed tasks which were regarded as "filthy and despicable under the tenets of Buddhism."[11] Discrimination against the *burakamin* was legally ended in 1871; however, even today they face discrimination in all aspects of their lives. The Japanese maintain elaborate records on ancestral origin.

Besides discriminating on the basis of class and caste, the Japanese discriminate on the basis of race and national origin. In addition to the 600,000 Koreans who live in Japan as permanent residents, Japan has a small but increasing number of Indians and Pakistanis who work as skilled or semiskilled laborers. In the city of Kawguchi, which depends on foreign labor to run its small factories, the local police put out a report that suggested these subcontinental Asians were dirty, smelly, diseased, fast-tempered, and deceitful. The same city barred a Pakistani from teaching because "there are a lot of communicable diseases and crime among Pakistanis."[12] Japanese perceptions of African Americans are no better. Japanese frequently refer to African Americans as *songoku*, "monkey."

Former prime minister Yasuhiro Nakasone in 1986 said that the United States overall has lower intelligence than Japan because of the large numbers of African Americans and Hispanic Americans in its population. In September 1990 the minister of justice, Seiroku Kajiyama, compared prostitutes in Japan to black Americans. He said that when Japanese prostitutes move into the neighborhood, it is like black Americans—they force white residents out because they ruin the atmosphere. A *Newsweek*/Harris poll noted that Nakasone and Kajiyama were not alone in their beliefs. It found that 31 percent of Japanese said that too many racial minorities and ethnic groups are a serious problem for the United States.[13] A toy company, Sanrio, after considerable external pressure, had to withdraw one of its leading new items, "Little Black Sambo." Considering these views about black Americans, it is not surprising that Japan has filled the trading gap with South Africa after other countries had withdrawn trade because of the imposition of U.N. sanctions.

In addition to Japan's racism toward different people of color, there has been, in recent years, an increase in anti-Semitic books there that suggest Jews are behind world problems. These books accuse Jews of anti-Japanese sentiment. One writer, Masami Uno, stated that Jews were "in control" of such U.S. companies as General Motors, IBM, and Exxon. A leading figure at the Ministry of Trade and Industry (MITI) was quoted as saying, "Japanese are geniuses in the factory and morons outside."[14]

The Japanese are bringing their racist practices to the United States in Japanese-owned companies. Employees of Recruit Co., a job placement firm, revealed that a secret code was being used by them to recruit for Japanese firms. The purpose of the code was to discriminate against applicants on the basis of race and gender, especially screening out African and Hispanic Americans and women.

Several Japanese companies, including Honda and Toyota, have been found guilty of discrimination and have paid millions of dollars to those who were discriminated against. Equal Employment Opportunity Commission officials have received numerous complaints about Japanese companies failing to promote minorities, women, and older people. Thus, it should not be a surprise that Japanese companies who locate plants in the United States avoid areas where there are large black American populations. In addition, Japanese auto and auto supply plants do not hire African Americans in proportion to how they are represented in the surrounding communities. For example, blacks represent 10.5 percent of the population around Honda's plant in Marysville, Ohio, but they comprise only 2.8 percent of that plant's work force.

There's also increasing evidence that the Japanese discriminate against white men in favor of Japanese employees. For example, NGK Spark Plug has been charged with having a two-tier reward system, a higher one for Japanese and a lower one for Americans. Two senior American executives filed suit against NEC Electronics Inc. for "anti-American bias" and for retaliating against them because they expressed concerns about Japanese employment practices that they perceived violated U.S. law.

A number of writers have noted that it is almost impossible for Americans, regardless of ethnic background or gender, to penetrate the upper levels of Japanese management. For example, Mitsubishi since the early 1970s has promised to open up their top levels to Americans; however, by 1988, only two of the forty-one division heads were Americans. Also, 31 percent of middle and above managers in Japanese companies in the U.S. are Americans. In Japan over 80 percent of the managers in foreign companies are Japanese.

The problem of racism in Japan will grow as immigration increases. The number of illegal foreign immigrants in Japan is officially stated to be 100,000, but, as is the case with the United States, some experts believe the accurate figure is three or four times that. Only about 100,000 legal immigrants are given permission to work in Japan, and most of these must leave Japan within three years.

The Japanese population is aging more rapidly than that of any other major industrial power. Japan has a shortage of workers, and future demographics indicate an even greater shortage, because of a low birth rate. And most Japanese executives believe that the shortage of labor and the aging of the labor force will be the most important factor holding back Japan's economic growth in the 1990s. Despite these facts, the Japanese are unwilling to let foreign workers come into their country to fill the shortage of workers. In the first half of 1990, fifty-one Japanese companies had to fold because they could not find workers, double the number for the same period from last year. In addition, 268 firms told the Ministry of Labor that they could not recruit all the workers they needed. The Japanese response to their demographic problems has been to tighten their immigration laws. They now limit immigration only to those with certain professional, entertainment, or sport skills. The law also holds businesses liable if they hire illegal immigrants. Finally, the Japanese will only issue two-week visas to foreign visitors and refuses to renew them when they expire.

Japan had and still has problems with an arrogant view of its Asian neighbors. In contrast to Germany, which has apologized and agonized over its aggression in World War II, the Japanese have not officially apologized. They prefer to sweep the entire matter under the rug.

The *Wall Street Journal* stated that Japan has been working on short- and long-term plans to economically transform the Asian-Pacific region into a prosperous economic power, as the Japanese perceive it. They intend to do this by providing technical and financial assistance to targeted countries in order to build the infrastructures needed to produce and deliver goods. They also will provide funding for those industries they have determined to be the most appropriate for the country, but more important, for Japan and its business strategies. Japan has determined that Indonesia will focus on textiles, forest products, and plastics, Thailand will concentrate on furniture, toys, and die-cast molds, while Malaysia will make sneakers, copiers, and television picture tubes. Probably the key to this strategy is that Japan will open its doors to those products from those countries.[15]

One must wonder to what extent Japanese decisions are based on racist attitudes. Kotkin and Kishimoto noted that a Japanese theorist, Ishiwora Karfi, in the 1930s saw four races in Asia and a clear division of labor in the new Japanese Empire that would emerge after Japan won World War II. Japan would be on top, followed by China, Korea, and Manchuria. The Japanese would be the political and industrial leaders, the Chinese would be the laborers and the small entrepreneurs, the Koreans would produce food, especially rice, and the Manchurians would raise the animals necessary for the empire.[16]

While many of these countries welcome Japanese assistance, many people have grave concerns. They remember that resource-poor Japan has coveted its neighbors' vast material resources for many years. During World War II, Japan killed thousands of Asians through war, forced-labor camps, and outright murder to achieve its Empire.

The superior attitude of the Japanese and their distrust of foreigners have prevented longtime non-Japanese employees from learning and understanding the businesses they work in. For example, S. Duthie, a Malaysian who worked for a cable plant for seventeen years, was barred from entering one of its plants in Japan because he was a foreigner. He said, "The plant was working on optic fibers. And I was told that it was top secret, even for someone like me, who had been with the company for so many years!"[17]

Kotkin and Kishimoto sum up how the Japanese operate in host countries. They noted that Japanese companies and business people behave in an extremely offensive manner. They set up their own schools and even golf clubs. They—like the "ugly Americans" of the previous generation—have tended to remain separate from the world around them. A former Japanese diplomat was cited as saying "the Japanese tend to treat Asians with a superiority complex."[18]

Looking more closely at the Japanese relationship with Koreans during the twentieth century will help readers better understand the depth of racism in Japan. Between 1910 and 1945, Japan forcefully removed Koreans to work in labor camps in Japan and other countries dominated by Japan; expropriated Korean property without due process of law; and tried to destroy the Korean culture by forcing Koreans to speak Japanese and to adopt Japanese names.[19] After World War II, the Japanese did not modify their attitudes toward Koreans, especially toward the 600,000 Koreans living in Japan, many for several generations. It was not until 1965 that these "visitors" received special permanent residence status and not until the 1980s before Koreans were granted full social welfare benefits.

Finally, for the brutality Japanese visited upon Koreans during the occupation, Japan apologized 45 years later, on the Koreans' insistence. Koreans living in Japan are still faced with discrimination in jobs, housing, and marriage, and they have only in recent years felt fairly comfortable using their Korean names. The Japanese still require Koreans to carry an identification card, and many still are denied citizenship despite generations of residence in Japan.

Sexist Attitudes in Japan

While Japan wrote in its post-World War II constitution that it would treat women and minority people equitably, women in Japan have not had the opportunities the constitution promised. Japanese society as a whole still believes that a woman's rightful place is in the home, raising children and waiting on her husband. They are considered second-class citizens.

Girls and boys are socialized into strict female and male roles at the earliest ages. The Japanese have institutionalized gender differentiation in schools. The higher women go in the educational sphere, the clearer it is that women are not valued as much as men. Thirty-eight percent of the men go on to higher education after high school. Ninety-five percent of them go to four-year universities, and only 5 percent to vocational schools. After graduating from high school, about 33 percent of women go on to higher education; 25 percent to universities. Women make up 90 percent of students in junior colleges. In addition, women are led into traditionally female majors such as home economics, art, and literature, while men are led into studying engineering and other sciences.

Even after obtaining their degrees, Japanese women generally hold low-level clerical jobs. Their pay is intentionally pegged at lower levels than men's. Sugimoto and Mouer write that women are not counted in unemployment statistics and many are not eligible for retirement benefits. There is even a curfew that prevents women from working overtime. Many women are expected to join the labor force instead of going to high school and then to leave the factory by age 24 to raise a family. Despite the fact that the Japanese work force is made up of 40 percent women, very few are in management positions.[20] Brinton notes that although Japanese women and men enter large firms at equivalent rates upon leaving school, 71 percent of men who start out in large firms are in career-track positions, compared to only 23 percent of their women peers.[21] Also, most positions in Japanese companies are reserved for women or men. One study found that about four to six hundred thousand jobs go unfilled in top-tier companies because they are reserved for men. No matter how high up a woman is in the company, she must serve tea if she is in the same meeting with men.

In addition, Japanese female employees are faced with numerous forms of sexual harassment, from having to put up with nude pictures of women on men's desks to actually being sexually assaulted. Sexual harassment in most Japanese minds, especially men's, is normal and appropriate. All these forms of discrimination persist despite the enactment of an equal employment law in 1985, which prohibits gender discrimination in all phases of recruitment, employment, and retirement. The catch in the law is that there are no penalties for employers who violate it. The blatant violation of the law is demonstrated by the fact that some Japanese companies still run employment ads in newspapers specifying the gender and age of candidates, and many positions in corporations are closed to women.

No wonder this is the case. Finance Minister Royutaro Hashimoto said in 1990 that Japan's declining birth rate could be attributed to the government's encouraging women to obtain higher education. He suggested that the government should discourage women from pursuing higher education so they could stay home and have more babies. The head of the Japanese Socialist Party, a woman, Takako Doi, was slandered during the Spring 1990 campaign by a leader of the Liberal Democratic Party. He claimed that the populace should be suspicious of her because she is unmarried and has no children. In the home, the situation of Japanese women is no better. Even if the wife is working (most women who are married do not), she is solely responsible for caring for the children and the house; for managing the finances; and for looking after the general welfare of the family.

When Japanese companies establish branches in the United States, they bring these sexist attitudes with them. Japanese companies are increasingly facing lawsuits from women. For example, the Sumitomo Corporation of America fought a twelve-year battle to not comply with U.S. civil rights laws. However, the U.S. Supreme Court ruled that our civil rights laws apply to U.S. subsidiaries of foreign companies. Sumitomo was found guilty of favoring Japanese and American men over women. The company agreed to pay $2.6 million in back pay and to develop and implement new employment policies.

An Equal Employment Opportunity Commission official told us that American firms have almost twenty times more women in management than Japanese companies located in the United States. The Japanese attitudes toward women can only increase conflict in their homeland and in countries like the United States that place a high value on the equality of women.

Japanese Views about Americans

The previous sections have discussed the nature of Japanese attitudes and practices regarding employees, foreigners, ethnic background, and gender. The Japanese attitude of superiority is applied toward Americans and Europeans as well. In this section, we focus on Japanese attitudes toward Americans.

Throughout the years of American and Japanese relationships, the Japanese have switched between feeling superior and inferior. For example, immediately before World War II, Japan developed an air of invincibility because of its military successes in Asia. They believed that with a quick surprise attack on Pearl Harbor they could defeat the United States. They also felt their victory would be secure because they did not believe the United States had the will to fight. Immediately after World War II, the Japanese felt inferior, and many were appreciative of American efforts to help Japan rebuild. However, as Japan's economic power grows, there are signs that many Japanese are openly returning to their historically superior attitude.

Leading Japanese businessmen, politicians, and scholars are saying openly that the United States is in decline, like many great empires. According to a 1990 *Newsweek*/Gallup poll, Japanese believe Americans are spoiled crybabies who have lost their competitiveness because of the corporate bottom-line orientation and not enough long-term investment. They see our workers as lazy and self-centered. They believe our school systems, cities, and social structures are crumbling. They perceive our streets to be filled with large numbers of drug and alcohol users. Finally, they believe our society has too many racial and ethnic groups.[22]

The same poll found that 33 percent of the Japanese respondents had less respect for the United States today than five years ago and that 54 percent believe Japan could again become an enemy of the United States.[23] A 1989 *Business Week* poll had similar findings; for example, it found that only 42 percent of the Japanese respondents had a fair or great amount of admiration for America as a nation, and even fewer, 32 percent, had such feelings for American people.[24]

Shentaro Ishihara, a right-wing politician, and Akio Morita, chairman of SONY, in their book *The Japan that Can Say No* put forth some views that are probably felt by more Japanese than are willing to admit to it. A key point is that Japan should think about changing the balance of military power by selling advanced semiconductors to the Soviet Union. Another key point is that the United States is becoming angry with Japan because the United States is racist. The essential argument of the book is that Japan no longer needs the United States but vice versa; thus Japan should act in a more forceful, self-interested fashion.

Clearly, such views can only lead to increased resentment toward the Japanese.

American Attitudes toward Japan

It is important to know that over the centuries the Western world has feared and misunderstood Asia. The U.S. has always taken the European view; thus any potential successes of Asian countries have always been viewed with discomfort and concern. We agree with Ishihara when he says that the United States has a racist attitude toward Japan. He argues, we think correctly, that the United States interned over 100,000 Japanese Americans and dropped the atomic bomb on Japanese cities in large part because of this racist attitude. The chapter on Asian Americans discusses in detail the history of American attitudes toward people of Japanese heritage in the United States. It will help readers have a better understanding of American attitudes toward current-day Japan.

That some American views of Japan are still racist is correct. A poll conducted by *Fortune* magazine in 1990 found that 44 percent of the American respondents believed Japan is our least trustworthy ally, compared to 29 percent for Germany, 18 percent for France, and 5 percent for Britain.[25] Note that British companies own far more property in the U.S. than the Japanese do, yet one hears very few comments about the British "taking over the country." The mention of Japanese purchases brings out fearful, hostile feelings in many Americans. *Business Week* found in a 1989 poll that by a 3-to-1 margin Americans believe Japan's economic challenge is a greater threat to the United States than the Soviet military.[26] Considering how U.S.-Soviet relations have improved, that observation is correct.

What are some of the facts about the Japanese presence in the United States which cause concern?

- Japan funds about 30 percent of the U.S. budget deficit.
- The United States buys 36.5 percent of all Japanese exports, up from 24.2 percent in 1980.
- Japan has a $50 billion dollar trade surplus with the United States.
- Japanese automakers will soon control at least 40 percent of the total U.S. automobile market.
- In 1989, Japanese owned almost $60 billion in U.S. real estate.
- Two Japanese purchases of U.S. property brought out hostile reactions from many Americans: SONY's $3.4 billion purchase of Columbia Pictures, and Mitsubishi's $846 million purchase of a controlling interest in Rockefeller Center. Just recently, the Japanese purchased a large segment of Pebble Beach, California for over $1 billion, and Matsushita paid $6.1 billion for MCA.

We believe that, despite American racism, the Japanese presence would be less of an issue for Americans if Japanese markets were not closed to so many U.S. products. Sixty-five percent of respondents in the *Fortune* study said Japan unfairly restricts sales of U.S. goods to Japan, and 63 percent said the United States should discourage Japanese investment in America. *Business Week* found similar news; for example, 69 percent of the respondents believed the United States should limit the amount of Japanese goods allowed into the United States.[27] Thus, while we agree with Ishihara's basic contention—the United States is racist—we also believe some of the negative attitudes toward Japan are based on legitimate concerns about the ability of the Japanese to play fair in the economic game.

Many Americans understand that Japanese firms have strategic advantages over American firms, both in Japan and in the United States. The Japanese government funds extensive research, gives low-interest loans, and has numerous protective tariffs, policies, and practices that limit the importation of foreign goods. The result is that Japanese manufacturers have the financial and strategic backing of their government. They also have guaranteed markets that form a base for their exports to the world. Japanese government and business work together as integral partners. The U.S. government and business are usually at odds.

Two stories epitomize the problems U.S. firms have entering Japanese markets. It took Texas Instruments twenty-nine years to be granted a patent on a basic integrated circuit. The request was filed in 1960 and not granted until 1989. This gave Japanese chip makers a 29-year start to develop their industry.

Another example was cited by Edward L. Hennessy, Jr., chairman of Allied Signal, in a *New York Times* column. Over a decade ago, Allied wanted to enter the Japanese market in a joint venture with a Japanese business group. Allied had developed a high-tech amorphous metal alloy that it believed would be a very good product in Japan. The company selected a Japanese-born and -educated executive who worked for Allied Signal in the United States to head the effort in Tokyo. He was fluent in Japanese and well aware of the nuances of doing business in Japan. Twelve years later, after running into roadblock after roadblock, the manager returned without the deal having been consummated. Incidentally, Japanese friends of Allied cautioned them that their "aggressiveness" was disturbing the harmony of their markets.

The real danger to the United States is Japan's increased influence in Washington. Japan is determined to buy access to the United States and to any country it targets. Pat Choate, in his book *Agents of Influence*, notes that the Japanese have more companies and government agencies working for them in Washington than any other country. It had 152, compared to 61 for Canada and 44 for Britain. Many high-level Reagan appointees now lobby for Japan. Choate notes that Japan spends $400 million a year to lobby and influence U.S. policy. In addition, Japan finances the majority of all university and think-tank programs that study U.S.–Japan relations.

Europe and Japan

Many Japanese élite in government, business, and academia believe that because of its "unique classless society" it will always be able to adjust to the times and stay ahead of the rest of the world. Some leading academics in Japan hold the view that Europe is degenerating and cannot compete because it is a materialistic, class-oriented society. Needless to say, this view is also based on the prejudiced attitudes Japanese hold toward non-Japanese.

While Japan faces hostility from the United States, we believe Japan will have greater problems entering Europe than the United States, not only because Europe has a more protectionist mentality but also because it is more ethnocentric than the United States. Since the days of the Tartars, Europeans have always had concerns about Asiatic invaders. Leading European government officials and business leaders have expressed concern about Japan. Weisse Dekker, chairman of the Dutch electronics firm Philips, said, "Japan is destroying American industry, and if we're not careful, it will destroy European industry as well."[28] A leading French official characterized Japan as an enemy who is out to conquer the world. A former Swedish minister of trade said that the West is very uneasy about the successes of Asian Pacific countries. He believes they are a threat to the living standards of the West. In a recent *Business Week*/Harris poll, 50 percent of European respondents, 28 percent of U.S. respondents, and only 13 percent of Japanese respondents believed Japan is the number one economic power today.[29]

The Europeans demand that if Japan wants access to European markets, all European Community (EC) countries must have access to Japanese markets. In other words, if Japan wants to sell cars in Germany and Germany wants to open banks in Japan, then Japan can sell cars in all EC countries, but all EC banks must have the right to open banks in Japan. Because of this stand by the EC, there is fear among Japanese that a new reunified Germany and the EC will leave them on the outside looking in. They correctly note that the EC was not formed to benefit anyone except EC countries. According to Kirkland, the Japanese will not be able easily to staff their European subsidiaries with all Japanese managers, as they have done in the United States and Asian countries. European firms are demanding European leadership at the top of Japanese companies located in Europe.

Last year, Japan increased its European investments by 74 percent over previous years. It invested almost $15 billion in the European Community. Much of these efforts have been concentrated in England, where language and culture are more similar to those of the United States than to those of the rest of Europe. In sum, while Europe is a potentially lucrative market for the Japanese, Japanese ethnocentrism, trading, and staffing practices will be barriers to Japan's success in Europe.

Conclusion

Japan is a country faced by an increasingly hostile and competitive world. Its reliance on imported natural resources leaves it particularly vulnerable to world opinion. Japan's competitors are becoming much smarter about the emerging global marketplace. Japan also has demographic, historical, and cultural disadvantages. Specifically, the Japanese population is growing older faster than that of any other society. The low birth rate will continue to create an insufficient number of Japanese people to run its economic machine. There are potential serious cracks in the Japanese social structure, such as Japanese workers' increasing dissatisfaction. Its sexist and ethnocentric attitudes will hinder it in utilizing female and foreign workers to replenish its work force.

It is evident that these attitudes are carried over to Japanese-owned companies in the United States and Europe. Neither continent is in the mood to overlook Japan's aggressive economic colonization. In addition, the Japanese still have to combat resentment that originates in the American and European suspicion of Asians.

Cetron wrote that Japan is heading for a nose dive, which will occur in the 1990s and then will level out. However, he believes Japan will not regain the dominant position it held in the 1980s because of "growing social service demands from an aging population, the strain of total reliance on imported energy and raw materials, and intensifying competition."[30]

5

Europe

A great deal has been said about the potential economic power of the European Community (EC). The twelve countries that will make up the EC are Belgium, Denmark, France, Germany, Greece, Ireland, Italy, Luxembourg, the Netherlands, Portugal, Spain, and the United Kingdom. In 1992, the EC will remove all tariffs, capital fund barriers, and people movement barriers among its member nations. It will create the largest trading block in the industrialized world and comprise at least 327 million people. This compares to 285 million for the Soviet Union, about 250 million for the United States, and 122 million for Japan. Silva and Sjögren observe,

> The more complete unification of Europe in 1992 adds another dimension to the flow of international consumption, the dimension of sheer numbers. . . . The impact of EC92 on reciprocity means trading as separate nations and then suddenly combining into one big trading and consumption machine. The offensive and defensive potential of this unification would alter the international scene.[1]

In this chapter, we suggest why we believe that the EC will have difficulty achieving the dominant economic position so many have predicted. Our hypothesis is that the EC will have problems achieving its dominant position not because it has been unable to deal effectively with issues like economics, trade, and the environment but because it will have difficulty dealing with the issues of race, ethnicity, religious differences, language, culture, and gender. It has taken Europe more than twenty-five years to reach agreements on "hard issues." They still have more than half the directives (agreements) on which to concur before 1992. It seems to us that when working people begin to make use of the new freedoms granted by the EC there will be tremendous potential for conflict based on such issues as ethnicity, language, and so on. There have been significant ethnic, linguistic, and religious conflicts occurring in most EC countries with immigrants primarily from the Third World. Add onto these the historical conflicts among European nations over ethnicity, religion, and language, and one can begin to imagine the potential problems the EC will face around issues of diversity.

During the eighteenth and nineteenth centuries, because of advances in medicine, the European population expanded rapidly. As a result, many left their native lands to colonize the Americas and other parts of the world. Many also emigrated during periods of famines and poor economic conditions. In the late twentieth century, the European population is rapidly aging, birth rates are very low, and the population is beginning to shrink. These trends will accelerate during the first half of the next century. For years, countries like Germany have had a birth rate below 2.1, which is the replacement rate to sustain the population. While the United States has large numbers of illegal and legal immigrants to replenish its aging population, European countries are implementing strict immigration laws to severely limit further immigration. In addition, there are movements, particularly, in France and Germany, to send non-native people, especially North Africans and Turks, back to their home countries.

EC92: A Closer Look

The main reason for the formation of the EC is not the love of one European country for another but the fear that unless such an alliance was made, the United States and Japan would dominate the separate European nations. Silva and Sjögren note that by means of a mere three hundred directives, twelve independent and richly diverse nations with a thousand-year history of conflict and tension will come together as a united economic power to satisfy "an explosion of world consumerism. Europe faced two choices: remain the battleground of consumer superpowers Japan and the United States, or forge a single consuming and production entity that could offer the world a third alternative to U.S. and Japanese product domination. The answer was the EC."[2]

Kiplinger and Kiplinger write that the annual trade flows and current fixed assets between the United States and the EC amounted to over one trillion dollars in 1988. For example, the United States exported $76 billion worth of goods to the EC countries, and they exported $89 billion worth of goods to the United States. The value of the U.S.-owned plant and equipment in the EC countries was $122 billion, and the value of direct investment in the United States was $158 billion. Finally, the sales of U.S. affiliates of European companies were valued at $340 billion, and EC sales by divisions of U.S. firms amounted to $450 billion.[3]

There are some significant differences between the free market systems of the United States and the EC countries. There are also differences among EC countries in this respect; however, overall, the United States has a much freer competitive market system than any EC country. European economic arrangements have been directed primarily by an élite group of national bureaucracies, staffed by technocrats.

European governments play much more intrusive and controlling roles than the U.S. government in their economies. In addition, government spending in European countries is substantially higher than in the United States. Finally, governments in Europe protect their industries and provide social welfare programs much more so than the U.S. government does. One can trace this centralized control by government to the remnants of the feudal system.

These characteristics of the EC countries' economies are detrimental, according to some observers. Kotkin and Kishimoto see little evidence that most of the European governments will change their centralized control policies and suggest that such controls have a "dampening effect on entrepreneurial development in Europe." They believe these policies favor large, well-established, politically well-connected companies and people as opposed to small entrepreneurial companies that are the key to a competitive economy. They cite numerous government-sponsored inter-European initiatives designed to combat the United States and Japan but rate most of them as failures.[4]

The structural nature of EC economics can have a detrimental effect on the EC's achieving some of its primary goals. Following are some key elements of the EC.[5]

- Citizens can set up businesses in any other country just as they can in their own countries.
- There will be a free flow of people, goods, capital, and services among the nations.
- U.S. and other non-EC citizens will only pass through customs once, even if they visit all twelve countries.
- There will be mutual recognition of university degrees.
- Citizens of one EC nation will be able to deposit money in banks in another EC nation.
- Banks can become partners and fund projects outside their native countries.
- Companies can bid for government contracts in other countries.
- Companies can compete as freely in other countries as in their own countries.
- Standards will be set for products considered vital to create a uniform continental market.
- Key environmental standards on water and air must be followed by all members along with safety for nuclear energy plants.

While the EC holds tremendous potential, there are several unresolved issues other than the people and economic structural issues that could get in the way of its success. One is the issue of currency. Will the EC have a common currency that is accepted in every country? Currently a person could start off with $100 in one EC country and after visiting a number of them end up with about half of the value without spending a penny. This could occur because of the charge for exchanging money from one currency to another and the fluctuating exchange rates. The main obstacle to a common currency was the United Kingdom's resistance to it and its opposition to a political union that would give the EC control over certain governmental decisions impacting all EC countries. It is not surprising that, being accustomed to insularity, Britain still perceives itself as separate from the European mainland. That Margaret Thatcher lost her job in part because of these policies might be a boost to the EC.

Another issue is that of the numerous tariffs that each country has established over the years to protect indigenous industries from cheaper or better foreign imports. The EC recognizes these must be standardized or eliminated; however, there is difficulty reaching this goal. A related issue is what to do with the value-added tax, a cost added to goods before consumers buy them. These taxes go to the governments' treasuries. Those countries with high value-added taxes are battling those who have lower taxes.

A third issue is what will be the impact of a reunified Germany on the EC. Will the EC be viable with such a dominant employer? Germany's economy is double the size of the next biggest economy, that of France. A final problem the EC will face on an ongoing basis, if it is successful, is which countries should become members. For example, the EC is showing some of its racial, ethnic, and religious biases as it considers the admission of Turkey, a poor, relatively uneducated, Muslim country. Many EC members argue that their main reason for being cautious in admitting Turkey is its poverty; however, we believe that the real reason is that the EC is concerned about cultural and ethnic clashes with a Muslim Asiatic nation.

More difficult to resolve than the preceding issues is the EC's ability to create an atmosphere where people from different races, ethnic backgrounds, genders, religions, and cultural and linguistic backgrounds can be treated with respect, dignity, fairness, and equality. Not only will there be conflicts among EC countries' native populations but also among these and the immigrant minorities from North Africa and former European colonies. Many have lived in EC countries for years, and many are still coming in every day despite EC countries' restrictions on immigration. A final issue is immigration from Eastern Europe. Simply because they are Europeans does not mean they will be received with open arms. They bring in skills and knowledge but also their own ethnic likes and dislikes.

EC Demographics

The key factors influencing demographics in Europe are its aging population and its low birth rate. Since the mid 1970s, many EC countries' birth rates have fallen below the population replacement rate of 2.1. In 1990, the birth rate among all EC countries on average was 1.58. Only Ireland had a rate slightly above 2.1.

European populations are aging at a rapid rate. Currently, the percentages of the population sixty years of age and older are as follows: Spain 17.3 percent, France 18.5 percent, Italy 19.1 percent, Belgium 19.9 percent, West Germany 20.5 percent, and Britain 20.6 percent. By 2010, the percentages in this age group will be Spain 20.5 percent, Britain 22.2 percent, France 22.6 percent, Belgium 23.9 percent, Italy 24.4 percent and West Germany 26.9 percent. These figures suggest that about 100 million of the EC's 327 million people are over fifty years of age.

It is a well-known fact that there is tremendous bias against older workers in Europe and that there are few laws to protect them. Anyone can pick up a European paper, look in the want ads section, and see ads requesting employees of certain ages, usually under forty years of age. In addition, many employees are fired because of age or forced to retire at the age of fifty-five.

Ethnocentrism in Europe

Not only must the EC eradicate age discrimination but it also must eradicate discrimination based on race and ethnicity. For the EC to remain viable, it must look outside of its boundaries for a labor force. Even if the Eastern Europeans are officially allowed to emigrate, their nations also face population declines in the coming years; therefore, the governments of Eastern Europe are unlikely to encourage their younger workers to emigrate. However, while Europe's population is declining, Asian and African populations are booming. The birth rate in North Africa, for instance, is more than three times higher than in EC countries. Yet, because of ethnocentric attitudes, Europeans do not consider people of color to be desirable workers and citizens.

One could accurately describe European nations as prisoners

of culture and ethnic identity. While over the centuries there has been cross-fertilization, each European nation has its own distinct culture based in large part on its language. This is in direct contrast with the United States, which has numerous people from different cultures, speaking different languages, who have influenced U.S. culture. No European country has had, as the United States has, large numbers of racial minorities or ethnic groups welcomed as immigrants from other countries. In addition, European countries have not been as tolerant as the United States in accepting religious differences.

Finally, European nations have gone through two major World Wars this century and numerous other wars in the hundreds of years before. The animosities associated with those wars are still seething under the surface. We believe they will be more evident as the EC becomes a reality. The recent firing of Nicholas Ridley, Britain's secretary of trade and industry, because he openly expressed views that have been expressed privately by many British is an illustration. In discussing the possibility of monetary union, he referred to the Germans as "uppity" and said giving up monetary rights is like giving Britain up to Adolf Hitler. While he was fired for making these comments, there was an internal government report that essentially said the same thing.

We can envision various ethnic, linguistic, and religious groups perceiving other groups as having advantages over them. For example, it is conceivable that large numbers of poor Europeans from Spain and Portugal could migrate to Germany for higher-paying jobs. It is also conceivable that after their numbers reach a critical mass or the German economy begins to falter and unemployment rates begin to increase, German citizens will begin to be hostile to these southern Europeans, who have different languages, cultures, and religions and who look different.

A scenario linked to this one could be if there were a great influx of poor Third World people trying to escape their countries for better lives in southern Europe. When these Third World people reach a critical mass (they seem to have already, despite their small numbers), conflicts will arise.

Silva and Sjögren note that the EC is finding it difficult to address such "soft" issues. "The soft obstacles encompassing the cultural and social methods, morals, and mores that have kept Europe a patchwork of separate states since the decline of the Roman Empire are the hardest for the EC to address."[6]

The EC countries have 327 million people, about 12 million of whom are immigrants or descendants of immigrants. France has the highest number of foreign immigrants, 4.5 million. Many are from North Africa and Portugal. Britain has 2.5 million, primarily from India, Pakistan, and the West Indies. West Germany has about 4.7 million foreigners, primarily from Turkey and Yugoslavia. Italy has over one million, primarily from North Africa. In addition, Belgium and the Netherlands have significant immigrant populations from their former colonies. Sweden has about one million foreign immigrants, but many of them are from other Nordic countries, which allow citizens from one country to live and work in another. Spain has slightly less than one million foreigners, mostly from North Africa and Latin America.

Despite the relatively small numbers of immigrants living in the EC countries, their presence has created sufficient conflicts that one must wonder what will happen as their numbers increase because of legal or illegal immigration. One of the greatest fears among EC members is that if illegal immigrants successfully enter any of the EC countries, there will be nothing to stop them from moving to another country because there will be no place to check the papers of illegal immigrants. There is grave concern that after EC92 the influx of illegal immigrants will rise significantly.

Problems Arising from Ethnocentrism

What are some of the warning signs of impending conflicts? What are some of the attitudes of the ordinary European citizens toward foreign immigrants, especially Third World people?

England

- England in the 1980s had a number of serious racial riots between white Britons and immigrants of color.
- A government report found that one of four people of

color in East London faced racial harassment during the past twelve months.

- Not only has Britain imposed tough limits on new foreign immigrants from nonwhite Commonwealth countries but it has ruled that no more than 250,000 Hong Kong Chinese will be granted British passports before the British colony reverts to China in 1997.

- A recent poll of British citizens found 90 percent agreeing that Britain discriminates against people of color. In the same survey, 30 percent of the participants favored laws to send the immigrants back to their native countries.

As a response to this hostile attitude, Ms. Thatcher placed tough limits on new immigration from nonwhite Commonwealth countries. Her justification was that since the British are so fearful of being swamped by people with different cultures, the best way to maintain good race relations is to cut back on the numbers of nonwhites allowed into the country. One must wonder what the British position will be if for some reason there is a great influx, let's say of Spanish, Portuguese, or Italians, after 1992.

France

- In the past year, violence against Muslim North Africans in France has increased greatly. For example, several of these immigrants were killed because of their origins in 1990.

- Arab youths recently rioted in Vaulx-en-Velin because of racial discrimination and poor living conditions.

- Three Muslim girls were expelled from school for wearing head scarfs, but reinstated after a ruling that they had a legal right to do so as long as it did not constitute religious propaganda. While this was a victory for the girls, the issue released a great deal of anti-immigrant feelings.

- Young French citizens of North African origins have been dismissed from school because local officials imposed a limitation on foreign North African students in the schools.

- Anti-Semitism is also on the increase. In the town of Carpentras, 34 tombs in a Jewish cemetery were desecrated. Six other cemeteries were vandalized and painted with swastikas. Attacks on Jewish businesses have also occurred, along with personal attacks on Jews.

- In a recent poll, 16 percent of the French people favored sending immigrants of color back to their countries, and 68 percent favored an end to new immigration. In another survey, 76 percent said there were too many Arabs in the country. It should be noted that the French have no such problems with the large number of Portuguese immigrants living in France. They are more similar than North Africans to the French in language, religion, race, and ethnicity.

As a result of the racist feelings just cited and the increase in popularity of Jean-Marie Le Pen's National Front, a racist political group, the French government has endorsed the end of new immigration.

Germany

- The largest immigrant group in West Germany is Muslim Turks. To find out about the problems of Turks, a West German journalist lived as a menial worker for two years disguised as a Turk. In his book *At the Very Bottom*, he described the extreme discrimination, abuse, and harassment Turks face.
- West Germany calls foreign workers "guest workers." They make it clear that the workers are there only for a short time and at the behest of the Germans; however, many have been there for years.
- It takes ten years to apply for German citizenship.
- In East Germany since the end of Communism, young racist skinheads have violently attacked foreign workers from Angola, Vietnam, and Cuba, Mozambique and Jews and homosexuals. On Hitler's birthday, the skinheads and their Nazi allies assaulted foreign Turkish workers in Berlin. A Vietnamese and his friend were viciously attacked.
- Before German reunification, all foreign workers in East Germany were to be sent back to their countries.

- Attacks on Jews have begun to occur with alarming frequency throughout Germany.

As was the case in France and Britain, the response of the German government to such racist acts has been to impose severe restrictions on the immigration of foreigners. Some of the right-wing German groups want to send all foreigners, especially Turks and nonwhites, back to their own countries.

Italy

- Italy is experiencing increasing racist acts against North Africans. For example, Italians in Milan have protested against housing for North Africans. Mysterious fires have been set to homes of North Africans.
- In Florence, masked Italians ran through the streets clubbing and beating North Africans.
- In Genoa, over a two-day period, Italians attacked North Africans.
- There are many jobs that Italians do not want and that are very desirable for North Africans; however, because of Italian racism, many of these jobs go unfilled.

The Italian government, like others, has tightened up its immigration laws under pressure from its own population and in response to EC desires. It has established severe penalties for hiring illegal immigrants and is looking at ways to limit immigration.

Spain

- Spain has seen an upsurge in racist attacks on the North African and Latin American immigrants, who represent about 800,000 of Spain's 40 million population.
- In the past year, Spanish police attacked and beat ten Africans who were sleeping in a downtown plaza.
- Job discrimination is rampant against immigrants, even in jobs which Spaniards refuse.
- Because of the stereotype that crime is associated with these immigrants, Africans and Latin Americans are frequently harassed by police.

- While only 14,000 Jews currently live in Spain, there have been several anti-Semitic incidents.

Primarily because of pressure from the EC and from its own people, Spain is considering tightening its immigration laws. The EC sees Spain and Italy as the two main entry points for illegal immigrants from North Africa. After 1992, immigrants who can illegally enter one EC country will be able to travel to others.

Sweden

- Sweden has had the reputation of being the most racially tolerant European nation, but Sweden has seen an increase in racism and anti-Semitism.
- In 1990, during a several-week period, young Swedish toughs firebombed refugee camps eight times. Twelve immigrants had to be hospitalized. The immigrants were primarily from Latin America, the Middle East, and southern Africa.
- Recently Sweden has had a difficult time deciding to give asylum to 150 Soviet Jews. A newspaper article said "Real Jews Should Go to Israel."
- In a recent poll, 50 percent of Swedes said their country should let in fewer immigrants and 10 percent said Sweden should take no more immigrants.

Early in 1990, Sweden tightened its immigration policies after receiving a large number of Turks fleeing Bulgaria. Thus, in the most liberal, open-minded EC country, problems are occurring.

The previous examples suggest that the EC will have problems dealing with its labor shortage because of the increasing racism, ethnocentrism, and religious biases of its people toward foreign immigrants, especially nonwhite, non-Christian ones. It seems to us that Europeans are taking a reactionary step, which the United States took in the late nineteenth and early twentieth centuries, to exclude nonwhite people. They are trying to slam the door shut on workers they will need to keep their economies healthy and viable. Some of the EC countries were pleased to see the destruction of the Iron Curtain and the downfall of Communism. At first, some saw Eastern Europeans as an abundant source of young white workers; however, the realities are that while the Eastern European countries have higher birth rates than EC countries, they are not that much higher and these populations are not much younger than those of EC countries.

Even though they are considered white, many Eastern Europeans are different from EC people in terms of language, religion, culture, and ethnic origins. All these factors will lead to additional conflicts, especially if the numbers of Eastern Europeans become large or the EC economies take a downturn. Several recent news articles have reported increased intolerance of Eastern Europeans in Western Europe. Finally, the EC countries could be faced by conflicts among Eastern Europeans who move to the EC countries. Some illustrations are the ongoing conflicts between Czechs and Slavs, Hungarians and Romanians, and Serbians and Croatians.

Even if the EC countries did not have any immigrants from Third World countries or Eastern European countries, they would have conflicts among ethnic groups who live in the EC countries. One only needs to remember the situation in Northern Ireland and the increased nationalistic feelings of the Welsh in Wales. Spain has been battling the Basque separatist movement for years, and the Catalonians in the Catalonia region are becoming more nationalistic. The northern Italians believe they are superior to their poor southern Italian neighbors. Belgium has an ongoing conflict between those who speak French and those who speak Flemish. Not only does the EC have these conflicts but also there are the superior feelings of the British, Germans, and other northern Europeans toward their southern, poor partners, Spain, Greece, Italy, and Portugal.

A final note that will add light to the complexity of achieving a viable EC: In 1990, French farmers became violent against trucks bringing in imported English livestock. What will happen when 1992 rolls around and large numbers of people have the right to move from one country to another?

The Status of Women in Europe

While EC countries have more progressive family care programs than the United States, they are behind in providing women with equal employment opportunities. There are a number of social, historical, and economic reasons why the EC countries have adopted progressive family care policies. For example, Sweden's philosophy is socialistic, based on the concept of providing workers with the tools to be assets to society. The French and Germans were pushed into more comprehensive family care programs when a labor shortage after World War II made it essential for women to enter the work force. Thus, European women are not necessarily in the work force in large numbers because of their societies' support for equitability. For instance, in the Soviet Union, women complain that although most of them work outside the home, they are also expected to do most or all of the home-care chores.

The participation rate and the progress of women in European economies are far behind those of the United States. As far back as the early 1970s, the EC was under pressure from women's groups to require EC countries to pass laws providing women equal employment opportunities. It was not until 1980 that such a law was passed in the EC Parliament. Specifically, member nations were required to remove laws discriminating against women in access to jobs, training, pay, social security, and working conditions. While all nations have adopted such laws and regulations, Davidson and Cooper note, the laws are not complete and in many cases not enforced. There are no powerful sanctions for violations against member countries by the EC or by particular countries against its companies who discriminate, except in the case of Sweden.[7]

In Spain, only 27 percent of women aged fifteen to sixty-four years are work force participants. This compares to 38 percent in Italy, 52 percent in West Germany, 55 percent in France, 59 percent in Britain, and 75 percent in Sweden. Overall, 45 percent of EC women work in paid jobs, compared to 63 percent in the United States. Many women in EC countries do not work full-time. Of the 55 percent of French women who work outside the home, 85 percent work full-time, which is the highest percentage for EC countries. The lowest percentage of women working full-time is in Sweden; 50 percent of Swedish women who participate in the work force do so full-time. The United States has a higher rate of women workers than EC countries, more women working full-time, and a much higher percentage of women workers with young children. For example, in West Germany, only 16 percent of women with infants and toddlers, compared to 52 percent in the United States, are employed.

Many European women are channeled into traditional female occupations; few of them are in key management positions. Women represent only about 20 percent of elected members in the European Parliament. Hesse wrote,

> Even in fields where women provide a large percentage of the labor force, such as the textile and clothing industry or in the health service, they are still found in positions of dependence rather than in positions at the top end of the scale, which are predominantly filled by men. . . . The fact is that women still clearly have fewer opportunities to promote their careers than men, despite improved levels of education.[8]

It is clear that the European women are still perceived much more in traditional female roles than U.S. women are. That the EC has not taken significant steps to ensure the equality of women in the work force is just another sign of the lack of valuing diversity that exists in EC countries.

Conclusion

As one looks into the future of the EC and its competitiveness in the global marketplace, it is clear there will be serious problems because of religious, racial, ethnic, language, and cultural differences. These conflicts will become more evident as the EC becomes a reality and goes through its recession cycles.

If the EC does not deal effectively with these issues, we believe the EC will be somewhat like the Soviet Union, which is made up of fifteen republics of diverse ethnic, religious, racial, cultural, and linguistic groups. It has for years had to deal with maintenance of various cultural traditions; the question of what is the official language and which languages will be taught in schools; who has access, among numerous ethnic groups, to education and jobs; who has the right to limited housing, and so on. Since the dissolution of the existing Communist state, the Soviet Union has seen a resurgence of hostility in its various republics.[9]

- In Dushanbe, protesters demanded that Islam be declared the official religion of Tadzhikistan.

- In Samarkand, gangs of young Uzbek thugs roamed the local marketplace, slashing the faces of women who wore makeup.
- Anti-Semitic incidents have increased. Pamyat, a right-wing pan-nationalist group, vowed to drive Jews out of the Soviet Union.
- Conflicts between the Azerbaijanis and Armenians are based on ethnicity and religion, the latter being primarily Christian, the former Muslim.
- In almost all of the Soviet republics there have been numerous protests for separation from the central union.
- The Georgian Republic, which has about a dozen ethnic groups, wants to become independent from the central union, but the small ethnic groups in Georgia also complain about discrimination from the Georgian majority.
- Conflicts of the three Baltic states, Lithuania, Latvia, and Estonia, with Russians living in their countries have been well publicized.
- Kazakhstan has conflicts with native Russians, and young thugs have attacked migrant workers from other republics.
- In Uzbekistan, the majority Uzbeks attacked the more prosperous Turks, which resulted in 99 deaths.

For the EC to survive and prosper, there must be not only an economic union but also a political union that will enforce the equitable, fair treatment of all EC citizens and immigrants living in EC countries. A tremendous effort will be needed to get all these different people to recognize, appreciate, respect, and value their differences. The place to start is a political union with laws to protect the rights of all human beings, such as exist in the United States.

We would be remiss if we did not note that as EC countries compete in the global marketplace, their prejudices will greatly affect their abilities to work effectively with Asian and nonwhite people. Even though the United States is a Western nation, the EC's ethnocentrism also interferes with effective interaction with Americans. The fact that half of U.S. managers either resign or are fired within eighteen months of foreign takeovers suggests the degree of the problems.

United States: Women

The previous two chapters present considerable evidence that Japan and Europe are faced with severe conflicts over the issues of accepting, respecting, and appreciating people of diverse cultures. Japan has had little history in dealing with "foreigners" on an equal basis, and Europe's experience with other nations has often been as colonizer rather than as equal. It seems clear that Japan and Europe lag behind the United States by several decades in giving equal place to minorities and women.

The United States has had over 400 years of history working at accepting, respecting, and appreciating people who are different. Although its record in this regard is imperfect, the United States as a nation has come to terms philosophically and legally with the diversity of its people. Because of this, we believe, the United States will have a competitive edge in the new global economy. People are, and will increasingly become, the key to a nation's success in the new global village. As Kotkin and Kishimoto observe:

> In sharp contrast to both Europe and Japan, the United States is blessed by a diversity perhaps unprecedented in world history. Although many have traditionally regarded the Chinatowns, the Hispanic barrios, and the Little Italys of America as sociological sore spots, in reality these communities—with their special family and cultural ties—represent some of the nation's greatest assets in the emerging world economy.[1]

While ahead of Europe and Japan in the fair treatment of women, U.S. employers still have much to do to ensure women full work equality in their organizations. Futurist Joe Coates cites a survey of 1,200 executives indicating that 68 percent were eager to promote women to top executive levels and 85 percent were eager to promote them to middle management. In addition, only 29 percent said women are not likely to be promoted as quickly as men.[2] However, these views do not reflect the real problems women face in the corporate United States today and will continue to face in the coming decades unless a more serious commitment is made to eradicate sexism.

Women hold 35 percent of the executive, administrative, and management jobs in the United States, almost double the 1972 level. However, only slightly more than 2 percent of general manager jobs are held by women. *Fortune* magazine found that in eight hundred public companies, only 19 of 4,012 people serving as the highest-paid officers and directors were women. Of 599 managing directors at five prominent investment banks, only 15 were women. In addition, only one woman is chief financial officer at any of the top 250 industrial corporations.[3] These statistics are true despite the fact that women represent more than one out of three business school graduates.

In the broadcast area, women are 36 percent of the employees, but they represent only 13 percent of the key editors, 6 percent of publishers, and 6 percent of the top officer and general manager positions.[4]

The Burden of Sexist Traditions

Sexist attitudes originated tens of thousands of years ago, as noted by Harris: "Male-supremacist institutions arose as a byproduct of warfare, over the male monopoly of weapons and the use of sex for the nurturance of aggressive male personalities. And warfare . . . is not the expression of human nature but a response to reproductive and economic pressures. Therefore, male supremacy is no more natural than warfare."[5]

At one time, war was conducted with hand weapons whose effectiveness was a function of physical strength. The less rugged physique and the child-bearing duties of women rendered them less physically powerful, so males dominated in war and in hunting for food. Male babies were preferred, since they added to the defensive team, and they had first choice of available resources. Women did drudge work and provided food not requiring vigorous hunting. Their subordination and devaluation followed from the need to reward men at the expense of women and to provide supernatural justifications for the whole male-supremacist structure. Thus, the origins of sexism are tied to the exigencies of cave and village life. Later, sexism was culturally induced, made permanent by laws, and when necessary rationalized with religion.[6]

The Bible is traditionally interpreted to show that men are superior to women: man was created first, and woman was created from and for man. This definition of women as inferior and subservient to men was reflected in early English law. The oldest written English law, Ethelbert's Doom of A.D. 600, and the laws that followed it in Western civilization were written and interpreted by men who subscribed to this definition of women and who used the Bible to justify their outlook. We should also remember that over the centuries the Bible has been translated by men.

In 1873 the U.S. Supreme Court found that the state of Illinois could deny a woman a license to practice law. In the opinion of Supreme Court Justice Joseph Bradley,

> The civil law, as well as nature herself, has always recognized wide differences in the respective spheres and destinies of man and woman. Man is, or should be, woman's protector and defender. The natural and proper timidity and delicacy which belongs to the female sex evidently unfit it for many of the occupations of civil life. The constitution of the family organization, which is founded in the divine ordinance, . . . indicates the domestic sphere as that which properly belongs to the domain and functions of womanhood. . . .
>
> It is true that many women are unmarried and not affected by any of the duties, complications, and incapacities arising out of the married state, but these are exceptions to the general rule. . . . And the rules of civil society must be adapted to the general constitution of things and cannot be based upon exceptional cases.[7]

This attitude was still in effect in 1961, when the Earl Warren Supreme Court upheld a Florida law, similar to laws in many other states, that gave women special immunity from jury duty so they could remain at "the center of home and family life."[8] This decision was overturned by a later Supreme Court decision.

It has been suggested that the Civil Rights Act of 1964 included nondiscrimination provisions for women only because some Southern congresspeople thought such a ridiculous idea would easily defeat the bill. However, their strategy backfired. During the 1970s many state laws that discriminated against women were challenged, often upheld at the state level, and sometimes overturned at the federal level.

One instance where such a discriminatory law was upheld is the 1970 case of *Reed v. Reed*, in which a woman challenged an Idaho statute stipulating that men must be given preference over women as administrators of estates of persons who died without making a will. The Idaho Supreme Court found the statute constitutional, giving this feeble opinion:

> Philosophically it can be argued with some degree of logic that the provisions of I.C. 15-314 do discriminate against women on the basis of sex. However, nature itself has established the distinction, and this statute is not designed to discriminate but is only designed to alleviate the problem of holding hearings by the Court to determine eligibility to administer. . . . The legislature, when it enacted this statute, evidently concluded that in general, men are better qualified to act as an administrator than are women.[9]

The most recent and important proposed legislation pertaining to the rights of women is the Equal Rights Amendment to the U.S. Constitution, which states, "Equality of rights under the law shall not be abridged or denied by the United States or by any state on account of sex." But many women opposed the passage of this amendment; years of traditional socialization prevented many women from endorsing this legal protection.

The English language itself—with its traditional use of masculine words like "he" and "mankind" to designate both genders—embodies the traditional sexist views. And male-supremacist stereotypes are often perpetuated in fictional and nonfictional characterizations of women. The following are examples given in a dictionary to illustrate definitions: "She burst into tears upon hearing of his death, but it was only a grandstand play." "She always wears a crazy hat." "Women with shrill voices get on his nerves." "You could see him turn off as she kept up her chatter."[10] One author counted approximately two hundred words to describe a sexually passive woman and only twenty to describe a sexually passive man.[11] And even in 1990, a thesaurus for an Apple Computer software package "offers only a few synonyms for woman, including 'female partner in marriage, wife, lady and Mrs.' but for man, the list runs on and on: "member of the human race, human being, body creature, individual life, mortal, party, person, soul, mankind, flesh, humanity, humankind . . .'"[12]

Sexist attitudes have also filtered into scientific thinking. Some psychologists have deemed women mentally ill if they are not dependent, emotionally expressive, and passive but rather display "male" characteristics like independence, stoicism, and aggressiveness.[13] Results of medical studies done only on men, like one that found aspirin lowers the risk of heart attack, have often been generalized to women, although women were not included in the study population.[14]

In sum, this legitimization of the second-class status of women by religion, law, language, and science has ancient roots. Ruth Benedict has aptly summed up the power struggle implicit in racism and sexism:

> Social change is inevitable, and it is always fought by those whose ties are to the old order. Those who have these ties will consciously or unconsciously ferret out reasons for believing that their group is supremely valuable and that the new claimants threaten the achievements of civilization. They will raise a cry of rights of inheritance, or divine rights of kings, or religious orthodoxy, or racial purity, or manifest destiny. These cries reflect the temporary conditions of the moment, and all the efforts of the slogan makers need not convince us that any one of them is based on external verities.[15]

Women's Participation in the Work Force

The view that women do not need to work is contradicted by past and present fact. Most women have always worked to help sustain their families; what has varied has been the location and conditions of their labor.

Before the Industrial Revolution, both men and women performed most jobs, and all members of the family had to work at income-producing activities. Little distinction was evident between men's work and women's work: "No work was too hard, no labor too strenuous to exclude women. Among the masses of people still emerging from serfdom and existing in terrible poverty, the family was an economic unit in which men, women, and children worked in order to survive."[16]

The Industrial Revolution tolled the knell for the cottage industries that had been preferred for women expected to bear and raise children while also producing marketable products.[17] Based on the exploitation of the working class, this revolution resulted in a labor situation not much different from serfdom. Women, and children as young as age six, were forced to work fourteen-hour days, seven days a week, in factories and sweatshops for less than subsistence wages. Heating, lighting, and ventilation were inadequate. Anyone who missed a day's work for any reason was automatically fired.[18] In his 1906 revelation of the inhuman working conditions for women in Chicago's meat-packing industry, Upton Sinclair described how they stood all day long, ankle-deep in briny water, freezing in winter and sweltering in summer.[19]

The emergence of the middle class accompanied the Industrial Revolution. This development allowed some men to provide for their families single-handedly. Women, increasingly freed from menial home labor by the new technology, were able to pursue other tasks. These tasks were limited and clearly defined, that is, only certain types of work were acceptable for these women. Their primary social role was to care for their families, and all work they performed had to improve their power to fulfill this role with precision.[20]

While the Industrial Revolution created a multitude of jobs for women in both factories and offices, few women, especially middle-class women, saw their employment as anything but temporary in order to meet some immediate need. The message of that time was that women were not to think about careers; their full-time job was properly in the home.[21] Encouraged to think of themselves as temporary or part-time workers, women did not expect or press for advancement and equal pay. But the fact is that for many minority and lower-class women, income-producing work was not a temporary expedient; it was permanent and necessary.

Throughout history, men have determined when and at what kind of jobs women could work. Usually the social policies shaped by men have resulted in women's working in positions that men, because of social class, education, gender stereotypes, or national needs such as a war, were either unwilling or unable to fill.[22] This basic concept was demonstrated during the Depression and World War II. Female workers were the first, along with the racial minorities, to be fired or laid off during the Great Depression. High rates of unemployment led to pervasive efforts to circumscribe the work of women who appeared to be depriving the male heads of households of their livelihoods. Women were still welcome to work in specified low-paying fields, but any woman presuming to compete for a "man's" job met with hostility and resentment. Government policy during the Depression was to "get the men back to work" and to spread the impact of the few available jobs. In 1932, a "married persons" clause for federal civil service workers specified that the first employees to be dismissed during personnel reduction were to be those who had spouses holding another federal position. Three-quarters of those dismissed under this clause were women, even though the law did not specify that the husband was to retain his job. Under the New Deal, men received preference for Works Progress Administration (WPA) jobs, and single women, some lacking all other resources, were at the bottom of the list.[23]

World War II brought about a complete reversal of this attitude, and Rosie the Riveter emerged as a patriotic folk heroine. Women poured into the labor force and proved to be competent laborers in many areas until then restricted to men. The nation had little choice. Women were needed to fill all kinds of jobs. In steel mills, women were found pounding typewriters in the offices and rolling steel next to the furnaces. These war jobs, however, were seen as a temporary emergency measure. At the end of the war, women were urged to return home to make room in the labor force for the returning veterans. Employers were surprised to find that many women preferred to remain at work, even though they were often demoted from their wartime positions. Women had developed a new ethic, a new sense of self-worth, and a new independence.[24]

During this same period and for the next 25 years, a role allocation between mothers and fathers was sometimes explained in biological terms: "Mothers take care of children because they naturally produce and feed them and men do not." These theories helped popularize the Ozzie and Harriets and the June Cleavers of the 1950s. Mothers who stayed at home represented the ideal.[25] Auerbach wrote, "The dominant American ideology of mothering holds that children need the nurturance of their mothers at home to ensure proper physical, emotional, psychological, and moral development. Any mother who does not stay home and care for her children is a bad mother. . . ."[26]

Despite such notions, over the last four decades an increasingly large percentage of entrants into the civilian work force have been women. In 1960, they represented 33 percent of the work force; in 1980, they represented 43 percent. This trend will continue for the rest of this century: by 2000, women will represent at least 47 percent of the work force. An estimated two out of every three people who will fill the 21 million new jobs between now and the twenty-first century will be women.

These statistics are very important, but they do not tell the whole story. The greatest changes in the female labor force in the 1980s have occurred among women of child-bearing age. Ellen Galinsky, a noted child-care expert, estimates that 90 percent of working women are of child-bearing age. She projects that 80 percent of these women will become pregnant at some time during their careers. But having young children no longer means leaving the work force. In 1986, 63 percent of mothers with children under age eighteen were employed, compared with 9 percent in 1940. The most dramatic increase in the labor force in recent years has been the percentage of working mothers with children under one year of age—from 31 percent in 1976 to 54 percent in 1989.[27]

Women now receive more undergraduate degrees than men. In 1989, they received 52 percent of all undergraduate degrees, compared with only 42 percent in 1970. As the percentage of women pursuing higher education continues to increase, American society will have to develop new programs and policies to keep these valuable employees in the work force.

The Changing Family Structure

What effect has the increasing number of working women had on the American family? One of the most striking effects has been a questioning of the idea that the typical family is the traditional nuclear family, in which the husband works full-time outside the home and the wife stays home to care for the two children. Fifty years ago, 70 percent of American families were traditional in this sense. At that time, corporate policies and procedures were in harmony with the structure and circumstances of many people's lives. But today, fewer than 10 percent of all American households fit this description. Yet we have found in our seminars that a significant number of the participating men, between 35 percent and 45 percent, believe that this kind of family is still the norm. (For women, the figures are between 10 percent and 30 percent.)

Over the past twenty years, the number of dual-career families and single heads of households has grown enormously. Two-income couples made up only 28 percent of all married couples in the United States in 1960; but in 1985, they made up 49 percent. This rapid growth in two-income couples is projected to rise to over 60 percent by the year 2000.

At the same time, since 1971, the number of families headed by women with no husband has increased by 67 percent. Almost 20 percent of all working women are now single parents. In recent years, as many as 61 percent of all black children born were born to single mothers, as were 28 percent of Mexican American children, 58 percent of Puerto Rican children, and 20 percent of white children. Today, more than one-quarter of all American children live in single-parent homes, while half of all black children do.[28]

As a result of the escalating divorce rate and the growing number of births out of wedlock (5 percent of all births in 1960, but 23 percent in 1986), experts estimate that nearly half the children born in the 1980s will live with a single parent before they reach adulthood. Sixty percent of all single working mothers with children under 14 earn less than $15,000 annually, and only 15 percent make more than $25,000. More than one-quarter of children born in the 1980s will live in extreme poverty, that is, in families with an annual household income of less than $15,000. Economics and biology have historically been used to explain role differentiation, but many sociologists, including myself, believe that gender discrimination is better understood in terms of the power structure. According to Margaret Polatnik, "The allocation of child-rearing responsibilities to women . . . is no sacred fiat of nature, but a social policy which supports male domination in society and in the family."[29] Polatnik discusses child rearing as a task that offers low status and little pay. The task is assigned to women by men who don't want it and who wish to preserve their monopoly of the higher status and prestige that come from being the breadwinner in this society.

Stereotypes about Women in the Workplace

Numerous studies have shown that society's negative stereotypes about women are carried into the corporate structure, where they adversely affect women's careers. Between 1976–78 and 1988, negative stereotypes about women have increased. For example, our 1976–78 survey found that 16 percent of men and 7 percent of women agreed that women are not serious about their professional careers; in 1988, 25 percent of men and 20 percent of women agreed. This flies in the face of the increasing numbers of women entering the permanent full-time work force and the findings of an unpublished study (Fernandez) of high-tech companies that 82 percent of the men and 85 percent of the women in the study group categorize their careers as either extremely important or very important. In addition, 68 percent of the women and 53 percent of the men said career development is their top priority in life.

Women Working Outside the Home

We believe this increase in employees who agreed that women are not serious about a professional career is tied to their belief that women should not work outside the home.

Figure 6–1 shows employees' responses from our 1988 study. Marked differences exist between the female and male respondents in their agreement with questions representing stereotypical

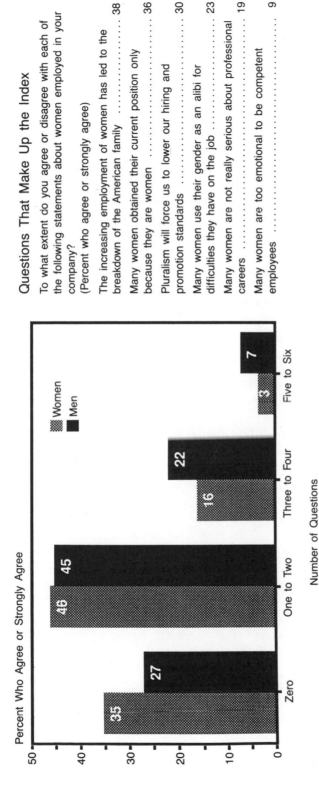

Questions That Make Up the Index

To what extent do you agree or disagree with each of the following statements about women employed in your company?
(Percent who agree or strongly agree)

The increasing employment of women has led to the breakdown of the American family 38

Many women obtained their current position only because they are women 36

Pluralism will force us to lower our hiring and promotion standards 30

Many women use their gender as an alibi for difficulties they have on the job 23

Many women are not really serious about professional careers 19

Many women are too emotional to be competent employees 9

FIGURE 6–1

Sexist Stereotypes and Attitudes

views of women. The responses to the statement "The increasing employment of women has led to the breakdown of the American family" are discouraging. Overall, 38 percent of the employees surveyed (29 percent of women and 49 percent of men) agreed with this statement. Men with grown or young children were most likely to agree. Married women with no children and unmarried couples without children were least likely to agree.

Here are some employees' comments bearing on this topic:

I personally do not feel I am taken as seriously about my work as I wish to be. (Native American, occupational, woman)

I have problems with child care and the erosion of the family unit. (White, occupational, man)

When conversing, I must suppress my true feelings about working mothers leaving their children in day care. (White, lower-level, man)

You and your entire group can't change the fact that a woman belongs in the home, no matter what "ism" you dream up. (White, occupational, man)

I like having a wife at home, mother at home. I see women in this role. (White, lower-level, man)

Results of mothers working—low morale, less respect in children. Little interest in men to be head of the household. (Black, occupational, man)

When women are the second income at home and have children and expect the company to always give them time off for the caring of children, I believe they are just there for the money. (White, middle-level, man)

The good old boys still think women should be home with the kids. (Black, lower-level, woman)

I feel most men are more qualified because they want to be the breadwinner in their homes and the women want to be at home. (White, occupational, woman)

Despite the fact that people often deny holding such prejudiced views or applying them to co-workers, it is clear that their effects are experienced by women workers.

Absence due to maternity leave can hinder one's chances for certain assignments or promotions. (Hispanic, occupational, woman)

There is discrimination against women who choose or value their families greater than the company in terms of amount of time given to work-related activities, both social and nonsocial. The company should recognize, women who both work and have families are the ultimate managers, rather than viewing them as insufficiently dedicated to the company. Active motherhood currently impedes promotability. (Asian, occupational, woman)

Women with children are allowed no leeway in taking time off work for sick children. They are forced to use vacation time. People who don't have children don't have this problem. Also fathers generally don't have this problem because the mother is usually the one who stays home with kids.
(Black, lower-level, woman)

Women have to make choices, and the company is not obligated to sacrifice performance in order to accommodate a woman's desire to have children. (White, upper-middle-level, woman)

Women's Psychological and Physical Characteristics

Women are often stereotyped as being less able workers or less suited to the workplace because of "peculiarly female" psychological and physical characteristics. The following employees' comments from our 1988 survey and our seminars illustrate this:

I have problems with discrimination based on emotional decisions made by female supervisors. (White, occupational, man)

Women are more moody and less consistent in approach to similar problems. (White, lower-level, man)

The majority of women I have worked with are too emotional and too hung up on petty bickering/gossip/fashion/cat fights and not focused on their jobs. The remaining *small* minority are the finest professionals in the field. (White, lower-level, man)

Some people think that women are inferior in science and mathematics. (Asian, lower-level, woman)

I do not believe that females are as technically able.
(White, upper-level, man)

I grew up in a society in which women usually are not expected to function very well technically or to act a lot in an open society. I found myself that I hold that prejudice to some extent, although not much. (Asian, lower-level, man)

Women often do not have the mechanical or physical backgrounds or the "rain in the face" discipline to get some job done. Once in a new job, they try to "catch up" on perquisites they missed.
(Hispanic, occupational, man)

Working with outside plant techs and their foremen over a number of years, it has been a very prevalent problem because it has been a traditionally male area. If a man gets mad and loses his temper, that's okay. If a woman loses it, she's a bitch or on her cycle. It's a problem that only time will solve. (White, occupational, woman)

Lots of testing of women, to see if they're as tough as men. Sometimes it goes to the point where a woman is set up because she's perceived as weaker. Generally, things are much worse than they were a few years ago. (White, lower-level, woman)

My boss told me it'd be hard for me to move up any higher in the company because I'm a small-structured woman (those of my ethnic background usually are). This kind of attitude exists in all places. It makes people like me hold a self-defeatist attitude that I'll never go higher than lower-level management. I'm not a real activist on these kinds of issues, but it disturbs me enough to try harder, work harder, to prove him wrong. So far, I've had no luck or opportunities to make a set up. Sometimes I wonder if it's worth the effort. (Native American, lower-level, woman)

Strong attraction to women; thus I must overcome a sexist reaction in the workplace. (Black, middle-level, man)

I can deal with every different racist/sexist. However, I have a little difficulty dealing with white young women.
(Asian, lower-level, man)

Some of the men I have worked around want us to be sweet and pretty to look at. (Asian, occupational, woman)

Women are forced to wear dresses before they are considered properly dressed. What's wrong with a jacket and slacks? Isn't that what men wear? (Native American, occupational, woman)

Gender Discrimination in the Workplace

All the data we have collected over the past twenty years indicate that sexist attitudes are translated into discriminatory actions against women workers. The protestations of some corporate managers that they can hold these beliefs privately without acting on them in the work environment is pure fantasy.

Employees surveyed in our 1988 study, both men and women, observed the following kinds of discrimination in their companies (see figure 6–2): Women have a harder time finding sponsors or mentors; women are excluded from informal networks and activities; women must be better performers to get ahead; women experience sexual harassment on the job; women's authority is not accepted as readily as men's; and women are often given jobs with "no future." To this we may add a notion that devalues women's real work achievements—the idea that many women got their jobs only because of their gender, perhaps through sexual favoritism or because of affirmative action requirements.

Not surprisingly, the women in our study perceived discrimination in all categories much more often than men. However, only 8 percent of men and 1 percent of women did not believe there is any discrimination. Almost six times the percentage of women (35 percent compared with 6 percent of men) believed there is a great deal of discrimination.

Between 1964 and 1972, the percentage of employees who believed that being a woman would be harmful to advancement in their companies decreased,[30] but between 1976–78 and 1988,

Questions That Make Up the Index

To what extent do you agree or disagree with each of the following statements about women employed in your company?
(Percent who agree or strongly agree)

In general, women have a much harder time finding a sponsor or mentor than men do 72

Many women are often excluded from informal networks by men 63

In general, women have to be better performers than men to get ahead 58

Many women are faced with some type of sexual harassment on the job 58

Many women have a difficult time initiating informal work-related activities such as lunch and socializing after work, because men misinterpret their behavior as a "come on" 48

In general, customers do not accept a woman's authority as much as they accept a man's in similar situations . 42

In general, women are often placed in jobs with no future 41

In general, women are penalized more for mistakes than men 33

How frequently do you hear language in your organization which you consider sexist? (Percent who said frequently) 29

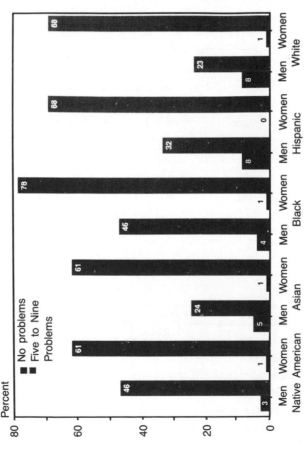

FIGURE 6–2
Gender Discrimination

the percentage of women believing this rose from 19 percent to 28 percent (white women) and 45 percent (minority women). During the same period, the percentage of men believing that gender would be harmful to advancement fell from 47 percent to 29 percent (white men) and from 15 percent to 13 percent (minority men). This is a clear sign that affirmative action efforts have slipped and that white males are feeling less threatened by even a perceived emphasis on preferential treatment for women.

Devaluation of Women's Achievements

In one of our studies, 59 percent of men and 33 percent of women stated their belief that women often get their jobs because of their gender alone.

> As a female, everyone says I'll be promoted quickly. I do not want to be promoted just because I am a female. I want to be promoted because I earned it. (White, lower-level, female)

However, situations in which corporations are legally required to hire or promote by gender are very few. Only 5 percent of all court cases mandate a quota system; all others order goals, timetables, and good-faith efforts to balance the work force. Thus, given the embedded gender discrimination in the corporate workplace, few women will obtain jobs or promotions just because they are women. And, of course, women (as well as men) would not be able to keep their positions unless they do their work well.

It is extremely important for women to recognize that the most important barrier to their advancement is not their ability on the job but gender discrimination. They must adopt a positive attitude and believe they have earned what they get. They must confidently reject the notion that the only reason they were hired or promoted was because of gender alone.

Social Interaction Problems Faced by Women in the Workplace

As noted earlier, the past ten years have brought no improvement in gender discrimination in the workplace, according to women in our studies. Although women who work for American-owned corporations may not find social interaction problems as pervasive as those who work for Japanese-owned corporations, it cannot be said that companies in the United States are doing a very good job in respecting, valuing, and appreciating differences.

In our 1976–78 study, 63 percent of women and 57 percent of men believed women managers were often excluded by men from informal work groups; in 1988, the figures were 71 percent and 43 percent. In 1976–78, 54 percent of women and 37 percent of men believed that women have difficulty finding mentors; in 1988, 81 percent of women and 55 percent of men believed this. Regarding sexual harassment, 62 percent of women and 47 percent of men in our 1988 study observed this occurring in their companies.

Some comments from our studies illustrate employee perceptions of various social interaction problems—exclusion from informal networks and activities, difficulty in finding mentors, sexual harassment—faced by women workers.

> Most of the discrimination women face from their male co-workers is a result of these men's wives. There is some discrimination from the men themselves, but their wives are very uncomfortable if their husbands work late and a woman also, or if they travel a lot and a woman does too. I am the only woman in premise sales in our office. My manager is also male, so that pretty much leaves me to myself. The men chum around and go to lunch together. I have not been invited along thus far. (White, occupational, woman)

> Older women have very few opportunities for advancement because they cannot attract sponsors or mentors.
> (Black, lower-level, woman)

> I believe women can more easily obtain or snag a sponsor but only certain jobs. I don't believe the problem is near solved.
> (Native American, middle-level, man)

> It gets lonely standing by yourself. Frequently, you have no department role models. Mentors are hard to find. It takes a lot of effort to establish relationships. Then the mentors retire, get moved, or die. You start again. (White, middle-level, woman)

> I'm the first female ever in this work group in a management position; the men I work with like me and think I do my job okay, but I'll never be their equal. (White, lower-level, woman)

Many important decisions result from the forming of bonds with a mentor or after-hours discussions with acquaintances. Often "the boys" go out after work to have a few drinks and discuss business (or pleasure). If a woman were to accompany them, it might be interpreted as a "come-on" or inspire jealousy and gossip at home or work. It has been argued that some men are also excluded from informal networks by other men, and this is true. However, men are much more likely to exclude women simply because they are women and not because of some factor that, as is the case for men, could be changed.

Women must make a conscious effort to establish themselves, while men almost always join the informal networks existing at their companies. Kanter suggested some reasons why men may exclude women from informal work groups: "Routine encounters become problematic: opening doors, pulling out chairs, shaking hands." Language is also a problem. Should women be called girls, ladies, gals, or females? Kanter concluded that because of an awareness of new standards for relations between men and women, and because behavior once taken for granted is no longer considered necessarily correct, men sometimes feel tense around women in new situations, particularly if the men want to make a good impression.[31]

> Many white men use sexuality to their advantage to get the job done, like hugging a [female] service representative to say good job. (Native American, lower-level, woman)

> When complaints are lodged because of language about "tits and beavers," most male supervisors can't get what the problem is. (Black, occupational, woman)

> Sexual harassment is alive and well, especially in this company, which does the most preaching. (White, upper-level, woman)

Oddly enough, we have had reports from both men and women that men, too, are the victims of sexual harassment. But in fact sexual harassment—unwanted attentions from colleagues or superiors on the job—is primarily a problem for women.

The heightened consciousness of people's rights in the work environment and the evolution of Equal Employment Opportunity case law have resulted in recent court decisions that bring incidents of sexual harassment into the realm of gender discrimination. Books and articles on this topic indicate that sexual harassment has been the rule rather than the exception for all women who work.

Men (and women) in this and most other societies have been socialized into thinking of women primarily in sexual terms. On television and in magazines, everything from cars to cake is sold by attractive women. This way of thinking does not begin or end at the corporate doorstep—it is present consciously or subconsciously much of the time. Some women workers manage to handle the problem of unwanted sexual overtures delicately, but the question arises of why they should have to handle them at all.

Men who expect a sexual response from co-workers tend to become enraged if rejected. Can you get fired if you refuse a superior's pass? You can. LaRouche and Ryan explain,

> Some women are hired for a dual function. The boss hopes to obtain not only an assistant but also a sexual companion. If the woman is cooperative, he can have his sex paid for by the company. He can offer his employee a salary increase for her sexual services without it costing him a personal dime. In such circumstances, excellent performance at work and in bed are part of the job requirements, and if you won't do both jobs, you get fired. In most cases, however, you are likely to be fired only if your rejection is demoralizing or hostile.[32]

Yielding to sexual overtures can be risky for women interested in careers as managers. Consultants warn against personal emotional involvements with work associates. B. Harragan states,

> What the unwritten and unverbalized canon of male ethics adds up to for women is clear: Any corporate woman employee who engages in intercourse with a fellow employee has jeopardized her chances of significant advancement within that particular corporate

structure. She is irrevocably labeled inferior and must go elsewhere to move upward with a clear path.[33]

But a middle-level woman manager has this to say: "The phrase 'she slept her way to the top' is male chauvinist slander, whether it's said by a man or a woman. The fact that a woman sleeps with her boss doesn't mean she doesn't have ability, any more than it means he doesn't."

Corporate policies cannot, and should not, stop sexual relationships arising out of work as long as such relationships are based on free choice of both participants and do not impede productivity. Unfortunately, unless both individuals have equal power and status, genuinely free choice is hard to obtain. Thus, corporations are obligated to provide a work environment free of sexual harassment that constitutes part of gender discrimination.

Strategies to Deal with Social Interaction Problems

How should women react to social interaction problems in the workplace? Women handle these problems depending on the individuals they deal with, the specific situations at hand, and their personal goals. However, a number of suggestions are applicable to most situations. With regard to exclusion from informal work groups, we suggest that the only time women should concern themselves about this is when participation in the informal work group will clearly influence their job success. In this case, the most practical and realistic way of gaining entrance is to gather the power and status through information, resources, and political connections to make men want to include women. Trying to be liked as "one of the boys" puts women at a disadvantage and at the mercy of such "boys." Women should recognize that the only reason to become part of an informal network is to gain an advantage, not to give an advantage to the informal network.

Women should also recognize that several different informal networks exist. The best strategy is not to participate in as many as possible but to take part in several *key* groups. In addition, women should form their own informal networks.

As women find it difficult to obtain mentors and sponsors, it is incumbent upon them to sponsor and support one another. In addition, they should seek out companies with formal or informal mentor programs that emphasize moving women up the corporate ladder.

Concerning invitations to work-related social occasions, women should recognize that these situations offer some of the best ways to gain insight into the people they work with. Thus, we suggest that women never stop initiating such work-related activities despite possible "misinterpretations." If they have a bad experience because of some sexist behavior on the part of their male co-workers, they should chalk it up to experience and learn from it. The only real protection women have is their ability to know themselves and to understand the people they are dealing with. In addition, they must have confidence in themselves when the rumor mill starts spreading gossip about "love affairs" and so on.

Finally, with regard to sexual harassment, the only real defense is to know that there is no reason why women should put up with this kind of behavior. Harassment happens; take action—the law is with women. LaRouche and Ryan state,

> Often women who complain of sexual harassment on the job are accused by their peers of bringing it on themselves. But I don't accept this view. A man's behavior toward a woman is determined by his own history and personality rather than by a woman's style of dress or manners. [She] doesn't control his behavior; he does. Otherwise how can one explain the difference between one man's macho wisecracks and another man's respectful invitation?[34]

Discriminatory Evaluation of Women's Capabilities, Authority, and Performance

According to our studies, workers perceive that women's authority is not accepted as readily as men's, that women must be better performers than men in the same job to get ahead, and that women are often placed into routine jobs because of gender stereotyping.

In 1976–78, 72 percent of the women surveyed believed that women must outperform men to get ahead; in 1988, this percentage had increased to 76 percent. In both studies, one-quarter of the men agreed. In 1988, 54 percent of women and 17 percent of men believed women are often placed in jobs with "no future." And in 1986, only 9 percent of women and 25 percent of men expressed a belief that women have the same power and authority as men in the workplace. The following comments are from employees in our studies.

> The majority of women workers are still assigned clerical jobs. Apparently, little has been done to give them opportunities and advancements. This applies to both white and colored people. (Asian, occupational, woman)

> Much of the discrimination is cultural and therefore extremely subtle. There is a tendency to channel women into database manipulation jobs and a willingness of women to be channeled in that direction. Not much is done to develop truly technical women who know why things work. We need to see more technical women managers. (White, occupational, woman)

> Women are held back and not given the opportunity to show their potential. They are labeled as noncompetitive and not aggressive. (Asian, lower-level, woman)

There are two main sources of power and authority at work— institutional (vested in the position) and personal. But, because of sexist attitudes, the authority inherent in a position if held by a man does not necessarily apply for a woman. The higher a woman advances in the company, the less likely she is to believe that she has the same power and authority as a man in her position would.

The effect of this lessened authority (as the jobholder and others perceive it) is to stifle a woman's confidence and effectiveness. Then if her performance worsens, some co-workers feel justified in their original sexist evaluation of the jobholder—a vicious circle. In this manner, companies who do not address gender discrimination fail to encourage and utilize the talents of the women they employ. "All people are more productive in a supportive environment," said a female lower-level manager. "The subtle everyday messages women receive telling them they are not competent are not supportive and cause an enormous loss of production." This does not bode well for success in the new competitive global economy.

Another serious problem women face in the workplace is the dual standards used to evaluate men's and women's performance. Schuller argued that society has classified jobs as "male" and "female." For instance, management is traditionally considered a male job and nursing a female job. Men who are managers and women who are nurses are in congruent types of jobs. People who hold congruent (traditional) jobs will usually receive better performance evaluations than those who hold incongruent jobs because society has imposed the stereotype that their abilities and skills are better suited to the congruent position. Put another way, sex role socialization has made people believe that men, not women, have the requisite abilities for managerial work. Thus, if a woman is in a managerial job, her performance will not be considered as effective or as good as a man's in the same job because of the sexist assumption that she lacks the necessary abilities. The converse would be true if a man were a nurse.[35]

One of the studies that found sex discrimination in performance appraisals was Deaux and Emswiller's evaluation of male and female abilities. They asked male and female college students to evaluate, on the basis of taped interviews, the intelligence and competence of one of four stimulus persons. The sex of the subject, the sex of the stimulus person, and the level of competence of the stimulus person were alternated. Highly competent men were evaluated significantly better than were highly competent women by both genders. In addition, the researchers found that men anticipated doing better than the person they evaluated on either a masculine or a feminine task, but women predicted a higher score for themselves only on the feminine tasks.[36]

Mary Cline et al. also produced some interesting findings. Forty-two male and forty-two female subjects selected from a large city, a small town, and a university campus were asked to evaluate four pen-and-ink sketches and four quotations. Two sketches and two quotations were associated with fictitious women's names and the other two were associated with fictitious men's names. Conclusions showed that, first, men devalued work produced by women relative to work produced by men. Second, women tended to devalue work produced by men relative to work produced by women. Third, the cross-sex devaluation was limited to the quotations and did not influence the evaluation of the sketches. The subjects did not generalize prejudice across all types of work produced by the opposite sex. Finally, these results were found in populations drawn from three very different settings, suggesting that sexism exists in all of society's institutions and geographic sectors.[37]

In brief, these studies suggest that gender discrimination plays a crucial role in performance evaluation. They also point out how sex role socialization has a negative effect not only on men's attitudes about women's performance but also on some women's attitudes toward their own and other women's performance.

We would be remiss if we did not state that social scientists have questioned the validity of studies such as those just cited. These researchers suggest that gender is not as significant as previous research had suggested. However, we strongly disagree with this, and so do many corporate employees. The prevalence of sexist attitudes has meant that women have had to be better performers than men to get ahead.

The notion of proof of ability has been discussed extensively in the literature. In our society, men are expected, and they themselves expect, to succeed in their chosen occupation, to receive financial rewards and satisfaction from their work, and to receive approval and support for their efforts from their families. When a talented man with demonstrated abilities does not succeed, for whatever reason, it is unquestioningly apparent to him and to those who know him that he has been the undeserving victim of injustice or rotten luck.

Women "have to prove by their performance that they do belong . . . they have to prove success, and on a continuing basis. They have to prove that their careers will not be dual, discontinuous, and consequently marked by a lack of commitment—a burden of proof to which a man is never asked to submit."[38] When to this sexist attitude is added an atmosphere in which, as tokens, women must perform every action under the critical scrutiny of the nontokens, it is neither surprising nor paranoid for many women to feel pressure to perform as superwomen.

Strategies to Counter Sexist Evaluation

To counter the inevitable refusal of some people to accord women the authority due to their positions, women must make certain that supervisors, peers, subordinates, and clients are aware of their sphere of responsibilities and their ability to take care of their job. This should be conveyed nonaggressively but firmly. Women must understand the different players and use different techniques to get the message across. What is important is that they appear confident, competent, and in charge. Rather than spending time and energy regretting that many co-workers will not willingly accord authority to women, they should concentrate on devising ways to obtain this authority to accomplish their career goals.

How can women combat dual standards of performance? There is no true solution to this problem. It depends on the circumstances and on the individual woman's goals. We do not agree with LaRouche and Ryan, who urge women not to protest injustices or discrimination because most people do not admit to their own sexism and will only become defensive. They urge women to find ways to dramatize their potential—the same potential bosses look for in management trainees. "Do new things in new ways. Walk around with a management textbook under your arm."[39] This is nonsense. How will a sexist boss recognize the efforts women put forth to be perceived as competent? The answer is, in a majority of cases she/he won't. Only when the corporate culture is committed to removing sexism, when the corporate culture values differences, and when leadership wants women treated equitably, will changes occur.

One positive strategy is to select a company with a track record and commitment to changing the sexist attitudes and behavior of its work force from top to bottom. This can be determined by finding out what types of "managing and valuing differences" workshops are conducted. How long have they been conducted? Are they a requirement for all people at all levels, or just a token gesture? Do the top officers, including the president, take time out of their schedules to deal with issues of equality? Where are the women in the organization in terms of levels and jobs? Does the company have a formal or informal program to provide mentors for women? Do internal women's groups exist with company support? Does the company actively support external women's organizations? Do the company's publications reflect a diverse work force? Answers to these questions will give women a good indication of the company's commitment to fair and equitable treatment in the workplace.

Here are some practical steps that women can take if they choose to hang in there. None are guarantees of immediate success in altering gender discrimination, but they may help.

- Until such time as things become fairer across the board, women must make certain that their educational credentials are superior or at least equal to those of the men with whom they want to compete.
- Women must develop and keep current with the latest skills, technology, and information in their field.
- Women must be familiar at some level with another language or two.
- Because it is so difficult for women to find mentors, they must be more concerned than men about managing their bosses (see Chapter 14).
- Women must be certain to give 125 percent effort, and never let down despite the negative situations they face.
- Women must take greater and more frequent risks to be recognized. They must also be aware that any failures will be blown up out of proportion.
- Women must take on additional responsibilities and tasks, which many men do not have to do to be recognized.
- Women must constantly be creative and think of new ways of doing things. They must recognize that they might not get credit for their ideas but that there is always the chance that they will.
- Women must deal with their own sexist orientation.

If women decide to move up in a sexist corporation, they might as well accept the reality that they must perform better than men in the same jobs. The higher women go, the more visible they become, the more eyes are focused on them, the more "perfect" they must be, and the more superior their performance must be.

The Impact on Women
of Balancing Family-Career Roles

One factor that clearly impacts a woman's career is how well she balances work and family duties. This conflict is rooted in the traditional arrangement whereby wives stayed at home and backed up husbands who worked as breadwinners. We have found that only 24 percent of women with children under age eighteen or under did not have problems balancing work and family, and only 22 percent of the women with elder care responsibilities said they had no problems.[40]

Most jobs are stressful, especially for the upwardly mobile. When this stress is added to family responsibilities and conflicting messages about proper roles, the total stress level, particularly for women, is extremely high. Having in effect two full-time jobs creates stress both at home and on the job. A certain level of on-the-job stress, caused by employment uncertainty, office politics, budget crunches, tight time frames, lack of corporate resources, and sometimes long hours, is a given for most employees. For upwardly mobile employees, factors such as employment insecurity, office politics, and long hours are added to extraordinary workloads, a great deal of pressure, and more than average responsibility. Ultimately, owing to the physical and mental problems that are its by-products, overload lowers corporate productivity.

J. Grimaldi and B. P. Schnapper made this observation on the eventual negative impact of stress on employees:

> The relationship between stress and illness is well documented. In fact, high blood pressure, ulcers, stomach disorders and heart disease are familiar examples of stress-related health problems. Low back pain and even colds and flu can result from stress. In fact, some medical experts have estimated that as many as 60 to 80 percent of their patients have stress related complaints.[41]

In 1989, we found that 60 percent of women, single or married, and 53 percent of single men reported experiencing stress on the job from balancing work/family conflicts, and similar numbers had stress at home for the same reason. But only 38 percent of married men with children age eighteen or under experienced stress at work and 42 percent experienced stress at home.

These figures suggest that many married men find themselves in a comfortable position. But that comfort may be short-lived. As career opportunities for women increase, and as the pressure of these careers intensifies, wives will become increasingly intolerant of the extreme imbalance in responsibilities at home, and more married men will begin to feel the stress of dual-career lives. Data from 1984 and 1989 surveys we conducted on child care showed 22 percent of the men having stress at home in 1984 compared to 39 percent in 1989.

U.S. law guarantees that women have an equal right to participate in the work force, yet society as a whole still manifests ambivalence about women working. Some individuals blame all family problems, including the high divorce rate, juvenile delinquency, and child abuse, on working women.

The socialization of women and men continues to project, to a certain extent, traditional role models in a time when they are outmoded. As a result, women experience a high incidence of missed days, tardiness, leaving work early, and dealing with family issues during working hours, and ultimately, more stress, which negatively affects their health and corporate productivity. Women have also become the primary care givers for the elderly, whose numbers are increasing. Many women try to make up for lower productivity on the job by taking work home and by coming to the office on weekends, but this effort, while laudable, further increases stress and family/work conflicts by consuming valuable limited time.

Women must get their companies to address work/family conflicts and child care and elder care issues. This will be no easy task. The main reason corporate America has failed to deal with these issues is that they are seen as almost exclusively women's issues. Corporations are still dominated by older men from traditional families who still believe, consciously or subconsciously, that women should be at home taking care of the children. Women who defy tradition and insist on working, they believe, must simply accept as their own responsibility the problems of balancing family and work roles and resolving the issues of child care. These corporate managers have not yet realized that most women are in the work force to stay and that their numbers will continue to increase.

At the same time, women should strive for more equitable division of home duties, child care, and elder care. Amelioration of these problems would give women more time to work on their careers and to improve their chances of advancement.

Women's Own Problems versus People Who Are Different

Part of women's success at work will depend on their ability to alter their own sexist, racist, or ethnic prejudices. It is clear, as the following employee comments from our studies show, that many women have problems accepting, valuing, and respecting people of different cultures or languages.

> I hear sexist remarks as much from women as I do from men. A certain stratum of women have become ruthlessly level-conscious. (White, lower-level, man)

> I have a hard time taking orders from men without thinking that they are being sexist. When someone has a heavy accent that makes them very hard to understand, I find myself treating them as though they were dumb. (White, lower-level woman)

> I don't like super-career women who act like men, the same men they criticize for being sexist. (White, occupational, woman)

> I've discovered that I tend to be in awe of white male supervisors but not of female, black, or Asian ones, no matter how high up they are. (White, lower-level, woman)

> I am not tolerant of women who dress and act slutty in a professional environment. I also have a mental picture of the perfect professional woman and judge all women by this picture. This

inhibits my ability to be supportive of other women and accept them as peers. (White, lower-level, women)

I have trouble communicating with many people for whom English is a second language. I find this a problem even with people who have good textbook English. I think it's due to cultural differences, and I don't know how to overcome it.
(White, lower-level, woman)

I grew up in a family where women were subservient. These attitudes and expectations are deeply rooted in myself. I fear I have become too militant in my militant striving, and I feel that I look down on women who choose to stay home and raise a family, for instance. (Asian, lower-level, woman)

For women to receive fair treatment in the workplace, they must learn to treat people who are different equitably. Women are both part of the problem and part of the solution in creating a competitive work force in the United States.

Building Positive Images

LaRouche and Ryan observe that women often seriously underestimate how much they accept a sexist view of themselves and their work without realizing that their accomplishments, seen through prejudiced eyes, are reduced to a distorted notion of "the way women are."[42] Unless women recognize the real impact of gender discrimination on their careers, they will allow prejudiced people to continue to blame them for their lack of success, to keep them feeling insecure about their abilities. Women spend enormous amounts of time and energy getting the right credentials and experience without understanding that sexist coworkers will never give them due credit, recognition, reward, or value.

One of the major reasons women have not been as successful as they might be in the workplace is that many have bought into the concept that hard work, keeping your nose clean, and ability are the keys to advancement. Many women want to believe that if there is discrimination, they will somehow be exempt; it certainly will not affect their own careers, only those of the less fortunate women. They even rationalize the failure of other women by holding the idea that these women must not have been "good enough."

Women in corporations face a demand for conformity. But doesn't everyone have to conform? Why should this be different for women than for men? The fact is that from their earliest days most women are socialized differently from men. As a result, women's operating and managerial styles are, in general, "naturally" different in some crucial aspects from those of men. Rather than understanding and attempting to adapt some of these positive qualities to the workplace, the male-dominated hierarchy attempts to make women conform to the male image. This effort has been helped along by business schools and self-help literature that tell women managers that they must be "one of the boys" to be successful. It is obvious at first glance that the most successful women in corporate America are those who have adopted the male style, down to the pinstripe suits and ties, the types of questions they ask, the mannerisms and language they use, and the "survival-of-the-fittest" mentality that characterizes most corporate men's cultural philosophy. If these same consultants and schools make similar suggestions for women who work in foreign-owned companies in the United States or in other countries, they may be giving the wrong advice on how women should behave in order to succeed. And it is not clear that in the American corporate culture such advice is best for succeeding in the 1990s.

M. Loden wrote that instead of valuing the varying styles women and men offer in their managerial roles, we have redefined equality to mean exact sameness according to traditionally masculine standards. "The result is that women who succeed in management often do so by adapting to male norms. Masculine bias, whether conscious or unconscious, continues to be the major obstacle." The feminine style is often not appreciated by male bosses and colleagues because they are not used to dealing with "the nontraditional approach."[43]

"I have noticed that women in management positions tend to have a hard exterior because they have to prove they are as tough as the men," said one of our female respondents. Women should not conform to meet male expectations. Yes, refusing to conform might for a time be detrimental to women's advancement, but it will do wonders for mental health—theirs and that of narrow-minded people around them. And in the long run, the refusal to straitjacket talents will be to the benefit of the corporation and to society as a whole. I have seen hundreds of women trying to become male clones and doing a very good job of it, but at what cost? Most of them will not be rewarded for behaving like males because they are not males, and men will continue to change the criteria for acceptance or will ridicule women who are trying. The definition of being "one of the boys" is one that the "boys" can always change the requirements for membership. In addition, the requirements vary from culture to culture, country to country, corporation to corporation, department to department, and work group to work group. Anyone who spends time trying to fit someone else's image cannot be spending as much productive time as if she were concentrating on doing the job well. If men had rewarded all the women who have forsaken their positive feminine style for the male image, the number of women in middle and upper management would be significantly higher than it is. "Women need to realize they are women and adopt a management style to fit their gender," one male middle-level manager noted. "Male management styles, which many women imitate, make them look silly and ineffective."

Loden supports this position. She wrote that many of the skills women have been encouraged to develop are the same as are needed to succeed in the new competitive global marketplace. These include intuitive management, interpersonal skills, and creative problem solving. Recently there has been growing appreciation of people-oriented skills, which "most women are taught to value and utilize from the time they are little girls."[44]

Not only do employees see women as being effective supervisors but also female bosses are consistently rated higher than male bosses in the important areas of career development and performance evaluation. Both male and female employees report that, at least to some extent, female bosses are more likely to give performance appraisals that are specific, useful, and clear as to what improvements are needed and how they might be effective.

Helen B. Lewis explains a major reason why female bosses may be preferred over male bosses:

Men, in keeping with the expectation that they will go into the world to earn their livelihood, are trained more frequently than women to understand the workings of inanimate objects or things. But more important, they are expected to accept, without thinking much about it, the idea that people may be treated as if they were things. . . . The majority of men also often take for granted that they themselves should be treated as if they were things—for example, units in a labor force.

Women, in keeping with the expectation that they will devote their lives to others, are trained—in fact, they train themselves—to understand other people. Men are also expected to understand other people (it's hard to prevent). But in our competitive, dehumanized, "business" society, men's dealings with other people are supposed to resemble their dealings with things and very often do.[45]

In short, women seem to be introducing a new style of management that, at least in some areas, may be better suited than the traditional one to modern employees and corporations.

Conclusion

We end this chapter with two wise comments from employees in our studies:

Talents and capabilities of women have always been great. Lack of recognition and self-worthiness keeps many women from development. (Hispanic, occupational, woman)

Women, like men, must realize they are able to achieve success. But it begins by knowing who she is and just how valuable her knowledge and contributions are. Self-esteem is the key to success. (White, occupational, woman)

Although U.S. law is progressive in its treatment of women, the U.S. workplace is by no means free of gender discrimination. Considering the growing number of women in the labor force, it makes good business sense to create work environments that fully encourage and utilize the talents of *all* employees.

United States:
Native Americans

While Native Americans are a small minority group in the United States, it is important to include them in any book on valuing differences. How the United States accepts and deals with the legitimate rights of Native Americans impacts on the nation's ability to become a truly fair, competitive, and diverse nation. While many Americans believe that Native Americans no longer exist as a distinct cultural group or that their problems have been solved, such a group does exist, and its treatment reflects our success or failure as a heterogeneous nation.

Historical Oppression of Native Americans

When Europeans arrived in the Americas, they found diverse Indian peoples who had populated the North and South continents for about 10,000 years. In North America, there were at least 200 tribes whose cultures varied greatly. Just over 150 years ago, Native Americans spoke 170 languages, few related. The Comanches, once an agricultural society in the mountains, became wandering warriors of the plains. The Mandans were a peaceful, communal, agricultural people; women owned all the land in their society. Their neighbors to the Northwest, the Blackfoot Indians, once an agricultural society, became fierce warriors like the Comanches and focused their lives around the buffalo hunt. Around the Great Lakes, there were the Potawatomis, who farmed, fished, and hunted. In contrast, Indians in the Southwest, like the Hopi, Navajo, and Apache tribes, had to learn how to use irrigation to survive. The Navajo, especially, lived in large settlements. In the East, where there was an abundance of food, elaborate systems of governance and cooperation existed among permanent settlements. The Iroquois Confederation was an excellent example of tribes with elaborate governance systems.[1]

The white settlers' treatment of the Native American population is a disgraceful story of murder, stealing, cheating, and lying to appropriate Indian land and resources. It is a credit to Native Americans that despite the devastation of their lands and cultures, they have survived to such an extent.

Competition for Indian land brought out racial stereotypes that supposedly justified stealing it. Berg has noted that as the Puritan population increased and its economic interest grew, it began to negatively change its conception of Native Americans. The whites' greed for land made the Native Americans victims of racism.[2]

After hundreds of treaties had been broken, most of their land stolen, their food supplies decimated, and their way of life destroyed, Native Americans became convinced that these treaties were not for their protection and best interests and they began to fight back. The fighting was ferocious and barbaric on both sides.

> Group by group, the Native Americans rose in rebellion only to be crushed—the Southern Plains tribes in 1874, the Sioux in 1876, the Nez Percé in 1877, and the Ute in 1879. The Apache tribe fought throughout much of the 1880s and 1890s until Geronimo finally surrendered with his remnant band of 36 survivors. The massacre of more than 300 Sioux, mostly women, children, and old people, at Wounded Knee, South Dakota, in 1890 marked the end of massive Native American resistance to white authority.[3]

All told, throughout the history of the whites and Native Americans, periods of peaceful coexistence were brief. From 1607 to the Wounded Knee massacre in 1890, the Native American population decreased from an estimated 2–5 million to 200,000. This was an attrition unmatched by the Black Plague, the Thirty Year War, or any modern war. During this period, about fifty out of two hundred Indian tribes disappeared.

Beyond this destruction, Native Americans at times were forced from their homes to be "civilized." White administrations developed programs that destroyed Indian values and religions, economic systems, political systems, and languages. In short, whites tried to forge an artificial amalgamation of hundreds of diverse and distinct Native American cultures. That these cultures could be regarded as a single one was a white people's idea, and because they possessed the power, they succeeded in making the concept a partial reality in the United States.

Following is an example of this forced adaptation to the majority white culture:

[From the late 1890s to the 1930s] tens of thousands of Native American children were "legally" kidnapped and forced to attend schools hundreds of miles from home. Often their parents could not pay for their transportation home during vacations, so the youngsters had to remain at school all year. The school curriculum made no concessions to the cultural history or needs of Native American children. Rather, it was designed and applied with the idea of eradicating all signs of Native American culture.[4]

The strength of the Native American peoples to resist majority-imposed values and culture has led the U.S. government to vacillate in its policies with regard to them. Policies have ranged in purpose from total integration of Native Americans into the cities and towns to their total isolation on reservations. More specifically, before 1887, most Indian people were settled on reservations. In 1887, the U.S. Congress passed the General Allotment Act (Dawes Act), whose purpose was to abandon a policy of separation and adopt a policy of blending Native Americans into the American mainstream. A key part of the act was to remove Indian children from their families and send them to schools. Another key part was to break up reservation lands into 160-acre individual farms in order to make Native American individuals self-sufficient. The final impact of the Dawes Act was to put valuable reservation land into white hands.

In 1934, the Indian Reorganization Act canceled and replaced the Dawes Act. It encouraged tribes to adopt constitutions to govern themselves. In the 1950s, the U.S. government returned to a policy of assimilation; it even tried to cancel the Indian constitutions. It encouraged Indians to move to cities/towns and to assimilate into the mainstream. Finally, in 1971, former President Richard Nixon returned to a self-determination policy, which was made into law by the Self-Determination Act of 1975.

Today, Native Americans still are one of the most oppressed people as well as among the poorest in the United States (23.7 percent live below the poverty level). The median income is $13,678, the lowest among racial minorities. Twenty-three percent of the homes are headed by females. Only 55.8 percent of those age twenty-five and older have completed high school, and 7.7 percent four or more years of college. Unemployment among Native Americans is more than ten times the national average, and as much as 90 percent of housing on some reservations is below health and safety standards. Fifty-six percent of Native Americans have no phones; 21 percent have no inside toilets, and 16 percent have no electricity. Finally, Native Americans are among the sickest in the country. They also have the highest rate of alcoholism and tuberculosis of any group in this country.[5]

The whites' desire to acquire Indian land and resources has never ceased, but Native Americans are now fighting back. As they fight back with guns and through the courts, they arouse a backlash motivated by profit. The 1.7 million Native Americans in a population of 249 million control 2 percent of the U.S. land mass. This includes much mineral-rich land whose importance has increased because of the energy crisis. Native American tribes own one-third of the country's easily accessible low-sulfur coal, one-half of its uranium, and substantial oil and natural gas deposits. Because of foreign-oil crises, these resources will become increasingly valuable in the future.

As noted in recent articles, Native Americans have won several favorable court decisions and settlements. These have dealt with matters as diverse as the right of a family to raise children on the reservation, rights to fish and hunt, the right to protect sacred ancestral lands, and rights to control water vital to the population and economic growth of the Southwest. Following are a number of examples:

- The sole Indian legislator in the Manitoba province of Canada filibustered important legislation to demonstrate

Indians' demand for more land, self-government, and educational improvement.

- The Passamaquorot and Penobscot successfully won an $81.5 million settlement against the state of Maine over a long-standing land dispute.
- The recent three-month standoff between the Canadian government and Mohawk Indians over the potential distur-bance of ancestral lands marks a new militancy.
- South Dakota Indians convinced the courts to rule that state highway patrols could not ticket Indians on their reservations. Also, a non-Indian family was placed in custody for several hours by reservation police because they were hunting too close to an Indian reservation.
- The U.S. Supreme Court recently ruled that the Shoshoni and Northern Arapaho tribes, under an 1868 treaty, have first rights to water on the Wind River. This gives them control over millions of chronically dry acres owned by whites.
- The Seneca Indians in New York State are demanding an increase in rent payments from $57,000 to $800,000 from residents of a town built 150 years ago on their reserva-tion.
- In Wisconsin, Chippewa Indians recently obtained the rights to log in state forests without paying state forest fees. They also in 1983 obtained the rights to fish and hunt freely in the northern third of Wisconsin.
- Because only 5 percent of county funds are spent on Native Americans' living areas in San Juan county, Utah, where Native Americans represent well over 50 percent of the county's population, Native Americans have developed a strong registration drive and all-Indian slate of officers to run for county seats.

It seems clear that Native Americans are developing a new consciousness about their rights and their culture. Is is important for the rest of the nation to recognize and appreciate what Na-tive Americans have contributed. For example, our governmental system of checks and balances was adapted in part from the Iroquois Confederation. As we become more concerned about our environment, we can learn from the Indian reverence for the earth. Finally, every time we eat corn and celebrate Thanksgiving, we can remember Indian help and hospitality.

Discrimination against Native Americans in the Workplace

As one might expect, because of population size and educational level, there are few Native Americans in U.S. companies. Those who have not assimilated into white society and who are dark-skinned are discriminated against more than those with light skins who have assimilated. Some stereotypes about Native Americans held by employees who took part in our seminars are that Indians are drunks, thieves, lazy, resentful and dogmatic; but also spiritual, stoic, independent, and respectful of nature.

One of the most perplexing findings in our 1976–78 study was that, despite their history of oppression by the U.S. government and people, Native Americans' responses to questions about equal employment opportunities, minorities, and treatment of women in their companies were more similar to whites' responses than to other minorities'. For example, in 1976–78, 11 percent of Native Americans, 10 percent of whites, and 57 percent of blacks believed that minorities are penalized more for work mistakes than whites are.

Undoubtedly, an operative factor in how workers are perceived in the workplace and how they perceive the company environment is the degree to which they identify with, and adopt the behavior and goals of, the majority culture. Our respondents may have been assimilated and may have seen themselves as a vanguard of their ethnic group who had had to work hard to attain their positions in the larger society; thus, they may have had little sympathy for other minority people who had not made it. We must remember that it was not until 1975 that the United States reversed a twenty-three-year-old policy of forced assimilation and that for sixty-seven years prior to 1934 a similar policy was followed. Millions of Americans who claim some degree of Indian ancestry do not profess an Indian identity. According to the U.S. government, only individuals who can demonstrate that they are biologically at least one-quarter Indian and who are actively associated with an American Indian tribe are officially recognized as Native Americans.

In 1988, when we asked the same questions, Native Americans' responses were more similar to those of other minority people, especially Asians and Hispanics, than to whites' responses. More specifically, 44 percent of Native Americans, 30 percent of Hispanics, 32 percent of Asians, 80 percent of blacks, and 14 percent of whites believed that minority workers are penalized more for work mistakes than white employees are.

Likely causes of this shift are: (1) that companies have become more vigorous in defining who is a Native American; (2) that Native Americans are becoming more aware of their situation in the United States since the government changed its policy in 1975 from encouraging assimilation to encouraging a return to cultural roots; and (3) as Native Americans have become more militant in their demands for fairness and their rights, they are more resented by members of the majority inside and outside the workplace.

A key problem some Native Americans face in corporate America, as we have determined from interviews and surveys over the years, is that, in general, their cultural style of dealing with people is the opposite of what succeeds in most bureaucracies. Almquist succinctly noted,

> Indians typically avoid several types of behavior that in white society are thought to be essential for "making it" in managerial and professional jobs. These behaviors include verbal manipulation, criticizing others. . . . Finally, most are reluctant to describe their personal problems or to seek assistance in solving them.[6]

Following are employees' comments from our studies that Native Americans have made about their situation in corporate America. Several reveal identification with the Native American ethnic group, but the last two suggest that the employees are responding as members of the white majority.

> I choose not to socialize with my non-Indian peers; my culture or orientation causes disagreement.
> (Native American, occupational, woman)

> For people who aspire to it—in seminars too many times minori-

ties are left out. The system is too Anglo-oriented. They should adopt some of our values—we would all be better off.
(Native American, occupational, man)

I am an American Indian and will speak my language with another person of the same tribe when other non-colored people are around; they get offended but it is my language.
(Native American, occupational, woman)

Several Indian employees believe nothing happens for American Indians in corporate America. They are the forgotten minority; the American Indian is overlooked.
(Native American, occupational, man)

Most Anglos are transferred around a lot to keep big salaries, but they don't do this for Indians.
(Native American, occupational, man)

When a person of color makes an error, an entire group of people is judged, not just the individual. This is unfair to American Indians and other people of color.
(Native American, lower-level, woman)

The company treats white men [like the respondent] like second-class citizens. They are saying "go the back of the bus."
(Native American, occupational, man)

I am an American Indian, but my culture is white.
(Native American, lower-level, man)

Conclusion

The history of Native Americans in the United States is one of which we cannot be proud. That the current conditions of Native Americans on reservations and, to a lesser extent, in the larger society are deplorable suggest that the United States still has a great deal to do to treat its minority citizens fairly.

If we as a nation do not learn to respect, appreciate, and value Native Americans' and other minorities' cultures, we will be in serious trouble in the new global village. We must appreciate the fact that Native Americans have the right to assimilate or to identify with their ancient and valuable culture. Whatever their choices, we must respect them. American society can learn from Native American culture and values.

United States:
Asian Americans

Much has been said about the success of Asian Americans. They are viewed as the "model minority." Nevertheless, they are faced with increasing discrimination as their numbers in the United States grow and as they begin to compete more vigorously with non-Asian Americans for education and jobs. The economic success of Japan has also brought out latent racism against Asians.

Over the years, American attitudes toward Asian groups have ebbed and flowed from positive to negative. Americans have been trained in the Western world view, which for centuries has feared and misunderstood Asia's various cultures and ethnic groups. Kotkin and Kishimoto note that Asians have been perceived as a threat as far back as the days of the Roman Empire. From these early days to the Middle Ages, "Europe lived in terror of Asiatic invaders." Western fears increased when the first Europeans to travel to Asian countries found their cultures to be far superior to the European culture, science, and societies. Let's not forget that the Chinese were the originators of paper, the printing press, and gunpowder. Kotkin and Kishimoto write, "Yet even after Europe's supremacy had been clearly established, Asia—its strange social and governmental systems, huge continental land mass and enormous population—loomed as a vague, dark threat in the European imagination. As early as 1873, English politicians fretted over the eventual industrialization of China as a potential challenge to European industrial supremacy.[1] Many Americans still operate from this historical fear toward Asians.

In this chapter, we focus on the three largest Asian groups in America: the Chinese, the Filipinos, and the Japanese. Before reviewing specified demographics, it is important to remember that before 1965, in all the major Asian groups, three out of four of immigrants coming to the United States were laborers. Since 1965, about 50 percent of Asian immigrants are highly skilled. This is due primarily to the change in the immigration law that gives preference to skilled immigrants and their family members. Note that, of the three groups only the Japanese have a majority of their current population native-born.

Another factor to keep in mind is that one of the reasons (besides education) for Asian Americans' higher family income on the average is that, generally, a larger number of family members work and contribute to family income; also, they are concentrated in states with high income levels. Nee and Sanders observed,

> Comparing the earnings of Asian Americans, who are concentrated in California, to whites, who more often reside in states where earnings are typically lower, gives the false impression of higher earnings for Asian Americans. In California, native-born whites typically report slightly higher earnings that native-born Chinese and Japanese Americans. Overall, Filipino Americans do not seem to be on the same road as Chinese and Japanese Americans. Filipinos' low income . . . appears to be consistent with a cost-of-ethnicity explanation.[2]

Filipinos are perceived by many Americans to be more like Hispanics than like typical Asians. Many are Roman Catholic, have Hispanic surnames, and are darker skinned than most Chinese and Japanese.

With these factors in mind, let's review Asian American demographics.[3]

Asian American Demographics

The trends for Asian immigration to the United States have varied a great deal over the past 140 years:

- Between 1851 and 1890, the largest group of Asian immigrants came from China.

- Between 1891 and 1930, the largest group of Asian immigrants came from Japan, but the greatest numbers immigrated before 1900.
- Between 1931 and 1950, few Asians immigrated to the United States because of racist immigration policies.
- Between 1951 and 1960, the Japanese were the largest Asian immigration group.
- Between 1961 and 1980, Filipinos were by far the largest group of Asian immigrants. During the same period a large number of Asian Indians, Koreans, and Vietnamese came to the United States.
- In 1985, the U.S. Asian population was 21 percent Chinese, 20 percent Filipino, 15 percent Japanese, 10 percent Asian Indian, 11 percent Korean, and 12 percent Vietnamese. In the 1990s Filipinos will be the largest group of Asian Americans, Chinese second, Vietnamese third.
- Asian Americans are 5.1 million people, or 2.1 percent of the population. By the year 2000 their numbers will be about 9 million.
- The percentages of Asian Americans who are foreign-born are 28 percent of Japanese, 62 percent of Chinese, 65 percent of Filipinos, 70 percent of Asian Indians, 82 percent of Koreans, and 91 percent of Vietnamese.
- Asians in the United States represent 4.1 percent of professionals and 3.2 percent of technicians but only 1.4 percent of managers in 1985.
- In the United States, 96 percent of Japanese, 94 percent of Asian Indians and Koreans, 90 percent of Chinese, 89 percent of Filipinos, and 87 percent of whites have completed high school.
- Sixteen percent of native-born white Americans age twenty-five and older have college degrees compared to 52 percent of Asian Indians, 37 percent of Filipinos, 26 percent of Japanese, 34 percent of Koreans, 36 percent of mainland Chinese, and 13 percent of Vietnamese.
- Of various ethnic groups in the United States, the Japanese have the highest average annual family income, $35,207, followed by Asian Indians, $29,961; Filipinos, $28,514;

Chinese, $28,377; non-Hispanic whites, $26,535; Koreans, $25,234; and Vietnamese, $15,859.

- The percentages of Asian Americans living below the poverty level are 4.2 percent of Japanese, 6.2 percent of Filipinos, 7.4 percent of Asian Indians, 10.5 percent of Chinese, 13.1 percent of Koreans, and 35.1 percent of Vietnamese.
- The percentages of female heads of households are 5.7 percent of Asian Indians, 8.5 percent of Chinese, 10.8 percent of Koreans, 11.8 percent of Filipinos, 11.9 percent of Japanese, and 14.8 percent of Vietnamese.
- There are extreme differences in the English language proficiency level of Asian Americans. The following percentages of these groups report they are very proficient in English: Asian Indians, 80 percent; Japanese 78 percent; Filipinos, 69 percent; Chinese, 50 percent; Koreans, 34 percent; and Vietnamese, 22 percent.

These demographics clearly show differences among groups in the United States who are considered Asian. With this in mind, we review the brief history of the Chinese, Japanese, and Filipinos in the United States.

Chinese Americans

The 1849 Gold Rush brought the first large influx of Chinese into California. As did other minorities, the Chinese came to the United States to find a life better than the depressed conditions they had left in their native country. Most of these Chinese, in the early stages of immigration, were recruited to work as miners and railroad laborers.

Initially, Chinese laborers shipped to California in the nineteenth century were locked into the holds of ships. Many suffocated or starved to death. Others stabbed themselves with pieces of wood or hung themselves. Yet, despite such tragic conditions, the Chinese population in the United States, almost exclusively in California, between 1850 and 1880 increased from approximately one thousand people to one hundred thousand.[4]

While the Chinese population was increasing, economic conditions in California were worsening. As early as 1852, the governor of California recommended that action be taken to stem the tide of "the yellow peril." The Chinese became targets of racism. These people, who had been regarded as desirable workers because they were a cheap and efficient source of labor, were subjected to the most outrageous expressions of bigotry.[5]

Not only were they stoned, robbed, assaulted, and murdered, but they were also the victims of discriminatory legislation. Political clubs were formed to force Chinese to go back to China. In 1882, the U.S. Congress passed the Exclusion Act. This was an anti-immigration law directed against the Chinese. It was the first U.S. law passed to restrict immigration on the basis of national origin. In 1900, at a rally in San Francisco, a sociology professor at Stanford University said, "These Asiatic laborers will undermine our civilization" and "The Chinese and Japanese are not the stuff of which American citizens can be made."

The Exclusion Act was renewed for another ten years in 1892 and extended indefinitely in 1902. The act was not repealed until 1943, when it was replaced by a new act allowing only 105 Chinese to enter the United States each year. This seems a less than magnanimous quota considering the important role the Chinese played in the Japanese defeat in World War II.

Another example of racism is found in the 1927 U.S. Supreme Court decision in the case of *Gong Lum v. Rice*. The court upheld the right of local school boards to force Chinese students to attend minority schools miles from their neighborhoods instead of permitting them to attend predominantly white schools in their own neighborhoods.[6] Other laws were passed barring interracial marriages between whites and blacks, Chinese, Mongolians, or Orientals. These laws were not overturned by the U.S. Supreme Court until 1967.

During World War II, the image of China and Chinese people changed to that of a valiant wartime ally holding their own against vastly superior Japanese forces.

After the war, while mainland China turned to Communism and fought the United States in the Korean War, Nationalist China was still a respected ally and became a valuable U.S. trading partner. These two Chinese nations greatly influenced

American attitudes toward the Chinese, both negatively and positively. More recently, the normalization of relations between the United States and mainland China has eliminated most negative attitudes Americans have toward the Chinese. In fact, as our trade with China increases, the need for Chinese employees is crucial. A number of U.S. companies have secured lucrative contracts from China because of the skills of their Chinese employees.[7]

At present, Chinese Americans are seen as a "model minority," an excellent example of an American success story. However, in reality, many Chinese Americans still suffer from racial discrimination. And their social problems—poverty, illiteracy, disease, broken families—have not entirely disappeared.

Japanese Americans

Between 1638 and 1868, few Japanese came to the United States, primarily because the Japanese government did not allow its citizens to emigrate. It was not until 1884 that Japan allowed laborers to emigrate. Almost all anti-Asian attitudes in the 1890s were directed against the Chinese, not the Japanese. In the late 1880s, as the demand for cheap labor increased and the Chinese, who had provided an abundant source of such labor, were prevented from immigrating to the United States, U.S. employers encouraged Japanese people to immigrate. While these new Asians were not warmly welcomed, because of the racism that had developed toward the Chinese, the need for labor and the characteristics of Japanese culture made the Japanese acceptable to white Americans. Marden and Meyer point out,

> The authoritarian character of Japanese social organization produced markedly obedient and self-effacing personality traits. The strong sense of subordination of the individual to the welfare of the group was reflected in the solidarity of Japanese subcommunities in this country. To conform punctiliously to elaborate social rituals was a major drive in the Japanese personality, accounting for the reputation for courtesy and good manners which the nineteenth-century Japanese acquired.[8]

In 1890, only several thousand Japanese were in the United

States. However, by 1900, there were around one hundred thousand, and this increase and the resulting competition with whites quickly kindled racist attitudes and behavior. As early as 1890, white male union members were participating in physically violent racism. Marden and Meyer give an example:

> Japanese cobblers were attacked by members of the shoemakers' union. In 1892, a Japanese restaurant in San Francisco was attacked by members of the local cooks' and waiters' union. From then on, anti-Japanese activity grew steadily in California, rising to a climax in the famous School Board Affair in 1906, when the San Francisco board of education passed a resolution requiring the segregation of all oriental children in one school. At the time, there were ninety-three Japanese attending twenty-three different public schools in San Francisco.[9]

Other racist incidents occurred. In 1905, the Hearst newspapers launched a major attack upon the Japanese. In 1907, President Theodore Roosevelt stopped Japanese immigration from Hawaii, Canada, and Mexico. He negotiated the famous Gentlemen's Agreement with the Japanese government that sought to put an end to Japanese immigration. However, these measures did little to halt the tide of Japanese immigration and anti-Japanese prejudice.[10]

With the antagonism toward them increasing in the cities, the Japanese Americans turned to farming. However, their success in this endeavor again posed an economic threat to whites. The California legislature responded by passing restrictive legislation regarding alien landholding. The first law, in 1913, said aliens who could not become citizens could lease land for no longer than three years, and they could not own it. Marden and Meyer note that when it was discovered that Japanese were buying stock in land-owning corporations and acquiring land in the names of their native-born children, a new law was passed, which in substance prohibited the leasing of land by any method to foreign-born Japanese. Similar laws were passed by other western states. Their constitutionality was upheld by the U.S. Supreme Court in a test case in 1923.[11]

The wave of racism against the Japanese culminated in the Johnson Immigration Act of 1924, which banned the immigration of persons who were ineligible for citizenship. This act was directly aimed at the Japanese and was not repealed until 1952. Throughout this period, Japanese Americans discovered that college degrees, a good work ethic, and middle-class values did not guarantee them first-class American citizenship.[12]

Anti-Japanese feeling intensified after Japan attacked Pearl Harbor in 1941. Japanese Americans, of whom seventy thousand were native-born American citizens, were interned in "relocation centers," although this violated their constitutional rights. Lt. General John L. De Witt, commander of the Western Defense Command, gave this "justification" for this action:

> In the war in which we are now engaged, racial affinities are not severed by migration. The Japanese race is an enemy race, and while many second- and third-generation Japanese born on United States soil, possessed of United States citizenship, have become Americanized, the racial strains are undiluted. . . . It therefore follows that along the vital Pacific Coast over 112,000 potential enemies of Japanese extraction are at large today. There are disturbing indications that these are organized and ready for concerted action at a favorable opportunity. *The very fact that no sabotage has taken place to date is a disturbing and confirming indication that such action will be taken.*[13] [Italics supplied]

Japanese Americans were sent to the Midwest and to the East Coast. Others joined the U.S. military to fight in Europe. Many Japanese who did not volunteer were drafted. In the exploitative tradition of racism, the same individuals who were locked up and denied constitutional rights were also subject to the military draft as citizens. The drafted Japanese Americans were placed in a segregated unit in Europe, where they distinguished themselves as one of the most-decorated units in any branch of the services. Others taught at U.S. Army language schools or worked for U.S. intelligence.[14]

Despite this shameful treatment, Japanese Americans remained more determined than ever to prove themselves and to succeed. This determination generated one of the most remarkable processes of upward mobility in U.S. history. The economic, educational, and professional achievements of Japanese Americans rank as high as, or perhaps higher than, those of any other ethnic group.

Filipino Americans

As a result of the Spanish-American War, the United States gained control of the Philippine Islands. It set out to Americanize the Islands, and English became the first language of many Filipinos. Part of the strategy was to educate a cadre of Filipinos in U.S. universities so that they could return to the Islands and assist in Americanizing it. By 1938, about 15,000 Filipinos had come to the United States to study under the Pensionado Plan, as this strategy was known.

When Japanese immigration was stopped by the Gentlemen's Agreement, the U.S. demand for cheap farm labor, especially in California, greatly increased the immigration of Filipinos. These early immigrants, mostly young unmarried men, were uneducated and had poor language skills in both Spanish and English. After working in the United States for a period of time, about half of them returned to the Philippines.

Over the years, Filipinos were stereotyped as being primitive, immoral, belligerent, unhealthy, and not smart. An Asian people, the Filipinos were ineligible for U.S. citizenship, and most of the anti-Asian laws, while directed against Chinese and Japanese immigrants, applied in most cases to Filipinos. In 1902, the Cooper Act said that Filipinos could exercise "all the privileges of American citizens," except the right to vote, to become citizens, to join the military, to own real estate, and so on. Filipinos did carry American passports, and could freely enter and leave the United States, but one must wonder what other privileges they actually did get.[15]

In 1918, the United States did offer any Filipino who served in the U.S. Navy or Marines for three years (they could only be stewards) the right to petition for U.S. citizenship.

Except for the previous concession, Filipinos were excluded from many professions and from the political process. They also could not marry whites until 1933, when California courts ruled that Filipinos did not fall under the anti-miscegenation law. Filipinos were considered Malayan, not Asian; however, the state legislature then passed a new law prohibiting Malayans from marrying whites. This law was overturned fifteen years later.

Anti-Filipino feelings surfaced in the 1920s and 1930s as whites saw Filipino Americans competing for jobs. On many occasions, whites attacked farms where Filipinos worked, burned their homes, and beat and killed them. In 1934, the Tydings McDuffie Act established a quota of only fifty Filipino immigrants per year and set a date for Philippine independence for 1944. This came about in 1946.[16]

Except for being stewards in the U.S. Navy or Marines, Filipinos were excluded from the military until 1942, when an all-Filipino battalion, led by white officers, was formed.

Filipino Americans are not viewed as a "model minority" and have met with perhaps more discrimination than Chinese and Japanese Americans because on the whole Filipinos are darker-skinned.

In concluding this overview of the Chinese, Japanese, and Filipino American experience, it is clear that the majority population accepts Asian minorities when they are needed to perform certain jobs, particularly those that majority workers do not want to do, and rejects or discriminates against them when they are perceived as no longer filling the economic needs of the majority society.

Current Discrimination against Asian Americans

At present, especially on the West Coast, in large East Coast cities, and in the Texas area, a trend of rising anti-Asian feeling is evident, in part because of the large influx of Asians after the immigration laws were changed to be more equitable and in part because of the successes of many Asian American immigrants. Another factor contributing to the increase in anti-Asian incidents is the economic success of Japan and, to a lesser extent, South Korea and Nationalist China in world markets. Loss of jobs to these countries and the importation of a large number of Asian goods have fueled negative reactions to *all* Asian Americans. Many non-Asian Americans do not distinguish among the different Asian minorities. A case in point was the death of a Chinese man in the Detroit area several years ago at the hands of an irate auto worker who thought the young man was Japanese.

In a recent survey conducted by the author, a majority of white respondents expressed hostile attitudes toward the Japanese; they made little distinction between native-born or foreign-born Japanese. In Rye, New York, some white parents removed their children from public schools because there were "too many Japanese children" in the classes. Many Japanese Americans in the New York City area, including some veterans of the Vietnam War, have reported an increase in anti-Japanese feelings. In Philadelphia, Chicago, and New York, black and Hispanic youths attacked Korean store owners; other Asian Americans have been attacked and reviled by blacks, Hispanics, and whites for no reason other than that they were Asians. Numerous articles have been written about Asians being attacked because they are Asian or are thought to be from a specific Asian group.

Asian Americans in the Workplace

Co-workers' Perceptions of Asian American Employees

Participants in our studies and seminars stereotype Asian Americans as diligent, smart, well-organized, motivated, well-educated, respectful, and family-oriented, but also as passive, quiet, short, humble, clannish, reserved, submissive, and sneaky. Despite the fact that high percentages of Asian Americans say they are fluent in English, the most frequent problem employees voice with regard to Asian co-workers is difficulties with language. They are also ill at ease with the different cultural characteristics. Following are some representative comments from our surveys of employees.

> Talk slowly and precisely to people with foreign accents. Don't trust groups that tend to be quiet [Orientals].
> (White, occupational, woman)

> I get impatient with cultures that cannot express themselves in the English language. The Chinese do not write documents with proper grammar. I feel I should not have to be subjected to reading these.
> (White, lower-level, woman)

> I have to work extra hard to work with an Asian female in my group and at understanding their [Asians'] contributions. They are very quiet and will do any task I ask without question, so I have

to make sure I go out of my way to get their feedback. This is frustrating because I prefer to work with forthright people who tell me what's on their mind. (White, lower-level, man)

Asians seem to take a "back seat" role when they could be more influential. They seem to work too much as a team.
(White, middle-level, man)

I feel that Oriental people do not lead effectively and communicate forcefully. I feel that Indian people are not articulate leaders.
(White, upper-level, man)

I hate to see "political behavior," which seems to be very prominent among Asians in the company, especially East Indians. I tend to view many things they do as political moves.
(Black, lower-level, man)

I don't like to be around anyone with personal hygiene problems. Unfortunately, this seems to apply to Orientals, Asians, though not all. (Black, occupational, woman)

I socialize rarely with Asians, because I'm afraid of making a mistake. (White, occupational, woman)

These comments indicate numerous potential areas of conflict between Asian and non-Asian Americans in corporate America.

Asian Americans' Perceptions of Problems Created by Discrimination

Many Asian American employees agree that their culture does not emphasize the aggressiveness, boastfulness, or outgoingness that they perceive are necessary to be properly rewarded in U.S. companies. On the other hand, some also say that success obtained through their emphasis on education, skills, and hard work is sometimes resented as well. They also agree that their use of English creates difficulties with non-Asian co-workers, despite the fact that they themselves feel they have mastered the language. Following are some comments from Asian American employees on how they perceive interaction in the workplace.

Communication with Americans is not very easy, since I didn't grow up here. Many times during conversations, I am reminded that I don't totally belong here. (Asian, middle-level, man)

I feel white males ignored me when I want to put my ideas or opinions forward in a meeting. Very hard for the outside world to believe that I am a technical person because of my lack of ability to speak in American English, though I have good English knowledge. (Asian, lower-level woman)

People here do not know how to discover the potential and ability of people who are simply modest. Everything here has to be vocal and visible. (Asian, lower-level, man)

My language, my size, my way of expressing myself—too direct; when asking other people to work, I was labeled too demanding; I am perceived as aggressive when acting assertive.
(Asian, lower-level, female)

My peers regard outstanding education and performance by a person of color as a threat to them. (Asian, lower-level, man)

We are more close-knit. We work harder and value things differently. (Asian, middle-level, man)

I sometimes find myself associating more with Asians in the work environment, because of fear. (Asian, lower-level, man)

When one compares the Asian American employees' responses about perceptions of discrimination in 1976–78 and in 1988, several interesting findings emerge. In 1976–78 they responded more like the white employees than like black or Hispanic respondents. For example, in 1976–78, the percentages who said at least four out of five elements of racism existed in their companies were Asians, 12 percent; whites, 9 percent; Native Americans, 7 percent; Hispanics, 20 percent; and blacks, 48 percent. However, in 1988, when we analyzed responses to three of the same questions, we found that Asian Americans responded more like other minorities than like white respondents. As an illustration, 44 percent of Asians, 52 percent of Native Americans, 41 percent of Hispanics, 83 percent of blacks, and 27 percent of whites believe minority managers must be better performers than white managers to get ahead.

Dr. Chalsa Loo, associate professor of psychology at San Francisco State University, notes that cultural differences may also explain the different responses: traditionally Asians are trained to be respectful of authority. She also notes in evaluating these data that Asian Americans may want to show themselves in a good light and to be seen as responsible, diligent, and nonresistant. She believes they may be disguising their feelings or frustration and discontent because it is more socially acceptable to be positive toward company policies. Expanding on these points, she writes,

> Culturally and traditionally, Asian Americans have tried to avoid confrontation with the Anglo society and Anglo authority, this being a means of survival in this country for them. . . . Historically, many feared that conspicuousness or resistance would result in harsher racist reactions from white Americans; thus their tendency to keep a low profile, accept whatever is handed to them, have few expectations of fairness and generosity from Anglos, be acquiescent toward authority, and work hard. . . . Through the product of one's work, one gains acceptance into American society. Intelligence and hard work are means of reducing or ameliorating attitudes of racism towards Asian Americans.[17]

Asian Americans' Perceptions of Other Ethnic Groups

Asian Americans too have expressed prejudices about people who are different than they are. In other words, just like any other group, they hold stereotypes that get in the way of their dealing with non-Asians. The following comments illustrate this.

> I have a problem when someone can't communicate and describe precisely what he or she means. I lose interest. I could be lenient to the progress of my wife if she got a more time-consuming job. I feel that sometimes women are not that hard-working.
> (Asian, lower-level, man)

> I have a very strong and negative impression over blacks. I know it is not right, but it is my impression over a group of blacks. That is one thing I'll have to deal with. (Asian, occupational, woman)

I tend to be intolerant with people with different life styles, for example, gays. (Asian, occupational, woman)

I must learn more about other religions. Although I have said that I respect the other religious people, I need to get to know more about African culture. I have to work on how to be more considerate and patient with the foreign accents. (Asian, lower-level, man)

I tend to judge people based on my own type of behavior and cultural norms, and have difficulty with some other types of behavior [especially loud/animated behavior].
(Asian, lower-level, woman)

I have this perception of white males in this country being too individualistic and for self-improvement without giving much attention to family concerns and others. (Asian, occupational, man)

Fear of having a woman boss. Some people I interact with do not understand me because I am an Asian male.
(Asian, middle-level, man)

I must understand that people not like me are simply different, not necessarily wrong or inferior. I think I should be more outgoing and try to learn more about others. (Asian, lower-level, man)

I feel blacks look down upon Asians/foreigners more than whites, so I tend to treat them just the way they treat me—a bit inferior.
(Asian, lower-level, man)

I have trouble understanding people who speak differently. I resent benefits available to minorities that are not available to me. I have low tolerance for foreign people who do not know how to drive.
(Asian, occupational, man)

I tend to be aggressive and brisk, hence am sometimes perceived as insensitive to women and minorities. Have been brought up in a macho environment, hence tend to relate to the more aggressive males in a group and sometimes ignore the more timid people. I tend to reach out to the power structure in a group to get support, since I may feel an inner need for support.
(Asian, lower-level, man)

We see that some Asian Americans have a host of dislikes for other people because of gender, language, culture, religion, and race. That these attitudes create problems for co-workers are demonstrated by the following comments.

I feel Indian/Oriental males don't value my opinion. Therefore, I tend to minimize interaction with these groups.
(White, middle-level, woman)

I have been affected by having an insensitive, biased (against blacks, black females, and Asian females) manager. I now feel I have to work harder when a male Asian is on the team to prove that I belong. (Black, lower-level, woman)

My Asian Indian supervisor does not believe that blacks are technically competent. (Black, lower-level, man)

I believe my Asian peers talk in their language about me. I get very upset! (White, lower-level man)

Asians act like they are taking over! They have a superiority complex. (White, middle-level, man)

Conclusion

Over the years, both positive and negative attitudes have been directed by Americans toward Asians. This minority group has sometimes been seen as a "model minority." However, as their numbers and their economic success increase, it is predictable that anti-Asian discrimination will increase.

It is important for the United States to recognize that as Asian countries increase their economic power, Asian Americans will be a valuable resource in assisting U.S. companies to form positive economic ties with Asian nations. But to take advantage of this resource that Asian Americans provide, we must deal with our racism and ethnocentrism, just as they must deal with their prejudices.

United States:
Black Americans

The minority group known as African Americans will comprise about one out of seven people in the United States by the year 2000. The umbrella name African American is often applied to several multiracial, multicultural, and multilingual groups— native-born people of African descent and immigrants from Africa and the West Indies whose languages are English, French, Spanish, Portuguese, Creole, or Swahili. These groups share one salient characteristic that defines their experience in U.S. society—they are dark-skinned. The majority society often does not distinguish one black American group from another, just as it does not distinguish among the different Asian ethnic groups.

Black Americans will become increasingly important to the economic success of the United States, not only as workers and entrepreneurs but also as consumers. They are also holding a larger share of political offices and becoming politically more astute and sophisticated. Another area of importance for black Americans in this decade is the role they can play in helping the United States to succeed in expanding African markets.

The legal rights and fair treatment of African Americans in U.S. society have improved, particularly since the 1960s, but there is still much to be done to eliminate discrimination by the white majority. Many of the problems black Americans face stem from discrimination, but some have to do with their own communities themselves.

Black American Demographics

Following are some key demographic trends.[1]

- In the year 2000, African Americans will represent at least 14.2 percent of the U.S. population.
- African Americans will represent 18 percent of the labor force growth between now and the year 2000.
- Black median income was $18,122 in 1980 and $18,098 in 1988. White median income was $32,003 in 1980 and $32,274 in 1988.
- Black Americans making less than $25,000 per year were 66.5 percent in 1980 and 65.1 percent in 1988. White Americans in the same category were 36.2 percent in 1980 and 36.3 percent in 1988. About one-third of black Americans live below the poverty level.
- Black and white Americans are currently graduating from high school at about the same rate (over 80 percent).
- African Americans are being elected to more local political offices: 300 in 1964; 1,469 in 1970; and 7,873 in 1989.

These demographics suggest that the African American population will grow and that in some areas it has made progress. However, the following sections suggest that equal participation in the majority society is still a goal rather than a reality for most black Americans.

Brief History of Oppression of Black Americans

Racism against black Americans as we see it in the United States today had its origins in the sixteenth century. The biblical story of Noah's curse on his grandson Canaan, "Cursed be Canaan, a slave of slaves shall he be to his brothers," was used by some to justify racism against black people. Canaan, according to the Bible, was the progenitor of the early Egyptians and other African tribes.

Just as male predominance is embedded in the English language, so are negative associations with the word *black*: it is associated in Western culture with evil, sin, death, despair, and ugliness, while *white* connotes purity, goodness, and holiness.

Schwartz and Disch state that the English colonists brought to the New World an association with the word *black* that "became important . . . in first defining and later justifying the status they desired for the non-white. Before the close of the fifteenth century, the words *soiled* and *dirty* first became linked with *black*. By 1536, *black* connotated 'dark purposes, malignant, deadly,'; by 1581, 'foul, iniquitous'; by 1588, 'baneful, disastrous, and sinister.' "[2] Jordan states that these negative associations with *black* preceded any contact between the English and Black Africa.[3] The negative connotations of *black* survive today in words like black eye, blacklist, blackball, and black knight (unfriendly takeover of a corporation) and, for instance, in the convention of the villain wearing a black hat and the hero wearing a white one.

Early U.S. legislators expressed racism in practice as well as in thought. The preamble to South Carolina's code of 1712 said that blacks are "barbarous, wild, savage and . . . they must be governed by special laws as may restrain the disorders . . . and inhumanity to which they are naturally inclined."[4] The tension created by the presence of a large downtrodden black population in a nation founded on democratic ideals of equality has haunted American dialogue, ideas, and leaders for more than three hundred years. Thomas Jefferson believed that a harmonious biracial society was inconceivable. "Deep-rooted prejudice entertained by the whites," he wrote, and "ten thousand recollections, by the blacks, of the injuries they have sustained," combine to make equal, peaceful coexistence between blacks and whites impossible. Jefferson believed that freed black and white people could end up in a conflict that would lead to "the extermination of the one or the other race."[5] Sixty years after South Carolina's code, when the U.S. Constitution was first written, a black man counted as only three-fifths of a white man for apportionment purposes; black women were not counted at all. Almost a century later, Chief Justice B. Taney wrote in his opinion of the Dred Scott case (1857):

> The question before us is whether the class of persons described in the plea for abatement compose a portion of this people and are constituent members of this sovereignty. We think they are not,

and that they are not included, and were not intended to be included, under the words *citizens* in the Constitution. . . . They were at the time considered as a subordinate and inferior class of beings, who had been subjugated by the dominant race, and whether emancipated or not, yet remained subject to their authority and had no rights or privileges but such as those who held the power and the government might choose to grant them.[6]

Such anti-black interpretation continued until the Thirteenth, Fourteenth, and Fifteenth Amendments to the Constitution granted black Americans equal rights of freedom, due process, and the vote. Higginbotham quotes from Mark Twain's parody in *The Adventures of Huckleberry Finn* to show that "as late as 1884 many white Americans still failed to perceive blacks as human beings." This is the dialogue:

Good gracious. Anybody hurt?
No'm. Killed a nigger.
Well it's lucky, because sometimes people do get hurt. . . .[7]

During this same period, the Ku Klux Klan reemerged, terrorizing and murdering blacks throughout the South and border states.

Thirty years after the Civil War, the U.S. Supreme Court ruled in *Plessy v. Ferguson* that "separate but equal" facilities were permissible. As with other minority groups, job competition was a major reason that white people developed racist attitudes toward African Americans. The fear that African Americans would compete for white jobs dates back even to slavery days. This fear has ebbed and flowed with the existing economic situation. Wilson describes the situation as follows:

In the antebellum North, where a more industrial system of production enabled white workers to become more concentrated and better organized, laws of racial oppression, especially in the nineteenth century, increasingly reflected the interest of the white working class. The demise of northern slavery was quickly followed by laws to eliminate black competition, particularly economic competition. However, the economy of the South gradually drifted toward industrial capitalism. In the last quarter of the nineteenth century, the white working classes were finally able to exert some influence on the form and content of racial stratification. White working class efforts to eliminate black competition generated an elaborate system of Jim Crow segregation that was reinforced by an ideology of biological racism.[8]

The "separate but equal" doctrine allowed states, especially southern states, to legalize the system of Jim Crow that effectively put many black Americans back into slavery, but legally.

During World Wars I and II, the lack of sufficient labor opened up opportunities previously closed to African Americans. However, they still faced racial discrimination in all aspects of their lives. Earning a living became easier during World War II, but racist constraints on how and where one lived and spent one's money remained as strong as ever.

McLemore observed, "The continuation of conspicuous discrimination in the midst of still another global war 'to make the world safe for democracy' enraged many African Americans. Two forms of discrimination were particularly galling, discrimination in war production and in the armed forces."[9]

Throughout the military services, Jim Crow practices were common. And since many military training camps were in the South, black servicemen faced segregation when they left the camps. They were frequently in danger of physical assault, not only by local citizens but by officers of the law as well. "For instance, a black soldier was shot in Little Rock, Arkansas, because he would not tip his hat and say 'sir' to a policeman. Another African American soldier was shot by two police officers because he had taken a bus seat reserved for a white in Beaumont, Texas. In Centerville, Mississippi, a sheriff obligingly shot a black soldier in the chest merely because a white MP asked him to."[10]

It was not until 1954 that the separate but equal doctrine was reversed, at least in education, in *Brown v. Board of Education*. Chief Justice Warren, speaking for the court, argued that to separate children "from others of similar age and qualifications solely because of their race generates a feeling of inferiority as to their status in the community that may affect their hearts and minds in a way unlikely ever to be undone. . . . We conclude that in the field of public education the doctrine of 'separate but equal' has no place.[11]

The 1950s and early 1960s saw the emergence of the civil rights movement led by Martin Luther King. It also saw the emergence of a new militant faction led by the Black Panther Party. While their tactics differed, the King-led movement and the Panther-led movement were both fighting for the true freedom of black Americans. These movements had tremendous impact on the next phase of the fight for racial equality. With the Civil Rights Acts of 1964 and 1965, African Americans and other minority people were legally given equal access to work, public accommodations, and so on.

Much racism has been founded in our academic institutions. In September 1990 a group of Harvard Law School students took their school to court, accusing the law school of hiring practices that discriminated against black women and other minorities.

One of the most suspect concepts coming out of academia is the suggestion that African Americans as a group are intellectually inferior by reason of heredity. The scientist William Schockley, one of the inventors of the transistor, was noted for his claim that I.Q. tests prove black Americans to be intellectually inferior to white Americans. He suggested that black people with an I.Q. below 100 have themselves sterilized.

Thomas and Sillen give the opinion that in the psychiatric and behavioral sciences, "students, research workers, and professionals—like members of the clergy and educators—are no more immune by virtue of their values and training to the disease and superstitions of American racism than is the average man."[12]

While African Americans made progress throughout the 1950s and 1960s, the rate slowed considerably in the 1970s. During the mid-1960s, black people in this country had a strong feeling of change in conventional racial patterns. This feeling was expressed in both their perception of increased contact with white people and their sense of "real change" in their situation. This sense of change for the better, which seemed strong during the 1960s, diminished during the 1970s and reversed in the 1980s.

Current Discrimination against Black Americans

Today, overt and covert racist acts still occur daily against black Americans. The expectation of continuing progress toward equality was not fulfilled in the 1980s, as evidenced by a variety of publicized events and statistics.

- In 1978, 30 percent of black Americans were living below the poverty level; in 1988, 33.1 percent were.
- In 1988, black median family income was $18,098, which was 56 percent of white median income.
- Congressional hearings recently confirmed that black Americans are rejected for mortgages twice as often as white Americans, even when income and other relevant factors are equivalent.
- Life expectancy of white Americans reached a record high in 1989 of 74.8 years; that of black Americans decreased to 69.4 years.
- A recent study found that black Americans are less likely than white Americans to receive coronary bypasses and kidney transplants, even allowing for equivalent income, insurance coverage, and state of health.
- Another study found that as a result of previous generations of poverty, black middle-class women are twice as likely as white middle-class women to have children of low birth weight.
- Black American men under forty-five years of age are ten times as likely as white American men to die of hypertension.
- In Los Angeles county, where black Americans make up 13.8 percent of the school population, blacks were victims of racial attacks 624 times in a year.
- In September 1990, at the Yale Law School, black law students received hate mail with racial slurs.
- According to leading criminal trial lawyers, at least 3 percent of white people convicted of crimes are innocent, compared with 20 percent of African Americans.
- The F.B.I. recently settled out of court a suit filed by a black agent who alleged racial harassment by his white peers and supervisors.

- In Wellesley, Massachusetts, a well-known black player of the Boston Celtics and his white girlfriend were forced by almost a dozen police officers, half with drawn guns, to lie down on the pavement because he "looked like a robber."
- Boston police, media, and the public were excoriated for being so quick to believe Charles Stuart, a white man, when he said that a black man had robbed and murdered his pregnant wife, Carol Stuart, while their car was stopped at a traffic light. It later came out that Stuart himself had shot his wife and blamed it on a black man.

These examples show the variety of ways racism impacts on the African American community. While some similarities exist between the social history of African Americans and those of other minorities in the United States, there are some crucial differences. The dual liabilities of a history of slavery and dark skin color have made their climb toward equality steeper and more arduous. To emphasize the violence and oppression visited upon African American people in the United States is not to ignore the discrimination other minority groups have suffered but rather to argue that the African American experience has been different in kind, not just in degree, from that of any other U.S. minority group. Kovel has noted that of all the various exclusions practiced in the United States—including those based on religion, sex, age, national origins, and economic status— none approaches in strength that of African Americans by white people, "the distinction of superior self and inferior other according to race, particularly as is revealed by the mark of skin color.[13]

The majority society in the United States has never wanted to be black. Unfortunately, African Americans, particularly those who have no other national identification, whose ancestors have lived in the United States for many generations, have incorporated this majority view as a negative self-concept. Thus, they have suffered a violation not only of their outer world (equal opportunities for safety, livelihood, education, and so on) but also of their inner psychological space. It took the Black Power and Black Is Beautiful spirit of the 1960s and 1970s to reverse this negative self-concept to a certain extent.

Pettigrew wrote that approximately 15 percent of white adults in the United States are vehemently racist out of authoritarian impulses. Another 40 percent are "conforming bigots," who reflect racist norms that remain as historical vestiges even as they embrace the newer, equalitarian norms. Only about 25 percent of white adults predictably support equal rights and fair treatment for people of color and refrain from exhibiting anti-black behavior under most circumstances. These strong anti-black feelings are based on a variety of stereotypes that are still held, even by many sophisticated white people and some minority groups.[14]

Of all minority people, African Americans are least likely to have positive stereotypes applied to them. Sociologist Leonard Gordon, in a comparative study of traits attributed to black Americans by white college students, found that from the 1930s to the 1960s the number of negative traits decreased greatly; however, in the 1980s they increased and new stereotypes emerged such as loud, aggressive, and sly.

Black Americans in the Workplace

Employees' Perceptions of Black Americans

In our studies and seminars from 1988 to 1990, employees described black Americans stereotypically as being poor, defensive, paranoid, antagonistic, aggressive, bitter, emotional, loud, pushy, inconsiderate, lazy, dumb, drug dealers, criminals, and welfare recipients. Positive stereotypes were that African Americans are rhythmic, good dancers, good athletes, proud, smart, and hard-working.

Meanwhile, African American employees used the following adjectives to describe their own group: poor, proud, good athletes, paranoid, "together," hard-working, smart, and discriminated against. Lambert and Taylor cite a survey in which African Americans saw others of their own group as being smart, wanting to succeed, unfairly treated, likable, intelligent, and practical but also as aggressive and untrustworthy.[15]

The following comments from employees in our studies and seminars reveal that the respondents hold negative stereotypes about African Americans, although there is some evidence that they are aware of the need to stop stereotyping.

I am afraid of black males, particularly dark-skinned, until I have an opportunity to get to know them as a person.
(White, middle-level, woman)

I was raised to fear black Americans without any direct experiences of my own to support this fear. (White, middle-level, man)

I have to overcome the fear I have when I walk in a black community. (Asian, middle-level, man)

I basically believe that the African American culture, on average, is not compatible with technocratic/academic institutions.
(Asian, middle-level, man)

When I see an African American person, I feel they are less likely to be intelligent and serious about technical work.
(Hispanic, middle-level, man)

I tend to automatically associate lack of education or lack of intelligence with African Americans as a group.
(Hispanic, lower-level, man)

I was conditioned to think that African Americans are not as intelligent as whites. (White, lower-level, woman)

As I try to give African Americans a chance, I feel they do not want to be a part of our society but want to be superior and take charge. (White, upper-level, man)

I have a problem working with minorities that have a chip on their shoulder about their lot in life and are always complaining about their injustices. (White, lower-level, woman)

African Americans think they are owed special treatment because they are black. (White, occupational, woman)

A manager is afraid to discipline a poor, lazy African American worker because he may be accused of racism.
(White, lower-level, woman)

Black Americans' Perceptions of Problems Created by Racism

If we compare the response of black Americans about discrimination in the workplace over the twenty years we have been studying these issues, in most cases they saw little change, and when they did, it was usually in the wrong direction. For example, in our 1976–78 study, 88 percent of African American employees, compared to 87 percent in 1988, believed minority workers must be better performers than white workers to get ahead. In 1976–78, 70 percent of African American employees believed that being excluded from informal work groups was a problem; in 1988, 87 percent believed this. Following are some comments about how black Americans perceive discrimination in the workplace.

My plan is to obtain director level. However, I feel there is no opportunity for promotion. (Black, middle-level, man)

You must be a favorite of the higher-ups to have a career. (Black, occupational, man)

I personally feel that as an African American male, I have not been properly advanced, based on my performance and qualifications. I have been a lower-level manager for all of my eight years in spite of having substantial experience as president and director of outside corporations. (Black, lower-level, man)

I feel I have the ability to perform any task given to me, but I don't feel my supervisor is supportive of that opinion. I don't feel as though I'm given the opportunity to prove that I have valuable skills or to improve on my skills. (Black, occupational, woman)

People of color have to be three times as competent as whites in order to be recognized as competent and capable. (Black, lower-level, woman)

People of color are rewarded half the reward of white and punished twice as hard as white. (Black, occupational, woman)

Some of the peers don't even speak unless I speak first. Some avoid eye contact, and it appears that some try to avoid any contact at all. (Black, occupational, woman)

The U.S.A. is a racist country; it has a racist past. Company employees reflect the same prejudices exhibited by society in general. (Black, middle-level, man)

While overt racism seems to have declined, there is a considerable amount of subtle racism which continues to exist in the company. (Black, middle-level, man)

If I have any bitterness towards anyone, it is a response to what this society has done to me throughout my life. Some unaffected people have no concept of what it is like growing up in a society such as this one. Minorities are confronted verbally, physically, professionally. In some cities, every aspect of one's life is affected because of one's race. (Black, middle-level, man)

As a result of these perceptions and feelings, we have found over the years, African American employees are by far the most critical of corporate treatment of minorities. For example, 87 percent of African Americans, 57 percent of Asians, 54 percent of Hispanics, 44 percent of Native Americans, and 35 percent of whites believe that minorities have a more difficult time finding a sponsor or mentor than white employees do.

The majority may feel more threatened by African Americans than by other minority groups because African Americans are the largest minority in the United States and compete more intensely in all areas with the majority. For example, African Americans have been competing in the labor market on a much broader scale and over a longer period of time than any other minority group. Most Native Americans are geographically limited, primarily to the reservation. Hispanics are found mostly in particular areas of the United States and are primarily limited to certain jobs (although this is changing). Asian Americans have been more narrowly restricted both in the American labor market and in geographic location. Thus, nonambivalent attitudes and the size of the African American population have made African Americans the biggest threat to the whites' dominant position in this society. As a result, African Americans face more types of discrimination and more severe discrimination.

Clearly, for this society to be competitive in the global marketplace, it must deal with these problems of discrimination more vigorously than it has so far. We would like to stress that the truth of discrimination lies somewhere between the extreme responses of black and white Americans.

Black Americans' Perceptions of Other Minority Groups

All the stereotyping and discrimination that occur make a diverse work force more difficult to manage, not only because of these factors negatively impacting on African Americans but also because of the negative feelings (primarily toward white people) that are generated in African Americans. Some of the following comments show the distrust, defensiveness, and cynicism black Americans feel.

> Sometimes being overly defensive in thinking that people will not perceive me as being as intelligent as they are because I'm African American. (Black, lower-level, man)

> Being viewed as being a person who excels in nonthinking activities (like sports) and not being taken very seriously causes me to become defensive at times towards whites.
> (Black, middle-level, man)

> I feel some white males tend to take it for granted that I am less knowledgeable and I am inferior because I am not white. So I tend to look at them and deal with them with some reservations.
> (Black, occupational, woman)

> One problem I have with some white people is that they always want to tell you what to do and how to do it even when you have more experience and knowledge concerning the job.
> (Black, upper-level, man)

> I feel I must work harder for a white man than I would ordinarily for a black man just because he is white and supposedly expects more. (Black, lower-level, woman)

> On the issue of racism, normally I wait until I feel a white person

is someone I can trust not to undermine, before giving them the benefit of the doubt. (Black, lower-level, man)

I decide on sight how I will deal with a person depending on what color they are. (Black, occupational, woman)

When I see a new white employee coming toward me, should I say hello or not? (Black, occupational, man)

I resent white male-dominated middle and upper management. I also feel resentment against Asian entrepreneurs who have taken over all the African American–owned businesses in my home area. (Black, lower-level, woman)

I have a difficult time living with and trusting members of my own race. (Black, lower-level, man)

I would have to deal with the stereotypes placed on myself from white America in two ways: doing whatever I can mentally to assure myself that I am not what I'm depicted as in the movies, news, and so on; verbally always portraying a positive self-image. (Black, occupational, woman)

As a child, I was never taught not to trust people, all people, or to question their intentions. I assumed always good. I learned to question people's motives through work and school experiences. I had been harassed when I was a child by cars full of white high schoolers. I had been called names by poor whites on street corners, but I wrongly believed that academia would free me from people with such attitudes, I believed that a professional working environment would do the same. But here I am not "nigger," I am an "AA [affirmative action] quota filler"; those attitudes remain. (Black, occupational, woman)

These reactions are not surprising, given the negative experiences of black Americans in the white society. Their lives have been infected by racism, they have faced isolation, and they feel they live in a hostile environment. Yet African Americans must recognize that regardless of this, the onus of responsibility is on them to overcome the barriers and to achieve. In the process of overcoming these barriers, they must not internalize the blame for their position.[16]

The African American Community's Own Problems versus People Who Are Different

While the discrimination visited on African Americans is real and serious, there are increasing trends of black people's turning on other minority and white people. The brutal attack on the Central Park jogger, a white woman, by a gang of young black men, as well as black attacks on Korean store owners and other violence illustrate the increasing hostility African Americans, especially poor African Americans feel toward other ethnic groups. Such violent racist attacks are counterproductive and inexcusable no matter who does them. African Americans, like other groups in the United States, must strive to become role models for the new diverse global village. Who can better show the way to accepting diversity than those who have been oppressed the most?

Conclusion

It is clear that African Americans are still having many problems because of discrimination. Noted African American educators like Walter Williams, Thomas Sowell, Glenn Loury, and William Julius want to downplay the issue of race discrimination; however, as we have seen, it is still extremely important. Yes, we agree to some extent with their philosophy that African Americans must solve their own problems. African Americans are gaining sufficient clout in key areas to develop an agenda. A key part of the agenda should be the elimination of the black subculture based on poverty, poor education, unemployment, drugs, and crime.

However, we need affirmative action, as much as we need cultural and value changes in the larger society and more African American self-help. We need these multiple approaches because even those African Americans who have succeeded face discrimination.

For example, John Gilbert, a black Harvard-educated linguist with degrees in international law and finance, has on more than one occasion been unable to hail a cab; but when his white secretary comes to his aid, she immediately gets a cab for her boss. Stanley Grayson, New York City's deputy mayor for finance and economic development, and his wife, Patricia, a vice president at National Medical Fellowships, have been confronted with racism in their exclusive apartment building. On more than one occasion, while she was in the laundry room of the apartment building, Mrs. Grayson has been approached by white residents to see if she would like to be their maid. Mr. Grayson has had white residents hurriedly close the elevator door in his face as he returned from work.

As one middle-level, female manager responding in one of our studies put it,

> My most important issue when looking at my own reactions to different groups is when dealing with minorities who believe that everything is okay and that they have all the same opportunities as the white world. These people do not realize that by thinking that they are equal in the eyes of white America they are naturally hurting minorities just as much as a nonminority.

In sum, African Americans must pick themselves up by the bootstraps and help other blacks without bootstraps get them. The United States must make certain that it is an active supporter of the rights of African Americans and that opportunities to prosper, to live peacefully, and as they wish are there. As the African American population increases, as Africa begins to move more toward the democratic capitalistic model, African Americans will become increasingly important to the success of the United States.

United States: Hispanic Americans

The Hispanic American population, which is very diverse in social, racial, and ethnic characteristics, will become the largest minority in the United States early in the twenty-first century. The major Hispanic ethnic groups in the United States are Mexicans (63 percent); Puerto Ricans (12 percent); Central and South Americans (11 percent); Cubans (5 percent); and other Hispanics (9 percent).

Especially in areas where Hispanic Americans are in large numbers, their contribution to the economic viability of those areas is crucial. U.S. businesses are beginning to recognize the importance of the Hispanic population. The importance of the Spanish-speaking population throughout Central and South America is also being recognized. While the European, Japanese, and North American populations are decreasing or not growing rapidly, those of Mexico and other Hispanic countries are. The potential of these nations, especially Mexico, to exert pressure for the equal treatment of Hispanic Americans will increase. Several recent articles in leading business magazines recognize these potential changes.

Hispanic American Demographics

Before analyzing the situation of Hispanics in the United States, we present some demographics.[1]

- In 1980, 14.6 million Hispanic Americans lived in the

United States. In 1987, there were 18.8 million, about a 30 percent increase. At present, they number 21 million and, by the year 2000, they will number 29 million.

- There are an estimated 3–5 million illegal Hispanic aliens in the United States.
- The Hispanic share of U.S. labor force growth between 1986 and 2000 is projected to be 29 percent.
- The Hispanic American population is much younger than that of the United States as a whole: twenty-five years is the median age for Hispanics compared to 32 years for the U.S. population.
- Twenty-eight percent of Hispanic Americans live below the poverty level (a 30 percent increase from 1980). Forty-six percent of Puerto Ricans do.
- The Hispanics' median income is $20,305 compared to the national median income of $30,221. Among Hispanic Americans, Cubans have the highest median income, $27,294, and Puerto Ricans the lowest, $15,185.
- Overall, 23.4 percent of Hispanic American families are headed by women. For Mexican Americans, the figure is 18.5 percent, and for Puerto Ricans, 44 percent.
- Almost one-third of Hispanic students drop out of school before the seventh grade compared to one-twentieth of non-Hispanic students.
- About 65 percent of Hispanics twenty-five to thirty-four years of age either dropped out of high school or graduated with limited skills.
- Cubans over twenty-five years of age are more likely than people of other Hispanic American groups to have completed at least four years of college. Puerto Ricans and Mexican Americans are least likely to have done so.
- While Hispanic Americans represent between 7 and 9 percent of the U.S. population, they account for 2 percent of scientists and engineers.
- Twenty-five percent of white men and women in America are managers or professionals; only 11 percent of the Hispanic men and 15 percent of the Hispanic women are in these categories.

- In 1980, Hispanic purchasing power was about $54 billion; in 1987, it was $134 billion; in 1990, it is estimated to be about $172 billion, and by the year 2000, $500 billion.

All these data show both potential assets and potential liabilities that Hispanic Americans bring to the economic table.

The following sections review the history of three Hispanic groups in the United States: Mexican Americans, Puerto Ricans, and Cuban Americans.

Mexican Americans

The first Hispanic Americans were Mexicans whose land had been ceded to the United States in 1848. Not until the following century did other large numbers of Hispanic people come to the United States. Large numbers of Puerto Ricans began emigrating to New York City during World War II; Cubans began fleeing to Florida in the mid-1950s to escape the Castro regime. However, the tone and stereotypes for all anti-Hispanic racism were set back in the nineteenth century in the Southwest.

Mexicans lived in and controlled large sections of the western part of what is now the United States for hundreds of years before Europeans and white settlers took most of it by conquest. In order to feel comfortable about the conquest of Mexican land, it was not difficult for Anglos (non-Hispanics) who were moving westward during the early nineteenth century to develop a host of stereotypes about Mexicans. They were much darker skinned then the average Anglo, and their religion was Roman Catholic rather than Protestant. Thus, some of the stereotypes that the majority society developed to oppress black Americans and "nonbelievers" were applied to Mexicans. Typical stereotypes were that Mexicans were lazy, dirty, drunk, ignorant, uneducated, and cowardly. Because of their religion, they were considered to be superstitious, disloyal, and subservient.

In 1848, Mexico signed the Treaty of Guadalupe Hidalgo, ceding to the United States a vast territory that encompassed what is now California, Arizona, New Mexico, Nevada, Utah, and portions of several other states. Mexico had previously approved the annexation of Texas. The total area was greater than that of France and Germany combined. Under the terms of the Treaty of Guadalupe Hidalgo, Mexicans would become U.S. citizens if they remained in the ceded territory for more than one year. Most of them remained.[2]

The United States would have taken over more Mexican land if large numbers of Mexicans had not been occupying it. As Steinfield observed, the belief in the superiority of American institutions and the implied assumption of racial inferiority of Mexicans functioned as a restraint upon territorial acquisition: the fear existed that this "alien race" would cause much difficulty if it were part of American society. According to this view, sparsely populated regions could be annexed with a minimum of difficulty because the American majority could populate them easily and become the dominant group. Mexicans were regarded with the same scorn as Native Americans and were often not differentiated from them.[3]

Once landowners and possessors of a sophisticated ancient culture, Mexican Americans soon found themselves powerless. Having been stripped of massive land holdings, large numbers of Mexican Americans were now available for exploitation on the labor market. In addition, after the Treaty of Guadalupe Hildalgo, there was a great deal of violence against Chicanos (as Mexican Americans were known). Throughout the ceded territories, between 1850 and 1930, more Chicanos were killed in the Southwest than black people were lynched in the South.[4]

Before and during the Depression, Mexican Americans who moved to the cities experienced only limited success in improving their economic condition. They did find some relief in the various welfare programs, but jobs were extremely hard to find. Anti-Mexican feelings were widespread throughout the Southwest in the 1930s, as illustrated by the following:

> In the face of hostility among minority groups and pressure from organized citizen groups, the federal and local governments tried to remove some of the surplus workers. . . . One-third of a million Mexican Americans were repatriated in Mexico between 1930 and 1933. Some people returned voluntarily. Others were politely coerced by welfare agencies, which preferred to pay the costs of

transportation rather than the costs of support, and many Mexican Americans were ruthlessly rounded up and deported. The officials who carried out the deportation orders did not always check to determine whom they were sending to Mexico. Longtime citizens of the United States as well as illegal aliens were driven or flown to Mexico.[5]

If people never learn to speak English properly and are poorly educated, they can be excluded from the economic mainstream. Many U.S. school systems managed to accomplish this exclusion for Mexican Americans. Zanden reminds us that Mexican American children were often segregated for purposes of instruction, in separate buildings or in separate classrooms. On the basis of pedagogical considerations, some educators insisted that this separation of Mexican and white students was a sound practice. Throughout most of the Southwest this segregation was considered desirable. Segregation of Mexican Americans was more a matter of custom than of explicit law—quite different from the southern whites' treatment of black people—but nevertheless, in some communities, Mexican American segregation was strict and total.[6]

World War II provided new opportunities for Mexican Americans, as for other minorities. The labor shortages of the war allowed them to enter into previously restricted higher-paying jobs. As did other minorities, Mexican Americans eagerly seized the opportunities. So great was the need for workers that the U.S. government approached the Mexican government to develop a contract program for Mexicans to work in the farms of the Southwest. Despite grave reservations because of past discrimination, the Mexican government concurred.

Racial discrimination did not completely disappear, and it continued to plague Mexican Americans during the war. Neither the segregated educational system nor the double-standard justice dispensed by southwestern courts was affected. According to Steiner, Mexican Americans did not obtain unbiased trials. In Los Angeles, after a young white youth was killed during a gang fight, twenty-four Mexican American youths were arrested and nine were convicted of murder. The judge, the prosecutor, and the jury were all white. Two years later, all the defendants were freed because lack of evidence.[7]

When the war ended, racial discrimination continued. Meier and Riviera noted that Mexican American veterans found, to their dismay, that little had changed in the way the majority society viewed them. They were still refused service at restaurants and hotels, and they still could not obtain jobs commensurate with their skills. Finally, they were still buried in segregated cemeteries.[8]

The problems do not go away. Job discrimination keeps Mexican Americans' income among the lowest in the United States. Health conditions and services in their communities are still poor. The housing situation is inadequate. In the schools, Mexican Americans are still treated as second-class citizens in too many areas. Educational facilities for Mexican American children in the Southwest are poorer than for white children. Their teachers are in need of more practical training for dealing with minority children. A pressing need also exists for bilingual classes.

In the late 1980s, some white people expressed fear that the rapid growth of the Hispanic population will make parts of the United States into an "extension" of countries to the south. But this fear is more mythology than fact, in part because Hispanic Americans are anything but a unified force.

This great influx of Mexican Americans, and the "Latin Dope Connection" brought out new racist stereotypes in the 1980s. For example, one hears increasing hostilities about Hispanic Americans not assimilating: "If they do not want to speak English, send them back!" This type of attitude has led to an increased movement toward making English the official language of the United States. Among anti-Hispanic stereotypes we hear are that all Hispanic Americans are drug pushers, are on welfare having lots of babies, or are "taking jobs away" from majority Americans.

Puerto Rican Americans

The second largest Hispanic group in the United States is the Puerto Rican. Puerto Ricans, as did many other immigrant groups before and after, came to America looking for better lives and opportunities. In 1987, Puerto Ricans represented 2.56 million Americans. Large numbers of them immigrated to the

United States, especially to New York City, to fill unskilled, semiskilled, and skilled job vacuums during and after World War II. However, in the late 1940s, there was a slowdown in the economy and a predictable decrease in Puerto Rican immigrants. In the early 1950s, the Korean War offered other excellent opportunities for jobs, and immigration increased again. About 40,000 Puerto Ricans volunteered to fight for the United States at that time.[9]

Since that war, well over 1 million Puerto Ricans have come to the United States seeking their "pot of gold." Sixty percent live in New York City, where many New Yorkers regard them as an undesirable immigrant group. This is despite the fact that Puerto Ricans can never be illegal aliens like members of other Hispanic groups because of their status as American citizens (since 1917, though without the right to vote for U.S. offices). As a whole, they probably suffer more discrimination than any other Hispanic American group because many Puerto Ricans are dark-skinned. In Puerto Rico, people are categorized in various ways, including by skin tone and class, but according to Almquist, skin tone is not a primary stimulus for discrimination:

> Racial prejudice on the mainland makes occupational and cultural assimilation difficult, in both direct and indirect ways. Many Puerto Ricans are black of mixed black and white ancestry. Mainlanders tend to discriminate against people who are not white, and Puerto Ricans suffer from this color prejudice. The severity of racial prejudice is somewhat surprising to Puerto Ricans, who are accustomed to making class distinctions but not race distinctions. In Puerto Rico, people who are of the same social class mingle at dances and parties regardless of color. On the mainland, however, they are ostracized for racial intermingling, and the tension surrounding black/white relations spill over into the Puerto Rican community. Puerto Ricans do not understand the severity of racial discrimination. They are reluctant to link up with blacks in the civil rights movement, and white Puerto Ricans are fearful of being labeled as black.[10]

Puerto Ricans living in the United States are shocked by this abrupt confrontation with majority prejudice based on skin color. There are several other special issues confronting Puerto Ricans as well. As noted earlier, they are U.S. citizens but do not have voting representation in Congress, and they cannot vote for President if they live in Puerto Rico. Those living there also do not pay income or social security taxes, but when they move to the mainland, all that changes. Loyalties are split between the mainland and the island. Are they Americans or are they Puerto Ricans? Where should they live—on the island or on the mainland, where they are perceived as welfare recipients, illegal immigrants, cheats, muggers, and just plain liabilities to society?[11]

Despite these conflicts, Lambert and Taylor found in their study of seven ethnic/racial groups' attitudes toward themselves and others, Puerto Ricans rated themselves most favorably of all ethnic groups: for instance, they saw themselves as likable, intelligent at school, smart with practical things, determined to succeed, intelligent, and law-abiding.

Looking at other ethnic groups, they perceived black people in the most negative light, as untrustworthy, not hardworking, and very aggressive or violent. White people were rated slightly better in terms of being trustworthy and hardworking, but "as significantly less intelligent and smart than Puerto Ricans themselves." Mexican Americans were also perceived as less trustworthy, law-abiding, and likable than Puerto Ricans.[12]

Because many Puerto Ricans have dark skin, they have suffered a similar racial oppression as black Americans. In our studies, Puerto Ricans, more than any other Hispanic group, responded similarly to black people on perceptions of discrimination. The other Hispanic groups responded more like the white group.[13] In addition, culture and language problems are more severe for many Puerto Ricans than for black people. As a result of these factors, Puerto Ricans are near the bottom of the economic totem pole in the United States, below all other major Hispanic groups and below black Americans.

Cuban Americans

The Cubans represent a major Hispanic group in the United States, numbering about 1 million people. Most Cubans—about 700,000—live and work in the Miami area. Many immigrated at the time of the Castro revolution (1959). They were mostly white (96 percent), middle- and upper-class, educated, and had been opposed to Castro's regime. Although wealthy in Cuba, they lost real and personal property in the new communist state. This well-educated, urban, high-status, primarily light-skinned Hispanic group received a much warmer reception in the United States than did Mexicans and Puerto Ricans. After the initial refugees, those who came in the 1970s and the Mariel Exodus in 1980 came predominantly from the working class; however, a high percentage were skilled workers. When they arrived, there were significant numbers of successful business people ready to extend a helping hand. Gann and Duignan point out that about half of the Cuban immigrants worked in Cuban-owned or -managed firms, for somewhat better wages than those who worked for non-Cuban enterprises.[14] Because of their relative acceptance, high-status backgrounds, and successful compatriots, Cubans compose the most successful immigrant group after Japanese Americans. Almquist wrote,

> U.S. citizens were especially receptive to [Cubans]. . . . The Cuban refugee held values that were very similar to their own. In addition, the Cubans who migrated brought qualities and skills which were usable in their economy: high educational levels, sophisticated occupational training, and a middle-class ethic and style of life. The ethic brought by Cubans included capitalistic values emphasizing "individualism, self-concern, personal right, and improvement of one's position in the stratification system as one's main worldly goal."[15]

Cuban Americans themselves practice ethnic, racial, and class segregation. Boswell and Curtes noted that Cuban immigrants living in Miami not only segregate themselves from Jews and from black people but also from Mexicans and non-Hispanic white groups.[16] In addition, within the Cuban community there is considerable segregation by class and skin color. The strong ethnocentrism of Cuban Americans has led to some well-publicized racial riots and attacks by Cubans on black people and vice versa.

One could conclude by saying that, of the three Hispanic American groups discussed, Cuban Americans are most likely to have identified with the conservative sector of the United States. That they are the most white of the three groups suggests that part of their success is based on the color of their skin.

Current Discrimination against Hispanic Americans

Despite the progress of the various Hispanic American groups, incidents of racial/ethnic discrimination against them happen daily.

- Rafael Riviera Garcia, a white-appearing Puerto Rican professor of art, was terrorized by a young white male until the professor shot him in self-defense.
- In Philadelphia, the Hispanic community, primarily Puerto Ricans, is up-in-arms because of discrimination. They represent only 2 percent of civil service workers but about 6 percent of the population. They claim that their neighborhoods are neglected by city services because they are Hispanic.
- In Los Angeles, a city with the largest concentration of Mexican Americans, a federal judge ruled that the Los Angeles Board of Supervisors intentionally drew districts in 1981 to stop Hispanics from gaining representation on the board.
- Increasingly, companies are forcing bilingual employees to speak only English on the job. While it is legal to restrict second languages on the job because of job-related performance reasons, the A.C.L.U. says it is happening for purely racial reasons.
- A young Puerto Rican woman at Bryn Mawr, a prestigious women's school outside of Philadelphia, was harassed by her white classmates, being called "spic" and told to leave the school.
- Recently, the Secretary of Veteran Affairs referred to illegal Hispanic immigrants as "wetbacks."
- The F.B.I. was found to discriminate against Hispanics in promotions and working conditions and is now in the process of correcting such discrimination, by court order.
- In New York City, minority students, primarily Puerto Ricans, walked out of school because a teacher constantly made derogating remarks about Hispanics' ability to learn.
- A successful Cuban vice president was fired from his marketing job by a younger white manager because "he was too uppity."

- Two white New York City corrections officers were charged with attacking with baseball bats two Hispanic males walking with a white woman and a Hispanic woman.
- Along the Mexican–U.S. border in California, there have been numerous violent attacks on Hispanics by white private citizens and U.S. border officers.

Hispanic Americans in the Workplace

Co-workers' Perceptions of Hispanic American Employees

We noted earlier that unfamiliar languages create conflicts for employees and societies. Lambert and Taylor observe that not only do Hispanic people have a high regard for the Spanish language but that speaking it is inextricably tied to a desire to maintain their own culture:

> Mexican American parents feel that they should not only maintain their own cultural styles of food, dress, songs, and dances but also maintain cultural values, for example, how children should behave with parents, how they should deal with dating, etc. . . . Both Puerto Ricans and Mexicans strongly supported bilingualism, and most of these parents spoke Spanish in the home.[17]

According to Rodriguez, 91 percent of Puerto Ricans, 90 percent of Cubans (and other Hispanic groups), and 64 percent of Mexicans speak Spanish in the home. Rodriguez also points out that 70 percent of Puerto Ricans, 60 percent of Cubans, 42 percent of Mexicans, and 55 percent of other Hispanic groups report they speak English well or very well. Self-reporting of language proficiency can be inaccurate, however, insofar as the speakers might believe they are proficient, but native English speakers might not agree.

Since most Hispanics are bilingual and proficiency varies greatly among individuals, language is a source of tension between the white majority population and the Hispanic community. Of course, this tension spills over into the workplace. The following comments from employees in our studies and seminars illustrate this.

I have difficulties in dealing with people when there is a language barrier and try to avoid this situation at times, especially with Hispanics. (White, middle-level, man)

My biggest problem are Spanish-speaking people who come to America and appear to make no big effort to learn English—to have their children go to a bilingual school and therefore display that no attempt will be made to learn English. I feel it is wrong and this form of education should be discontinued. An extension of this is I see that Spanish-speaking persons apparently feel they are owed this luxury to not have to learn English; therefore America should pay for their inabilities to get and hold jobs.
(White, lower-level, woman)

Language and accents are my biggest hangups. Living in a city where Spanish is becoming the main language, I have become very critical of people who do not speak the language of our country. It is very hard for me to see all of the information in Spanish when we are in a country where English is the chosen language.
(White, middle-level, woman)

Many of the Anglos I must deal with express resentment about Hispanics speaking Spanish at work; some even complain about it when they hear it in the company parking lot. I guess they tell me because they think I am Anglicized—I speak perfect English and have made it to this level. I speak fluent Spanish also.
(Hispanic, upper-level, woman)

In addition to stigmatizing them because of the language problem, some of their co-workers stereotype Hispanic Americans as being less intelligent, lazy, rough, too emotional, thieves, knife-carriers, illegal aliens, and welfare recipients. There were some positive stereotypes also: Hispanic Americans were characterized as being kind, quiet, friendly, lively, passionate, exotic, warm, musical, and culturally rich. Note that these positive stereotypes are very different from those used to describe Asian Americans: the latter are much more likely to be qualities that companies look for in employees. The positive stereotypes of Hispanic people are more likely to be irrelevant to the workplace.

I've always been conditioned that blacks are less motivated than whites or Asians, and Hispanics carry a stereotype with me of having less initiative than blacks. (White, occupational, man)

My city is being overrun by Mexicans. They are lazy and dirty. Everything is going downhill. (White, occupational, woman)

I feel that some others are not as capable of doing certain work— through poor education, lack of drive, etc. . . . Hispanics and blacks. (White, lower-level, man)

It's hard for me to accept the fact that minority groups bond together. . . . I understand why they do, but I feel sometimes excluded because *they* feel left out from the majority.
(White, lower-level, woman)

Fear of violence from inner-city non-white, Hispanic, and black people. When driving through a poorer section of town, I'm nervous about being assaulted. (White, middle-level, man)

Hispanic Americans' Perceptions of Problems Created by Discrimination

In our 1976–78 study, 30 percent of Hispanic American employees said that minorities were excluded from informal work groups; in 1988, 42 percent thought so. At both times, more than half agreed that minority workers have to be better performers than white workers to get ahead. A key problem perceived by Hispanic American employees was lack of opportunity.

I have a business degree in management, and I'm a top service representative in sales. I have asked to be promoted, and I'm very mobile. However, no offers. (Hispanic, occupational, man)

If anyone is missing out on opportunities, it is Hispanics, who I see only in janitorial positions. (Hispanic, occupational, man)

The supervisor did not "bond" to me (suggested I work for someone else). Doesn't like Mexicans. (Hispanic, lower-level, woman)

Although you can do something to progress yourself, you need help from others who could point you in the right direction and help get your foot in the door. Seldom does this happen. It has mostly been talk and no action. (Hispanic, occupational, woman)

Hispanic Americans' Perceptions of Other Ethnic Groups

As we found in regard to other minority groups, Hispanic Americans also hold discriminatory stereotypes of ethnic groups other than their own. Indeed, though the majority society classifies all Spanish-speaking groups as Hispanic, Hispanic people often express negative stereotypes about other Hispanic groups.

> Cubans and Puerto Ricans come to California and try to take over. Mexicans have been here for centuries.
> (Hispanic, occupational, man)

> Puerto Ricans need to get educated and work hard like us Cubans. They have a lot of advantages but don't use them.
> (Hispanic, middle-level, man)

Such reactions, though counterproductive, should not be surprising. Lumping together as "Hispanic" groups as diverse as Argentines, Chileans, Costa Ricans, Cubans, Dominicans, Mexicans, Puerto Ricans, and Spanish, who come from various racial and cultural backgrounds, is contravening reality as these people themselves perceive it.

The situation is complicated by a diverse welter of attitudes and practices with regard to race and color, both in the United States as a whole and within the various Hispanic communities. As previously mentioned, Puerto Ricans on their native island stratify people based more on class than on skin color, whereas the majority society in the United States has discriminated primarily on the basis of color. Among Cubans, stratification by color is more pronounced. In general, how government and different ethnic groups categorize and react to "white" and "black" appearance varies over time, place, and culture. But the racial classification and prejudice that Hispanic immigrants find when they come to the United States is extremely divisive and creates severe conflicts for them. The question of race and color then plays a role in their own rejection of other ethnic groups, both Hispanic and non-Hispanic.

Sixty years ago, the U.S. census had a category "Hispanic/Latino." In 1950, 1960, and 1970, Hispanic people were classified as white, but they could check a category "persons of Spanish mother tongue" in the first two censuses. In 1970, they could check "persons of both Spanish surname and Spanish mother tongue." In 1980 and 1990, Hispanics could specify whether they were Mexican, Puerto Rican, Cuban, and so on. In addition, they could specify "race": Aleut, Asian Indian, Black or Negro, Chinese, Eskimo, Filipino, Guamanian, Hawaiian, Indian (American), Japanese, Korean, Samoan, Vietnamese, White, Other. In this manner of counting, most Hispanics (97 percent) classify themselves as white, although many are dark-skinned.

Some of the Hispanic respondents in our studies and seminars had serious objections to considering themselves members of a minority or people of color. In fact, some of them expressed negative stereotypes about black Americans. But some also refused to categorize by color.

> I hate your "people of color." People should be people. White is also a color. I'm a white Hispanic, but I'm white.
> (Hispanic, occupational, man)

> I consider myself to be white; I am not a person of color.
> (Hispanic, lower-level, woman)

> Hispanics are considered white in the United States. Why do you classify them as people of color? (Hispanic, upper-level, man)

> I am a Hispanic, by your terms, and never knew I was colored. I see everyone as a creation of God, and God makes no distinctions, so why should I? I am an American, equal to anyone, and the same goes for everyone you entitle "colored."
> (Hispanic, occupational, woman)

> We Puerto Ricans are always lumped with blacks. I get very disturbed. We are Hispanic, not black. (Hispanic, occupational, man)

> I would be very upset if my child married a black.
> (Hispanic, lower-level, woman)

> I believe blacks are responsible for their position; they want everything handed to them. (Hispanic, occupational, woman)

A marked number of Hispanic employees expressed dislike of affirmative action and workshops that promote acceptance of diversity. We believe this is in part because they did not wish to see themselves as members of a minority.

Why make such a big issue. Everyone is human and that's all that counts. (Hispanic, occupational, woman)

Quit forcing it [workshop] upon people.
(Hispanic, lower-level, woman)

Stop pushing so hard. We're miles ahead of the rest of the nation. (Hispanic, occupational, man)

Conclusion

The Hispanic population is of growing importance to the U.S. economy. In the coming years, Hispanic countries will play significant roles in United States economic success. This will increase pressure on the U.S. government to ensure that Hispanic Americans are treated more fairly. For example, Mexico is the third largest trading partner with the United States—$45 billion per year; by the year 2000, this trade will triple to about $130 billion per year. In addition, it seems clear that regardless of the U.S. immigration policy, there will be increasing illegal immigration from Mexico and other Latin American countries as their populations explode.

Although some Hispanic Americans are reluctant to see themselves as members of a minority group, they are so in effect by virtue of the fact that English is their second language and that many Hispanic Americans are dark-skinned.

U.S. society must improve its tolerance of bilingual Americans, including people whose native language in Spanish. Bilingual Hispanic Americans will be a tremendous asset to U.S. society as we deal with Spanish-speaking countries. At the same time, Hispanic Americans should become proficient in English, the majority language of their adopted country, while keeping Spanish fluency.

As is the case for other minorities, affirmative action and improved acceptance of people who are different are important requirements if the United States is to utilize the resource of a diverse population in the global marketplace.

On their part, rather than rejecting black Americans and other groups different from themselves, the Hispanic groups in the United States should join with other minority groups in resisting discrimination and striving for equal treatment in the workplace and in the larger society.

11

Discrimination in the Workplace and Minority Strategies for Success

The previous chapters demonstrated that all ethnic minorities face numerous negative stereotypes over the years that lead to discrimination in all aspects of their lives. In this chapter, we discuss more specifically the stereotypes and discrimination against minorities in corporate America, and, more important, we give minorities some tools to assist them in dealing with discrimination.

As noted, economic issues are probably one of the most important factors in determining the level of race discrimination in this and most other societies. Although political and social competition are important, the competition for a finite amount of desirable land, money, and jobs largely determines the intensity of the threat felt by the dominant society. Once a minority group begins to take something to which the dominant group feels exclusively entitled, minorities become subject to all the manipulation, exploitation, and harassment—in short, oppression—that the dominant group can muster. The relative size of the minority population, as well as its skin color, also influences white America's attitudes and behaviors. Finally, the threat Americans perceive from non-white nations plays a crucial role in the formulation of American views toward minorities. The minority groups' responses to society, in turn, are thereby influenced.

The discrimination encountered by each minority group in this book is in some areas unique in kind and in degree. Each group has its particular legacy of both positive and negative stereotypes; some have more positive stereotypes than others, and vice versa. These stereotypes come not only from the white majority but also from the minority groups themselves.

As we noted earlier, black Americans in our surveys have always been by far the most critical about discrimination against minorities in corporate America. In our 1976–78 study, we found that Hispanics were significantly more critical than Asians and Native Americans. In 1988, we found that the difference in responses of Hispanics, Asians, and Native Americans to questions about discrimination against minorities were no longer significantly different. It seems that as the number of Asian Americans increases and anti-Asian attitudes increase because of Asian countries' economic successes, the amount of discrimination faced by Asians in corporate America has also increased. In addition, Native Americans, who in the past responded similarly to white people, are much more likely to respond similarly to Asians and Hispanics. This could be due to increasing resentment among white people as Native Americans become more aggressive in fighting for their legal rights. Thus, in the late 1980s and the 1990s, we no longer have significant differences among Hispanics', Asians', and Native Americans' perceptions of discrimination in the corporate world. We still do have significant differences between those three groups and African Americans. The latter's opinions about discrimination in the workplace have remained quite constant except for a dip in the mid-1970s.

A Review of the Data on Race Discrimination in the Workplace, 1964–1980

In 1964, Garda W. Bowman, in her study of two thousand corporate employees who were almost exclusively white, found that 77 percent believed that being black, 71 percent believed that being Chicano (Mexican), and 68 percent believed that being Asian was harmful for advancement in business.[1] In 1972, we found that 68 percent of black people and 58 percent of white people believed that being black was harmful to advancement in business.

In research conducted for the book *Racism and Sexism in Corporate Life*, which used 1976–78 data, we revised the question about the impact of race on career to ask specifically whether employees believed their own race would be harmful, irrelevant, or helpful to their own career advancement. African American men and women (46 percent) and white men (45 percent) were most likely to believe that their race would be harmful. From 6 percent to 16 percent of other race or gender groups felt this way. In 1988, the percentage of white men who believed their race would be harmful decreased to 39 percent and the percentage of black employees believing this increased to 50 percent.

In comparing data on a number of identical questions asked in 1972, 1976–78, and 1988 (for example, minorities have a more difficult time finding a mentor, minorities are excluded from informal work groups, minorities must be better performers than white workers), it becomes clear that most employees, regardless of race, believed that racial discrimination decreased between 1972 and 1976–78 and increased between 1976–78 and 1988. For example, on the question of whether minorities had to be better performers, 88 percent of the African American managers and 33 percent of the white managers believed in 1972 that the statement was true. These figures dropped in 1976–78 to 82 percent of the black managers and 17 percent of the white managers. By 1988, however, the figures rose: 87 percent of the black employees and 32 percent of the white employees believed that minorities must be better performers than white people to advance. In 1976–78, about 40 percent of the other minorities concurred, but in 1988, 58 percent did. What these data suggest is that when there is a national commitment to combat racism, racism declines. In the 1980s, the Reagan administration did not have such a commitment, and racism increased. President Bush's veto of the 1990 Civil Rights Bill suggests that a new survey would find an increase in racism also.

Race Discrimination in Corporate America Today

We constructed an index of six questions related to discrimination against minorities to test the extent to which discrimination is perceived. Figure 11–1 shows the index results. Note the striking difference between white people and people of color with respect to perceived race discrimination. For every group except the white, at least twice as many employees perceived three to six problems as perceived no problems. The same percentage of white women believed there were no discrimination problems as believed there were three to six problems. More white men (40 percent) believed there were no discrimination problems than believed there were three to six problems (31 percent). Among the other minority groups, black men (84 percent) and black women (90 percent) were, by far, the most likely to report discrimination. The other groups ranged from 44 percent (Native American men) to 52 percent (Asian women).

Most minorities and women at middle levels and above remain consistently critical of the treatment accorded minorities and women. Contrary to white men's responses, minorities and women do not develop a more optimistic evaluation of their careers and work situations as they move up the corporate ladder. One explanation is that managers from the dominant group feel more a part of the group that helped them get there. For women and minorities, group identity diminishes as they progress up the management ladder, because fewer same-sex or same-race superiors, peers, and subordinates are found at the higher levels. As their status becomes more obviously "token," they feel more isolated and thus become more alienated. Finally, as minorities and women move up the pyramid they are usually placed in less powerful staff departments. Naturally, they develop an increasing sense of powerlessness, in contrast to their white male peers, whose situations hint at a string of further advancement possibilities.

We have consistently found over the years that, on the whole, frequency of contact with minorities on the job does not significantly alter the responses of employees about race discrimination in the company. For white women, but not white men, the more frequently they have social contact with minorities outside of work, the more likely they are to believe that a great deal of racism exists in the company.

What this pattern indicates is that perceptions of racial discrimination on the job in many cases have nothing to do with

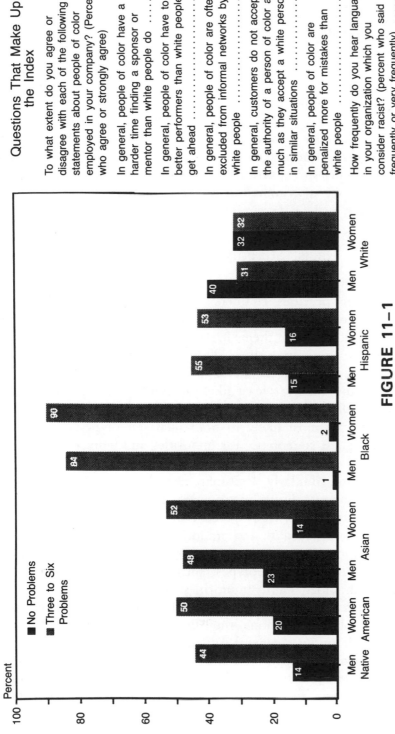

Questions That Make Up the Index

To what extent do you agree or disagree with each of the following statements about people of color employed in your company? (Percent who agree or strongly agree)

In general, people of color have a harder time finding a sponsor or mentor than white people do 39

In general, people of color have to be better performers than white people to get ahead 35

In general, people of color are often excluded from informal networks by white people 32

In general, customers do not accept the authority of a person of color as much as they accept a white person's in similar situations 28

In general, people of color are penalized more for mistakes than white people 14

How frequently do you hear language in your organization which you consider racist? (percent who said frequently or very frequently) 22

FIGURE 11–1
Race Discrimination

the actual experience of working with minorities but with personal feelings. The fact that social contact outside the workplace modifies white women's perceptions of race discrimination and not white men's suggests the tenacity with which white men cling to their subjective perceptions of racism, probably in large part because they sense that their privileged position is under attack. It is easier to reconcile the obvious inequities by believing that minorities face many problems as the result of minorities' own deficiencies. Yet we must keep in mind that 60 percent of white men see discrimination in their company, and 31 percent see a great deal of discrimination.

Racist Stereotypes by Participants

Discrimination is based on a complex set of stereotypes that we discussed in previous chapters. In this chapter, we develop a composite of stereotypes in the workplace and discuss how minorities can overcome them. In 1988, we found most people held stereotypes about minorities. This fact has not changed in the past twenty years. Figure 11–2 shows 1988 responses. Note that African Americans are least likely to hold stereotypes about minorities, followed by Hispanics and Asians. White and Native Americans are most likely to hold such stereotypes.

The toughest stereotypes for minorities and women to counteract are all related directly or indirectly to their abilities and qualifications. Similarly, legitimate complaints made by minority managers about discrimination are frequently discounted by white workers. Fifty-eight percent of white respondents in our 1988 study believed that a minority person could not be demoted without bringing on undeserved charges of discrimination. This leads to other stereotypes, such as "minorities have a chip on their shoulder," and "minorities are too aggressive."

Kochman made some comments bearing on the issues that allegedly follow demotions, the "undeserved charges of discrimination." He outlines general differences in black and white styles of emotional expression and states that black people incorporate their feelings more fully into decision making, business meetings, and negotiation sessions. Black people tend to feel freer than white people to react to "efforts to get them to set aside their

Questions That Make Up the Index

To what extent do you agree or disagree with the following statements about people of color employed in your company? (Percent who agree or strongly agree)

1. In general, an employee of color could not be demoted even for inadequate work without undeserved charges of discrimination being made.

2. Many people of color obtained their current positions only because they are people of color.

3. Many people of color use their race as an alibi for difficulties they have on the job.

4. Many employees of color come from different cultural backgrounds that are not conducive to their success in the company.

5. Pluralism will force us to lower our hiring and promotion standards.

6. In general, people of color are not as dependable as white employees.

7. What is your position on interracial marriage? (Percent who are not supportive)

Percent who agree or strongly agree

Question no.	American Indian	Asian	Black	Hispanic	White
1	44%	38%	9%	40%	58%
2	67%	35%	28%	24%	56%
3	44%	21%	26%	33%	42%
4	55%	38%	35%	27%	31%
5	11%	26%	2%	16%	33%
6	22%	5%	9%	3%	10%
7	38%	20%	27%	22%	48%

FIGURE 11–2

Racist Stereotypes and Attitudes

feelings as unrealistic, illogical, and politically devious." That is, efforts to deflect legitimate black anger "cut off valid feelings from their causes, thus discrediting the feelings as inappropriate or unwarranted."[2] Asians whom we interviewed during the past five years have noted that because of the "quiet, nonagressive, shy" stereotype that white people have about them, they are perceived as not "acting right" when they complain about perceived discrimination. A middle-level Asian male manager said, "When Asians defend their rights, Anglos don't know how to react. They perceive Asians' complaining about anything as abnormal."

Another important stereotype directly related to work qualifications is the concept that many minorities come from cultural backgrounds not conducive to being successful in business.

When discussing the present-day work force and cultural backgrounds, one must distinguish comments that may have more relevance to native-born American minorities or foreign-born minorities who have lived in the United States a sufficient period of time to become acclimated to U.S. culture than to those who are recent arrivals or who have not acclimated to U.S. culture. Much of what is written in the next several pages applies mostly to the first two groups (native-born and acclimated). An upper-level, white male manager wrote,

> I think that minority employees have a greater problem . . . succeeding in jobs because there are fewer who have had success-oriented backgrounds, i.e., succeeded in school, succeeded in engineering, accounting, computer science, and other more difficult curricula in college. Their measure of success may tend to be materialistic in more cases than for white people, rather than intrinsic.

Like many stereotypes, this comment contains a grain of truth about deprived and uneducated minority people, but it reveals a major flaw. Many people make distinctions about the poor and uneducated versus the educated and middle-class in their own groups, but they do not make these same distinctions when it comes to outside groups. This dual perspective is evident in the fact that over 90 percent of employees agree that most minority workers are as qualified as white workers, while at the same time 27–55 percent believe that the cultural backgrounds of minorities will interfere with managerial success. Over the years we have found about one out of three employees, regardless of race and gender, believing that minorities need special training to be successful managers. Is this a measure of self-doubt? Have some of these minorities internalized racist views about minority cultural deprivation? Are different minority groups referring to other minority groups but not to their own? For example, are African Americans saying "we are qualified, but Hispanics, Asians, and Native Americans are not"? In all probability, the answer is yes to all of these questions.

The persistence of racial stereotypes is more likely to be caused by lack of understanding, insufficient meaningful interaction, or simply the bias of unhealthy people than by vital cultural differences. Minorities are not given a chance to disprove an imputation of undesirable characteristics. Many minority managers interact effectively with white people every day, but many white managers are unable or unwilling to acknowledge effective interaction. Some white managers are not comfortable in these interactions, but they do not identify their own uncertainties as the cause. A white middle-level manager admitted, "The white community considers blacks to be different without really knowing them. Its lack of social and business contact with blacks has tended to segregate blacks in the minds of the white community. Therefore, it categorizes blacks into one group."

In addition, because of racist stereotypes and attitudes, the same behavior on the part of white and minority workers receives different interpretations depending on who is on stage. Minorities who are assertive, self-confident, and ambitious are characterized as being too aggressive, arrogant, and wanting too much too fast. A white male with these characteristics might be viewed in a very positive light.

The fact that white employees have great difficulty acknowledging their different interpretations of the same behavior by a minority person and a white person may relate to the social unacceptability of such attitudes in all but reactionary circles today. It has been pointed out that, in general, different minority groups have different styles of operating, and our earlier data attest to some of these differences. Asian Americans usually exhibit a less confrontational behavior style than do African Americans, for instance. Ethnic background also affects white operating styles. Italians, in general, are much more verbal and expressive with their hands than Anglo-Saxons. Looking more closely at the general differences in style between some blacks and some whites, Kochman wrote,

> Whites tend to avoid dynamic opposition. This is because they see confrontations as leading to intransigence, a hardening of opposing viewpoints, with the result that neither opponent will listen to the other's viewpoint, regardless of its merit, let alone concede the possibility of its validity. Thus whites equate confrontation with conflict. Their goal is "openmindedness": flexibility in approach and the recognition that no one person has all the answers. To realize these aims, whites place their faith in a mode of intellectual engagement that weakens or eliminates those aspects of character or posture that they believe keep people's minds closed and make them otherwise unyielding. . . .
>
> Blacks, in general, do not believe that the presence of affective and dynamic opposition leads to intransigence. Quite the opposite: They often use formal argument as a means of testing their own views. Thus they speak their minds with the expectation that either their views or those of the opposition will be modified as a result of a successful challenge, a point against which one or the other opponent has no effective reply.[3]

An example of a difference in style between Cuban and Anglo-Saxon people is also instructive. Many Cubans love a good argument, a Cuban vice president of marketing said. "Many Americans do not understand Cubans and other Hispanics who have a good argument. Anglos think we want to fight, but we just love a good argument. When it's over, it's over."

Of course, there are similarities in behavior among all Americans. It has been effectively argued that cultural differences among black, Asian, Hispanic, Indian, and white Americans are not significant in terms of objectives or means of reaching objectives. Put another way, we have more important similarities as human beings than we have dissimilarities because of ethnicity.

In order to survive in the majority society, minority people must develop bicultural competence. This ability is developed both consciously and unconsciously through all of society's institutions. Valentine explains the survival strength demonstrated by the development of bicultural competence:

> Most minority people are prevented from activating or actualizing their life-long socialization into white patterns, the same patterns which so many Euro-Americans easily use to achieve affluence and ease. Most minorities are reduced to peripheral manipulations around the edges of a system which might have crushed them entirely long ago if they had not acquired and developed such multiple competence as they could.[4]

In other words, the cultural argument against equality cannot be justified with logic. It is employed in a racist and a class-biased manner rather than on an individual case-by-case basis. Although many minority people come from lower-class backgrounds, many variations in life-style and attitude exist within a given class, and much more in an entire group. Further, more and more minority people are coming from middle-class backgrounds. Nevertheless, a minority who grew up in deprivation should have no more difficulty than a white person who has overcome an underprivileged status to be an effective manager. To think otherwise is to succumb to the values of cultural imperialism. Finally, we must recognize that there are significant intragroup ethnic and cultural differences among the various minorities.

In sum, the vast majority of minority people born in the United States or who have been here long enough to acclimate to the U.S. culture are bicultural and can operate effectively in the corporate structure if given the opportunity. Those foreign immigrants who are recent arrivals must be given a chance to acclimate themselves to their new society. When some minorities choose not to adopt an exclusively American culture, they are labeled as culturally handicapped. Many Westerners assume that Western culture is the only functional one for the business world and that other cultures are incompatible. They do not appreciate that, in different parts of the world, other cultures have as much meaning and value as theirs. This results in their trying to ignore, suppress, or reject foreign cultures. The problem is not just one-way. Many foreigners, because of the biases they bring to the United States about American culture, women, religions, and so on create their own problems. Their culture clashes with the United States' formal goal of treating everyone fairly and equitably. Thus, U.S. corporations find themselves confronted with serious problems related to low productivity and low employee morale. They would benefit from adopting some of the positive cultural and value differences that minorities bring into their companies. Also, foreign immigrants and minorities would benefit from appreciating and adopting some of the positive elements in the prevailing majority.

Strategies to Counteract Racist Stereotypes

What can minority people, regardless of whether they are recent immigrants or not, do about stereotypes in order to become full-fledged members of corporate America at all levels? First, they must achieve a sound understanding of racism and how it works in U.S. society and in corporate America. They must understand that there are still serious questions in the minds of many white Americans, especially white men, about minorities' ability to succeed in the corporate sphere. Because of stubborn and overwhelming negative stereotypes, minorities must clarify for themselves their own strengths and weaknesses so that they can readily determine what is racism and what is not. What are they contributing to their own and their organizations' problems? Part of the racist game is to blame the victims for their oppressed position. As long as minorities base their estimations of self-worth on the opinions of the majority society about them, they will be on a constant merry-go-round, trying to repair their so-called defects as defined by white people. As soon as one "defect," like needing the right education, is fixed, along comes another: "Minorities must improve their attitude." If the "attitude" improves, it will be, "Minorities need more experience to be really qualified." By the time racist society finishes "rounding out" and "polishing" the minority with the proper qualifications, the minority will be so well-rounded that he or she could be a basketball for the N.B.A.

Wasting energy by buying into racist stereotypes does not leave minorities time to develop the proper game plan, which could concretely enhance their chances of success in corporate

America. What is more, they begin to question the successes they do achieve.

Many minority consulting firms lately have been advising minorities to assimilate, to adopt the characteristics of white men as much as possible to be successful. We vehemently disagree with this approach. When I worked for AT&T, some came to me with proposals to teach minorities not only the "proper" hair style but also the right words to say, where to live, how to socialize, and so on. In other words, they guaranteed that they could make minority people into white male clones except for their color or perhaps gender. This, they believed, would ensure success. First of all, corporations have been run by people who are too similar in body, mind, and soul. Second, to be successful in the new global marketplace is to learn to appreciate, respect, and value differences. Thus, from the corporate viewpoint, manufacturing minority clones of white males is not the efficient, productive way to go.

From a minority standpoint, to believe that adopting the white male model is the ticket to success simply indicates a lack of appreciation of the tremendous power of race and gender in our society. Of course, there is a certain amount of conformity that all must maintain in order to be part of corporate life, but to strive to be other than oneself is destructive to the integrity and uniqueness of minority cultures and to individual minority group members. No matter how much a minority person tries to emulate the majority group, the fact is that racists will never value this effort at assimilation. Rather, they will misread it as an affirmation of their own superiority, to the detriment of pluralism.

How much more valuable it would be for all concerned if minorities could look at themselves in the mirror in the morning with genuine affection and respect for themselves and their own uniqueness. When they come home from work at night, they should be able to feel the same way. Research has shown that many women are developing severe physical and psychological problems as a result of trying to be like men at work. The same applies to minorities.

In sum, to combat racist stereotypes, faith in oneself and one's ability is crucial. Minorities must develop positive approaches to the challenges facing them. They must fight for their rights and put fear and doubt aside. They should give the best and expect the best.

As we noted earlier, stereotyping is a two-way reaction. Stereotypes are no more justifiable and no less destructive if they are held by minorities than by the majority culture. For corporate America to become a productive, global economic force in the coming decades, all stereotypes must be dealt with regardless of their source.

Dual Performance Standards

It is clear from earlier chapters that one of the frustrations minority workers face is that, in general, they simply have to be better performers than white workers to get ahead. Throughout our twenty years of survey research, this question has always produced one of the largest disparities in response patterns. Eighty-seven percent of African Americans, 67 percent of Native Americans, 58 percent of Asians, 53 percent of Hispanics, and only 32 percent of the white group agree that minority workers must outperform white workers to advance. Broken out by race and gender, more than 40 percent of the white women and only 25 percent of the white men concur. In addition, 80 percent of African Americans, 44 percent of Native Americans, 30 percent of Hispanics, 23 percent of Asians, and 14 percent of white respondents believe that people of color are penalized more for mistakes than white employees. "Black workers are asked for proof of their qualifications and skills," says a black female middle-level manager. "Caucasian workers are viewed in terms of their potential for growth and skills development."

How can minorities deal with this inequity? First of all, they must admit that it exists, get angry if they need to, and then put their anger aside and develop a game plan.

Second, minorities should get credentials from the best schools that they can and concentrate on developing those on-the-job skills that are in limited supply in their work group, so that others will be compelled to call upon them to ensure their own success. They must be sure to improve their oral and written communication skills, not only in their native tongue but in the majority language.

Third, minorities must understand that in order to be better performers they must be secure enough to take creative risks. They must seek exposure and alliances outside of their work group that could positively affect how they are perceived and evaluated. Fourth, minorities should try to get line jobs with numerically measurable results.

Finally, minority workers must assume primary responsibility for seeking equitable performance evaluations by making sure that, at a minimum, their supervisors review performance quarterly and potential yearly. They must strive to correct any weaknesses that they and their supervisors agree they need to work on. If minorities feel that they are being treated inequitably and dual performance standards are being used, they should pursue it up the hierarchy. If the issue is not resolved, they should file an Equal Employment Opportunity suit against the company.

Some minority employees will say, "But if I file a suit, won't that hurt my career?" The answer is yes, in most cases; however, unless more minority employees file legitimate suits against companies, why would companies change discriminatory behavior? We have seen minority workers who have not pursued their rights only to have their jobs terminated anyway in reorganization efforts.

The choice for minorities is to sit there and take it or to fight for equity. If they pursue the former path, nothing will change except that they could lose their jobs or fail to advance if they are right about the company's discriminatory activity. If they choose the latter, they might still lose their jobs, but they might have a chance to have their grievances redressed. In addition, if companies have sufficient suits filed against them, eventually someone in the hierarchy will begin to take notice and take positive steps toward ending dual standards.

Power and Authority Problems

Minorities must recognize that, because they lack certain institutional power and authority that white men acquire by virtue of their positions, they must be better performers than white men in similar jobs. This takes on added significance when one recognizes that the essence of corporate life is power and authority. In this market-oriented society, where customers rule, we found that 33 percent of Asian, Native American, and white employees, compared to 38 percent of Hispanics and 56 percent of African Americans, believe that customers do not accept the authority of a person of color as well as they accept that of a white person in a similar position.

In 1986, we found that 38 percent of black Americans, 9 percent of white Americans, and 16 percent of other minorities responded that minorities do not have the same influence as white people do with regard to clients and co-workers.

On the opposite end of the scale, 52 percent of white respondents, 10 percent of black respondents, and 29 percent of other minorities responded that minorities have the same power and authority as white workers. If this is the case, then corporate America is throwing billions of dollars down the drain in ineffective interactions. In addition, as markets become more global, to not give the same power and authority to minorities who are representing their companies in their country of origin or ancestry could be extremely detrimental, especially if the host country becomes aware of it. The latter could interpret the lack of power and authority as an affront to the entire country.

To deal with the power issue, minorities must recognize that while the power and authority inherent in a work position normally devolves to white males, it does not normally devolve to minorities. However, minorities can assume much more power and authority than the corporate world or their position inherently gives them if they only dare to do so. One way to increase your power and authority is to assume that you have it and act accordingly. It is better to beg for forgiveness than to ask for permission.

From the first day in a new position, minority workers must act decisively and with confidence. Any evidence of weakness, indecisiveness, and failure to take charge will only convince racist subordinates and peers that the minority worker is an easy target whose power and authority can be challenged at every turn.

Because they understand how their actions might be misinterpreted, many minorities are at times reluctant to go after or exercise the power and authority to which they are entitled. If white co-workers are not listening to their opinions, however, ultimately minorities must be forceful and deal with them in a straightforward manner or develop strategies to accomplish their job even if they are not being listened to.

Before taking any action, minorities must decide how important it is to their getting the job done. Note that we did not say how important it is to their ego but to their job. If other employees are not accepting their authority, a quiet private discussion often does the trick. For subordinates who will not listen to reason, minorities should try sending them some clear messages through pay raises, job assignments, budgets, promotions, and so on. If that doesn't work, get rid of them. Minorities cannot afford to have subordinates who are insubordinate.

A word of caution: Minorities must guard against overreacting to employees' bypassing them for reasons of expediency. Being in a competitive marketplace requires bypassing the chain of command. Secure bosses know their subordinates can determine when such bypassing is appropriate. Only if such actions are clearly based on racism or on no other legitimate reason should they become an issue.

Finally, minorities (and women) must recognize that retaining power and authority is an ongoing process. As minorities move through their careers, they will always encounter some white people who do not want minorities to have power and authority. Some will go to great lengths to render minorities powerless. To protect themselves, minorities can never become complacent with their current measure of power and authority.

Exclusion from Informal Work Groups

A great deal of power in the corporate structure rests in informal networks. Systematic exclusion from powerful, political, well-connected informal groups can seriously block access to the power and authority that one needs to perform at one's maximum. Just as women feel excluded by men, many minority workers, especially those who are dark-skinned, believe they are excluded from informal white work groups. A significant percentage of white respondents concur. In 1988, 87 percent of African Americans, 42 percent of the other minorities, and 36 percent of the white group believed that many minorities are often excluded from informal work networks.

What can minorities do about being excluded from informal work groups? To be successful, productive employees, they must have some access to these groups. If it is difficult for the majority to include minorities, minorities must not waste their energies trying to become part of groups that are more social than political. Remember, real informal networks exist primarily to enhance the power, influence, and careers of their members.

The way to become part of informal work groups is to have something, or appear to have something, that the groups want. Short of this, minorities must find ways to socialize at work and nonwork functions with the intention of making contacts and becoming part of the informal work group. Try to find something in common with the leader(s) of the group, and build on it.

Minorities must take the initiative to become members of informal work groups. In addition, they must begin to form their own informal work groups. Unfortunately, most minorities do not do very well at forming their own informal networks, largely because whites criticize them as being "racist." To refrain from forming informal work groups because of such perceptions is to allow racism to deny minorities access to a crucial strategy for success in the corporation. Minorities must recognize that the white power group does not view its own exclusiveness in the same light as it perceives exclusiveness in minorities.

Most networks have overlapping memberships. Each group has its "snitches" and "plants," and thus an informal work group must be used cautiously and strategically. This last point is critical, because many minority people tend to be more open, honest, and straightforward than many white employees. In addition, when the "old boy network" seems to let them in, they feel their acceptance is total, and they let their guard down. This is a false assumption and a fatal mistake.

One way in which minorities can be sure that the informal work group will be more useful than harmful to their careers is if sponsors high in the hierarchy introduce them and mentor them. However, as is the case with women, minorities have a much harder time finding such sponsors than white men do. A large percentage of black workers (87 percent), compared to 35 percent of white workers, agree with this proposition. Fifty-seven percent of Asians, 54 percent of Hispanics, and 44 percent of Native Americans concur. While there are few minorities in real positions of power to be effective mentors, minorities can still sponsor other minorities; therefore, minorities should not have the false notion, especially at the lower levels, that their mentors have to be white.

A most important strategy that minorities must undertake to enhance their overall situation is to overcome some of their competitive individualism and recognize that all their fates are ultimately wrapped up together. Minorities should do exactly what a white male lower-level manager complains about: "They create a lot of their own problems, once they are promoted; they try to pull only their brothers up."

As minority workers move up the corporate ladder they must make special efforts to bring minority co-workers along. A criticism of minority workers would be that the few who have made it into the middle and upper ranks have not made a concerted effort to assist others of minority groups. Minority workers should remember that if they do not assist each other, they cannot expect others to assist them. Minority workers should not refuse to bring along white co-workers with them—they must do so to be successful—but they should also make a concerted effort to bring along minority employees. Only when the middle and upper levels of management have a much larger number of minority occupants committed to recognizing their obligation to help the corporation change its racist attitudes and behaviors will minorities have a somewhat equal chance of advancing up the corporate hierarchy and help their companies operate effectively and competitively in the 1990s and beyond.

Language and Writing Skills

We have presented considerable information about the importance of language in defining culture and how people communicate. In the coming decades, it is absolutely essential for minorities (as well as whites) to become bilingual or multilingual. In addition, regardless of the company or country they are working in, it is important to be able to speak the dominant language used in the company or country.

With specific regard to working in the United States and in U.S. companies, the following applies. One can extrapolate how this applies to working in foreign companies in the United States or abroad.

It is perfectly acceptable to the white corporate structure for a white employee to speak with a strong accent or occasionally to use incorrect grammar; it is considered "cute." However, black English has no place in corporate America, and Hispanic and Asian accents are also a handicap, even though German, Swedish, or other European accents are considered chic. Our only advice is that minorities should try, within reason, to eliminate any accent. Those who have a natural uncorrectable accent can minimize negative reactions by using flawless English grammar.

By extension, it is clear that written skills are key to the success of minorities. Minority speech can be criticized subjectively, but what minorities write is a permanent record of their skills and conceptualization processes. Written material is much harder to judge subjectively than discourse. So minorities would do well to develop their written skills. One poorly written document can have a long-term negative impact on a minority worker's career.

In short, minorities must develop excellent written and oral communication skills, in more than one language, if they expect to be successful. Minorities must remember that we use these two skills more frequently, and more people observe them, than any other skills we have.

Organizing

Minorities should also do precisely what a majority group manager criticized—stick together: "Minorities, especially blacks, always stick together. They have all these groups which are only for blacks. . . ."

It is much easier for a ruling group to destroy one person than a group of people. Organizing, having lunch and dinner together, are important ways for minorities to assist one another. Forming organizations for self-help and to pressure and influence corporate leaders' behavior is essential for changing racism in corporate America. Many minorities avoid such tactics because they fear the reaction of white employers. Minorities should remember that in most corporations there are private dining rooms for upper-level managers and for middle-level managers, the majority of whom are white men. One hears no criticism of this practice as clannish. On the contrary, such arrangements are considered conducive to the development of personal bonds, the sharing of information, and doing business.

One of the main issues minorities must confront is that, consciously or unconsciously, white American society has engendered deep hostilities among different minorities and among white women and men who might support minorities. It is crucial for these groups to put aside their hostilities and recognize that the survival of their companies, in the years to come, will rest on their abilities to accept, respect, and appreciate differences.

Dealing with Paranoia

Our final point is that minorities cannot avoid some paranoia about racism and thus about white people. It is absolutely crucial, however, for that paranoia to be contained within the bounds of healthy skepticism. Minorities must be suspicious of white people until gaining sufficient evidence that they are "all right," that they have dealt with their racism or are in the process of dealing with it. It is exhausting and counterproductive to interpret every negative action on the part of white people as evidence of racism. We admit that at times it is hard to tell whether an action arises from racism, since this is no longer in most cases overt. Minorities should, however, always do some reality checking with themselves and others they respect before pouncing on racism as the reason for all negative actions. If minorities do not do this, they will not be successful.

Some psychiatrists warn that it is extremely difficult to keep this paranoia positive and not self-destructive. To maintain a high degree of suspicion toward the motives of every white person and at the same time never to allow this suspicion to impair one's grasp of reality, is walking a very thin tightrope.

Conclusion

Despite optimistic propaganda about the tremendous progress made by minorities in the past decades, few minority and white people find their companies free of racism.

Minorities (like women) are faced with a whole host of problems that white males do not have to face. They range from general factors such as combating stereotypes about their abilities to the daily necessity of being better performers than whites in order to get ahead. They must perform with the additional handicaps of not having the same power and authority to get their jobs done, being excluded from informal work groups, and having more difficulty finding mentors.

The essential ingredients of minority success in the 1990s and beyond are recognition and understanding of racism, and the development of a positive self-concept and expert technical, professional, analytical, and communication skills. Minorities must be creative risk takers and on the leading edge of new concepts, strategies, plans, and technologies.

While this is an individualistic competitive society, minorities must forge alliances among themselves and with their white allies in order to be empowered to change racist attitudes and behavior in corporations. They must recognize that none of them will have equal opportunity until all of them do.

It is absolutely crucial for minorities to deal with their own racism. A competitive and diverse work force will not come about until all its employees see they are both part of the problem and part of the solution.

Finally, minorities must realize that sitting around complaining about how bad things are will not change anything. Minorities must adopt a "must-do" positive attitude.

12

United States: White Americans with Emphasis on White Men

When people discuss managing differences, they often focus on the problems created by discrimination for people of color and women. In this chapter, we explore the problems that white Americans, especially white men, perceive. We also provide strategies for white men to employ to become positive members of pluralistic companies that will be competitive in the global marketplace.

The white population in the United States will become a minority by the middle of the twenty-first century. In two of our states, California and New York, white people will become a minority about the year 2000. Texas, New Mexico, and Florida will follow soon thereafter. While the majority of the white population believes in equal opportunities and fairness, there are dangerous signals that as the minority population increases and more white people see themselves competing with them for schools, housing, and jobs, old hatreds and animosities are reawakening.

White Employees' Perceptions of Problems in the Workplace

In general white Americans express the greatest number of stereotypes about minorities, but they are the most likely to say they do not bring them into the workplace. Thus, they do not see as much discrimination against minorities as these groups themselves do, but tend to attribute minorities' problems to individual inadequacies.

It makes me very angry to encounter a racist person, but it also makes me angry to encounter someone who uses their color [to obtain consideration in the company]. (White, lower-level, woman)

I know there are some people who think because of their race or gender the company should hand them good jobs, qualified or not. I believe I should only advance my position when I earn it and not because I'm a female purple midget. (White, occupational, woman)

Let time take its course. Just to promote a person of color or a woman [if they haven't earned it] doesn't do them or us any good. I don't respect them. I lose respect for the company. In time, those that show potential will be promoted and moved up with respect. (White, lower-level, woman)

That minorities are angry with the world and think that they deserve everything on a plate and not to have to work for it. People with foreign accents should try to speak English at all times, because this is the U.S. language. In doing this, they would just improve their English every day. (White, middle-level, woman)

Employees in the work environment who are underqualified and do not perform an adequate job still maintain their status as employees. Why? Because maybe they represent a minority? (White, occupational, man)

Indeed, many white workers, especially white males, believe that what they face now in the U.S. workplace is reverse discrimination. They believe that qualified white men are losing out to unqualified women and minorities.

Where's the white male organization? Oh no, that would be prejudiced. However, every other kind of person on the face of the earth has their own club. Talk about segregation! By the way, I'm a white female whose white male husband can't get a job because he's the wrong color. I guess white children don't need to be supported as much as children of color. (White, occupational, woman)

I believe that a total reversal in discrimination has happened. A white male and a black male with the same qualifications will not be judged equally because of the federal government. The company will choose the black male because they're afraid of being called a racist company. (White, occupational, man)

I personally have been turned down for jobs and promotions because I was not female or nonwhite. The explanation was "off the record" of course! (White, lower-level, man)

I am a White male. I am discriminated against because I'm not gay, I'm not a minority, I'm not a woman, I'm not handicapped, and I'm white; therefore I get no favoritism, only the opposite. Our company is so busy trying to be fair to those who say "you are neglecting me because I have this particular (whatever)" that they hold off the average white male, which is discrimination in reverse. (White, occupational, man)

While we make up for the lack of women in middle and upper management, many qualified white males will go unrewarded. Many females promoted are deserving. Others are obviously not nearly qualified. (White, middle-level, man)

We are all individuals regardless of our color or sex and we should all be treated the same, as far as promotions, raises, and opportunities go. If a white female and a black or other minority were both qualified for a position, the minority would receive the position. Whatever happened to seniority? (White, occupational, man)

Co-workers' Perceptions of White Male Employees

As is to be expected, minority workers and women see white men's position in the workplace from a very different perspective. Some stereotypes used by employees in our seminars to describe white people, and especially white men, are arrogant, crazy, ignorant, insensitive, out of control, spoiled, and selfish. The more positive stereotypes are privileged, shrewd, in control, dominant, powerful, and smart.

Figure 12–1 shows employee responses to several questions about white male workers. There are considerable differences among the various groups on many of these questions. For example, only 27 percent of white men, as compared to 42–83 percent of other groups, believe white men got their positions just because they are white men. Following are some employees'

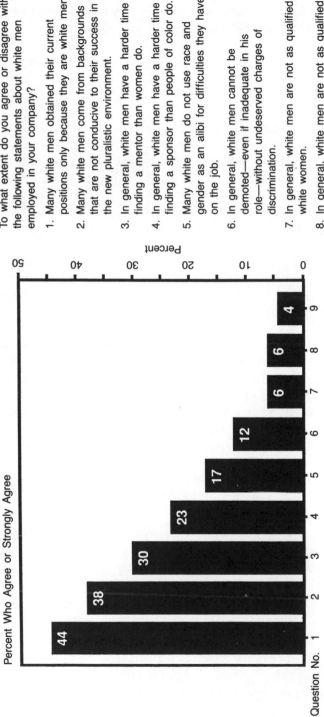

To what extent do you agree or disagree with the following statements about white men employed in your company?

1. Many white men obtained their current positions only because they are white men.

2. Many white men come from backgrounds that are not conducive to their success in the new pluralistic environment.

3. In general, white men have a harder time finding a mentor than women do.

4. In general, white men have a harder time finding a sponsor than people of color do.

5. Many white men do not use race and gender as an alibi for difficulties they have on the job.

6. In general, white men cannot be demoted—even if inadequate in his role—without undeserved charges of discrimination.

7. In general, white men are not as qualified as white women.

8. In general, white men are not as qualified as people of color.

Percent Who Agree or Strongly Agree

FIGURE 12–1

Co-workers' Perceptions about White Male Employees

comments from our studies regarding their perceptions of white people, and especially white men, in the workplace.

> The only problem white men face today is that they have been spoiled for too many years and are having a hard time adjusting to sharing. They've been raised to think they get the whole pie. (White, occupational, woman)

> White males have created their own problems. Many white males are very prejudiced against people of color and make no bones about it. Higher management men do not like women or people of color running the company. This makes it very difficult to work with them. (White, lower-level, woman)

> I generally think all whites have no respect for blacks, and I start with that notion. I respond to them from that point. I have to . . . demand respect. (Black, occupational, woman)

> I get angry at white males. Not only do they think that they're better than colored men and women, they think that they're the next best things to perfect. They can do no wrong. (Black, occupational, woman)

> I'm defensive and get mad at whites when questioned about data that I have done a lot of investigation on. I feel, if white, there would not be a second thought as to whether I knew what I was talking about. (Black, occupational, woman)

> The white man protects the white man politically or whatever. No demotion would be made; lateral move, yes. But still he is being taken care of. The white man supposedly does not have faults. They do, but these are not brought out openly and rapidly as they would be with a minority. (Hispanic, occupational, man)

> I believe that I see whites as "bull-shit artists." I see them make schedules that are not attainable, present them to the department, and when the schedules do not materialize, they are not penalized for them. But if someone who is not white does it, one has to explain why and the assignment will be given to someone else. I feel that whites can do sub-par work, present it to their buddies, and their buddies (in general) will look the other way. I feel that my attitude about white work ethics are biased. But I see nothing

to dispel the notion. Look close at our department and see how the whites take a lot of time off yet get promoted; they accomplish nothing spectacular at work yet get promoted.
(Hispanic, lower-level, man)

White males are still in control or in power positions. There appears to be a reluctance to share this control and become pluralistic. This creates anger and hostility against them.
(Black, middle-level, man)

Traditionally, white men have had hardly any problems in the company. In the last few years it may have been a little more difficult to be promoted because of jobs being filled by people of color, but they still have enough pull from friends or family to reach executive positions. (Hispanic, occupational, man)

There is some evidence that some minority people are beginning to act out their hostile attitudes toward white people, even those white people who have no problems with people of color. A personal example I had illustrates this. In April 1990, I was running for exercise. I noticed a large excited group of black children aged 5–14. In the middle of the large group were two thirteen-year-old white girls who were systematically getting spit on, punched, and kicked. I entered the crowd and told the black children to leave them alone. I was cursed and spit at but not hit. However, as the two white girls and I turned our backs to walk away, a fuselage of sticks, bottles, and small rocks hit us. I turned around and chased the black youths away. They dispersed. I escorted the girls safely to their home. What had the girls done to the black children? Nothing, except that they were white!

A recent survey showed that racial attacks on different groups in the Los Angeles school district have increased greatly. In 1988, white victims reported less than 100 racial attack incidents; in 1989, such incidents numbered 337. The districts speculate that as white children become a smaller minority (28.9 percent) of the student population, they are prone to more racial abuse. In Philadelphia, there have been a number of racial attacks on white students during the past year. In one case, a young white man was killed.

While minorities are generally not in positions of power to negatively affect white careers, the coming decades will certainly produce changes in demographics and thus in power relations. As has been shown in the Los Angeles county schools, minority students are taking out some of their anger on white children, who represent far less than a majority of the county school population. It is certainly reasonable to conclude that minority feelings must get in their way of working effectively with white people.

In fairness to white men, many are not insensitive, racist, or cry babies. The second most frequent comment we received from white men in our seminars concerned their fear of unintentionally offending minorities or women. This fear can be as nonproductive as racist and sexist views, because it inhibits open healthy communication among people. This in turn leads to misunderstanding and lower corporate efficiency. The following comments illustrate these feelings.

> When I'm supposed to be sensitive to some groups like blacks, I find myself ill-at-ease for fear of offending, and probably come off as cold or indifferent. (White, upper-level, man)

> While in a group such as this I am afraid of possibly saying something wrong that may offend somebody.
> (White, occupational, man)

> Feel that I must be careful about inadvertently offending someone of another race or the opposite sex (walking on eggshells). Sometimes I assume the other person is prejudiced against me because of my sex or race. We don't communicate.
> (White, lower-level, man)

> I worry that the other person automatically assumes that just because I am a white male I am prejudiced against them. Any statements made could be taken as prejudiced because the other person is very sensitive to the issue. Not sure how to "break the ice" sometimes. (White, middle-level, man)

> Fear of getting accused of picking on a minority person when I'm in the work environment. I was at a review, and the person who was giving the review was a minority person. I was giving good

feedback about the document. I felt some frustration about it and said to myself it looks like I'm picking on them. But before the review, I had asked myself, was it because of the document or the man, and it was the document. (White, upper-level, man)

Are white men accurate or are the minorities accurate in their assessment? Is the company treating white men unfairly and giving the opportunities to unqualified women and minorities? Or do white men, harboring a sense of entitlement perhaps, in Machiavelli's terms "expect more than they deserve"? What can white men do to enhance their career opportunities?

A Change in White Men's Advancement Opportunities

Whenever we give a speech on mobility in corporations, we like to start out by asking, "Would you prefer to compete for a promotion with thirty-three people or one hundred people?" Most respondents say they would prefer to compete with thirty-three people rather than one hundred because they would have a much better chance for promotion. To understand this is to understand the problem white men face in their desire to move up the corporate ladder, and the psychological turmoil that they increasingly experience as corporations move toward greater commitment to equal employment opportunity.

Until the Civil Rights Act of 1964, white men in corporations had to compete against only 33 percent of the adult population, for that is the percentage of the adult U.S. population that are white men. However, after 1964, white men, at least by law, had to compete on a more equitable basis with the other 67 percent, that is, women and people of color. Essentially this meant that white men who were average and below average in abilities began to have a more difficult time in advancing, because they were now competing with the entire adult population, which includes many with credentials and abilities superior to theirs.

Despite this, however, white men who are above average— especially those who fit the image of the promotable manager— have little trouble advancing in work. The most numerous and powerful decision makers were and are white men and even average and below average white men still, in many cases, have an advantage over above average women and minorities.

Terry has pointed out that although white male managers currently face greater competition for fewer jobs as a result of affirmative action policies, racism [and sexism] have sheltered them from the need to test their skills. The tacit discrimination practiced by upper-level management created the need for affirmative action, he explained. This discrimination leaves white men ill-equipped to deal with pluralistic competition once it is forced upon them.[1]

Greatly increased competition with large numbers of people whom white men believe, at some level, to be inferior or deficient in some way naturally leads to severe psychological dislocation, and to cries of unfair treatment and reverse discrimination. Corporations should recognize this as a normal reaction of people who are at risk of being displaced from a privileged power position. This is especially painful because white men, always a minority of the population, have perceived themselves to be a majority. As a white lower-level manager said, "The company in effect has produced a new minority—the white male."

Let's use an analogy to put the problem white men face into perspective. Suppose that you and your immediate friends had controlled this society for 500 years. During those years, you and your ancestors were brought up to believe that you are in control because you work hard, have the necessary credentials, and have the right values and attitudes. You were also taught that those other people (not your friends) failed to make it into the power positions not because of discrimination but because they were essentially inferior and did not have the right skills, values, and attitudes. Now, after 500 years, you and your friends are told by law you have to share your privileged position with large numbers of "inferior" people who greatly outnumber you. Do you think you would willingly share your position and power? Would you immediately stop believing, after 500 years of discriminatory socialization, that the others were inferior? Would you think that the law was fair? The answer to all of these questions is no. Neither you nor I would willingly give up or share something that we had been conditioned over 500 years to believe was rightfully ours because we had the right values, intelligence, and work ethic. Neither would white men.

What we would do, given the above scenario, and what some white men have done, is to become fearful toward people and programs that challenge our privileged position. In addition, we would begin to develop, consciously or unconsciously, an array of strategies to defend the status quo. The news media tell the populace about how terrible things are for white men and how women and minorities have it made. Academics write books about the terrible consequences of the new meritocracy and how this has negatively affected corporate efficiency and productivity.

By developing such theories that blame the victims and encourage them to accept the blame for their oppression, white men can feel more comfortable that they indeed deserve their privileged positions. In this way, they can concentrate on maintaining their bastion of power and privilege and avoid looking at their own deficiencies.

A crucial way in which white men have maintained their privileged position has been by keeping women and minorities divided, fighting among themselves for a small piece of pie. This keeps the oppressed occupied.

Some white men exhibit a siege mentality. This insecurity seems due in large part to the white man's upbringing, in which he was taught that he is the superior being and would never have to compete with people of color or women. Many white men are like fish out of water in the emerging, more equitable diverse environment. They are trying to figure out how things are changing.

Enhancing Career Opportunities

The most important step that white men can take to enhance their career opportunities is to accept reality so that they can better develop their strategies. If one insists on living in a world of illusion, one cannot effectively cope with the real world. Listed below are some of the realities that white men must recognize and accept.

Reality No. 1. Corporate America Is Unfair to All

Corporate America is an unfair bureaucracy that has never given promotions, jobs, rewards, or anything else strictly on the basis of merit, even to white males. In addition, it does not offer unlimited opportunities, as most white men have been brought up to believe.

Reality No. 2. Image Is Vital to Success

The higher a white man goes in the corporate structure, the more likely he is to be discriminated against by the white men in power if he does not fit the image of the promotable manager.

It is essential for white men to recognize not only on an intellectual level but on a gut level that there are numerous subjective reasons why people get ahead. Over sixty years of systematic research support this view.

Again, it seems that white men, because the system is theirs and because they see many successful role models, find it hard to see reality. As developers and owners of the system, most have totally bought into the rhetoric of meritocracy and as a result are having extreme difficulties with their perceived limited career opportunities.

Reality No. 3. Competition Is Keen

White men must recognize that most of them will not get the promotions or the jobs they desire—not because of reverse dis-crimination but simply because the selection pool has increased from thirty-three people to one hundred people. The odds against the thirty-three people, especially those who are average or below average in ability, are greatly increased.

Despite the prevalent belief among many white men that they are members of the superior group, each race and gender has a small percentage of outstanding people, a larger percentage of below average people, and a very large percentage of mediocre people. The vital question for white men is, now that they are competing with a larger pool of people, which of them will lose out to the increased competition. And in the new global market place, the competition will be greatly increased.

Reality No. 4. White Males Are Still Advantaged

In most cases, the below average and average white man still has significant advantages over women and minorities of the same ability. The same advantage applies to above average white men who compete with above average women and minorities. As Jones wrote,

> Much of the expressed antagonism toward affirmative action is based on the belief that standards are lowered by allowing "less qualified" minorities and women in entry positions ahead of "more qualified" white males. The historical fact is that minorities and women have had to be overqualified in order to obtain opportunities. An implication of the overqualification requirement is that, historically, white males have obtained positions with substantially weaker qualifications.[2]

Why is this the case? White men still dominate the U.S. workplace. They set the cultural tone, the standards, and the criteria for advancement. Human beings are most likely to select people like themselves to replace them, in this case white men. Researchers have clearly demonstrated that competitive choices favoring in-group members tend to dominate all other choices available to the study participants.[3] In other words, despite white men's concern that they are at a great disadvantage because of affirmative action, the basic concept of in-group bias suggests that, until the corporate hierarchy has many more women and minorities, white men will still be the favored group. However, as the chapter on Japan suggests, in Japanese companies white men are at a great disadvantage compared to Japanese men but at a great advantage compared to minorities and women.

One would suppose, with all the cries about reverse discrimination over the past twenty-six years, that women and minorities have substantially advanced into the corporate hierarchy. However, only a handful of women and Hispanic Americans and only one black American have risen to the top of a major U.S. corporation.

Reality No. 5. The Concept of Reverse Discrimination Is Based on Non-Truths

White men's sense of reverse discrimination is based in large part on the non-truths they hear from their own corporations, from the media, and from educational institutions.

Over the past twenty-six years, we have observed many white men who believe that they are victims of reverse discrimination because their companies and managers implicitly or explicitly do not tell them the truth. Some are directly told that their careers are going nowhere, or that they did not get a promotion or a lateral job, because of women and minority quotas. In fact, none of the companies in my studies ever had quotas; they had goals and timetables for management positions up through middle management. The goals and the timetables were minimal, and there was no penalty for failing to meet them. Most managers or occupational workers who believe they were discriminated against actually were not promoted because of lack of skills, ability, or potential, or because of some subjective evaluation on the part of their bosses or the company. Also, companies promise many more opportunities than they are able to deliver and have not developed ways of satisfying the high expectations of many workers. Since most white men believe they are being discriminated against, it is much simpler and easier to tell them that they are not going anywhere because of women and minorities than to tell them about their own limitations. White men, who feel much more in-group loyalty to the company than other groups, are less likely to take formal action against perceived discrimination than women and minorities.

When lack of mobility of white men is blamed on women and minorities, this should be a red flag. White male candidates should recognize that, by allowing their superiors to shift blame, they are allowing them to avoid discussing the employee's actual ability to do the job. Most bosses want to avoid uncomfortable situations, especially those related to giving employees bad news like why they are not getting a promotion. Therefore, bosses will pick the easiest way out. White men can commiserate with one another about how terrible it is now for them because of reverse discrimination; however, there is no commiscrating when one white man tells another, "I am not supporting you for a promotion because you just don't have it. I don't like your style or your personality."

Corporations have done a disservice to white men by not explaining the true facts about their opportunities. Society, which is controlled by white men, has done the same. New media, books, and articles have basically presented an image that all it takes to succeed is to be a woman or a minority person. The statistics, however, show just the opposite. Probably the one factor that has caused more psychological trauma in white men than any other is the Reagan/Bush administrations' constant attack on equal employment opportunities and affirmative action. How can white men believe they are getting a fair shake when the two most popular presidents in recent history say that they are being discriminated against? Bowser and Hunt summarize the impact of the Reagan administration in this regard. An erosion is evident in the federal commitment to initiatives and programs that, for almost fifty years, assisted the advancement of racial equality. Moreover, a number of occurrences reflect a mood of backlash and hostile reaction to the insistence on racial justice in America: "Our nation seems quite willing to countenance an era of benign neglect on contemporary racial issues."[4]

To deal constructively with the potential for reverse discrimination, white men should insist on quarterly written performance evaluations. They should also seek yearly written potential evaluations with career plans and development plans as integral parts of the evaluation process. Our book *Racism and Sexism in Corporate Life* discusses performance, potential, and career planning, and contains good commonsense advice on how to ensure that one is getting at least an even chance of being treated fairly in these processes. *Survival in the Corporate Fishbowl* has other survival tactics. This advice is useful not only to white men but to anyone trying to have a successful career in the corporate world.

White men should ask for a breakdown of all promotions by race, gender, and level. They should also demand to know specifically why they did not get a particular job. If they believe they are truly the better candidates and that they have been discriminated against, they should pursue the matter to higher levels. Sitting around complaining about reverse discrimination instead of insisting on the full story from the company is short-sighted and unproductive.

Having said this, let us also say that white men who say that women and minorities are "always crying" about discrimination are themselves some of the worst offenders.

To focus constantly on race and gender as factors holding up a career is to waste a lot of energy. White men, to be successful in the emerging heterogeneous corporation, must begin to face reality. If they continue to attribute their lack of success to reverse discrimination, they will not focus on getting the true story from the company, and thus they will be unable to develop realistic strategies to reach their goals, revise them according to the realities, or develop plans to correct them. They will doom their careers, because competition will get tougher as more people compete for fewer positions.

Reality No. 6. Nothing Excuses Poor Performance

With the increasing competition and limited opportunities, white men must not allow their frustrations to affect their performance. If they do this, it will give the company a solid reason to block them from reaching their desired positions. In 1988, 58 percent of white men in our studies agreed that many white men were not performing their jobs as effectively as possible because they were frustrated about their perceived limited opportunities. Figure 12–2 shows that white men are most likely to agree with this statement, and Asian women and black men are least likely to agree.

If white men or any other people really believe they are not being treated fairly, they should adjust their goals, fight for their rights, or leave the company. Poor performance benefits no one, especially those who are considered the poor performers.

Reality No. 7. White Men Must Adjust to Diversity

White men who attempt to change their prejudices will have greater promotional opportunities than those who do not.

Many minorities and women have been socialized somewhat

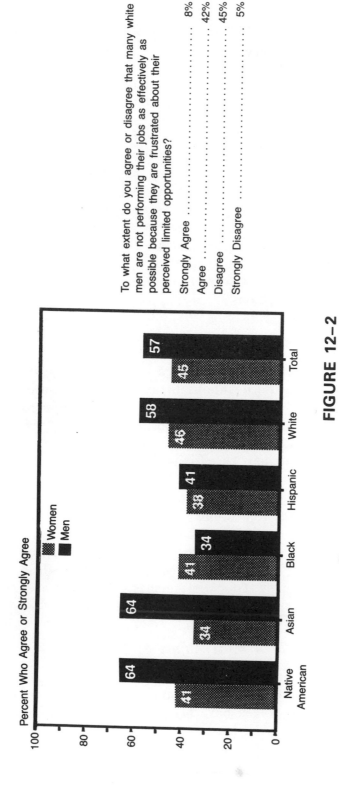

FIGURE 12-2

Perception of White Men's Performance on the Job

differently from white men. They have diverse cultural backgrounds. In some cases, they have different value systems and
different expectations than do the white men who currently
dominate the U.S. workplace. The coming together of these people of diverse backgrounds, in some cases for the first time in the
corporate setting, has created great tension for everyone.

This is not to judge which group has the correct background,
values, expectations, and so on. Each group has some unique
good and bad qualities. In addition, there are more similarities
than differences among Americans because of the American socialization process. What is important for white men to understand is that because of their power and dominant position, they
have not had to adjust to others; others have always had to
adjust to them. In 1988, we found that overall 39 percent of
employees believed white men's backgrounds to be not conducive to their success in a pluralistic environment. The percentages
varied from a high of 59 percent for black women to 34–47
percent for the other groups (see figure 12–3 for responses by
role and gender). If this is true, then many white men will be at
a great disadvantage. They have problems dealing with workers
who have different backgrounds, different cultures, values, and
norms and different languages and religions.

The U.S. workplace, out of competitive necessity, will become
increasingly heterogeneous. The employees who will have the
greatest chances of making it will be those who can accept and
feel comfortable working in this new work force. White men
who retain their prejudices will never be able to work effectively
with truly heterogeneous work groups. As a result, they will
never be able to help their organizations achieve the best results.
White men who can operate effectively in this new heterogeneous environment will have a definite advantage.

Conclusion

This chapter rounds out our discussion about ethnicity and gender in the United States. It is evident from the analyses in this
chapter that white people, especially white men, are beginning to
face hostile segments of minorities and women. Part of this hostility can be traced to the racist and sexist behaviors of white

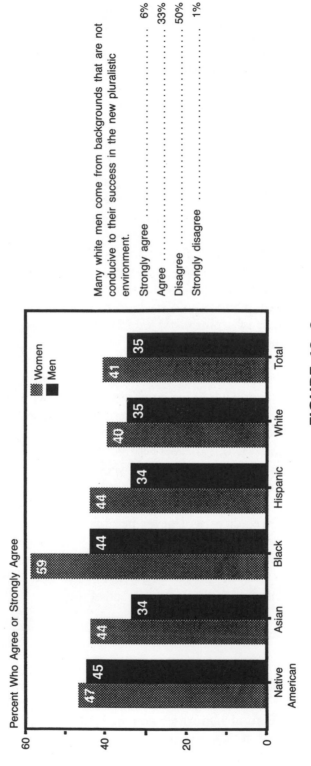

FIGURE 12–3
White Men's Background and Pluralism

men, and part of it can be traced to the fact that women and minorities have been socialized into stereotypes about white people.

For white men to be successful in the 1990s, they must deal with their own shortcomings. In addition, they must become more skilled at dealing with people who are different than they are. As we have suggested throughout, an important characteristic of any employee in the 1990s and beyond will be the ability to speak more than one language and to understand different cultures.

United States: Other Diversity Issues

Age, Religion, Sexual Preference, and Disabilities

Managing a diverse work force means not only being able to deal effectively with people of different ethnic groups, gender, culture, and language but also people of different ages, abilities, religions, and sexual preferences. Clearly, most people in our society will be in one or another of these categories.

Age

As demographics show, the U.S. population is aging, just as those of other industrialized nations are. As the "baby boomers" enter middle age and the "baby bust" contributes to a shortage of workers, older people in the United States are becoming more crucial to the economic success of the United States. In addition to being a source of labor, they wield a growing economic and political power. They have tremendous buying power and will change the youth-oriented marketing of this century to the gray-oriented marketing of the twenty-first century. Following are some of the demographics for the older population.[1]

- In 1987, the median age of Americans was 32.7; in the year 2000, it will be 36; by 2010, the median age will be 39.

- In 2010, 25 percent of the U.S. population will be at least 55 years old.
- In 1890, only 2 percent of people lived to 65 years of age; today 65 percent do.
- In 1900, 40 percent of the U.S. population was 17 years of age and under, and 3 percent was 65 years of age or older. In 1980, the figures were 28 percent and 11 percent, respectively; by the year 2030, the figures will be 22 percent and 21 percent.
- Between 1985 and 2000, the 20–34-year age group will decrease by 15 percent, the 40–54-year age group will increase by 59 percent, and the 55–69-year age group will increase by 25 percent.

People have been retiring earlier for the past two decades; the average retirement age for men is 62 years. The percentage of workers retiring before age 65 rose from 62 percent in 1978 to 84 percent in 1986. In a study by the American Association of Retired Persons, 46 percent of workers said they planned to retire at or before age 65, and 19 percent said they planned never to retire. A recent *Business Week*/Harris poll found that 20 percent of the respondents hoped to retire before age 55, 28 percent before age 65, and 21 percent between ages 65 and 70.[2]

As the "baby bust" continues to create a shortage of labor, a small but increasing number of companies are hiring older workers and retirees. Even though many older workers would like to resume work, or continue to work, they want to do so on their own terms. Some older employees want to continue working on a part-time basis. Furthermore, as women become more prominent in the workplace, they are less likely to want to leave their jobs, possibly influencing their spouses' retirement plans.

In a survey of 440 firms, 90 percent said they considered older workers cost-effective. Older workers were rated as being, for the most part, punctual, committed to high quality, and well able to perform their jobs. However, in another survey, older workers were rated the lowest in terms of accepting new technology, competitiveness, flexibility, and adaptability in learning new skills.[3] Even though a majority of the companies believed older workers needed skills training to make them more effective, only 30 percent of the workers had such training.

Some examples of how companies are employing older workers follow.

- Cigna Corporation has a program for retirees that allows them to work part-time, especially on short-term projects. The costs are lower than hiring temporary employees.
- Travelers Insurance Company has a job bank from which they hire for temporary work former employees who have retired. Their office of consumer information is staffed entirely by retirees.
- Arizona's Western Savings and Loan bank recruits older workers for teller positions because they relate better to the large older population there. Some of the older workers staff the bank's "customer clubs" for elderly people with big deposits.
- Kentucky Fried Chicken has a program called "The Colonel's Tradition," which has opened 1,500 jobs for older workers.
- McDonald's Corporation is another fast-food chain seeking older workers. The Masters program at seven regional centers trains older people seeking part-time work.
- At Kinder-Care Inc., the nation's largest chain of child care centers, 10–12 percent of the staff are over 55. This chain recruits older workers because of their reliability and their "way with children."
- Xerox Corporation allows older workers to select less stressful jobs as their ability to handle physically demanding jobs decreases. They get paid about halfway between the level for their previous position and that of the new position.
- Grumman Corporation hires retirees to fill its seasonal needs. Grumman finds them to be more productive than new hires.
- Of the 124 workers at Avanti, a manufacturer of custom-built cars, no one is younger than age 45. The company says they are reliable, meticulous, dedicated, and take pride in their work.

These examples show that companies hiring older workers find the experience positive. However, all is not perfection.

Age discrimination is becoming a more prominent issue as the U.S. population becomes middle-aged. A 1964 study by Bowman and our 1975 studies clearly show that substantial majorities of managers believe that being under 45 years old should be a helpful factor for promotions.[4] For example, 76 percent of the managers in Bowman's study and 62 percent in our study said that being under 45 years of age should be helpful for promotion, and about one-half of the managers in both studies said that being over 45 years old was harmful to advancement. Age was clearly seen as a factor in promotions.

In our 1976–78 study, 24 percent of employees believed their age was an advantage to their achieving their desired position, 47 percent believed it was irrelevant, and 27 percent said it was harmful. Thus, at that time, a majority of employees believe their age played a role in their advancement opportunities. The older the managers, the more likely they were to believe their age was an obstacle: 13 percent of managers aged 30 and under, compared with 72 percent of managers aged 50 and over, believed age was an obstacle to advancement.

In our 1988 study, 42 percent of employees stated their age would impact on their careers: 17 percent thought it would be positive, and 26 percent saw their age as a disadvantage. Thus, there seems to be a decrease in the relevance of age to advancement, but the decrease occurred on being an advantage, not a disadvantage. This decrease could be attributed to our work force's aging.

Employees were asked in 1988, "If you had a choice, what age group would you prefer your supervisor to be in?" One-half of the respondents did not have any preference, and only 5 percent preferred someone over 50 years of age. Forty-one percent preferred supervisors who are 31–50 years old.

Following are employees' comments from our studies about discrimination based on age.

Older women have very few opportunities for advancement because they cannot attract sponsors or mentors.
(Black, lower-level, woman)

It is evident white males over 50 are not considered in this company at the present time. (Native American, lower-level, woman)

Be serious; I am a white male, age 55. (White, lower-level, man)

My company has no interest in older employees, no matter how qualified. (White, occupational, man)

The signals are clear that white men, particularly 40 plus years of age will have limited opportunity for advancement beyond middle management. (White, upper-level, man)

There seems to be a lot of ageism in my company. More older employees could be promoted and questions like "When are you going to retire?" could be asked less often by younger employees. (White, middle-level, man)

I have a problem with people who are always talking about age, like it is a crime to get old. (Black, occupational, man)

We would like to note that, in our experience, age discrimination in companies is subtle. Corporations generally will find different covert reasons for discriminating against older workers. For example, they will tell older workers they are not being promoted, given lateral assignments, sent for additional training, and so forth, not because of age but because the older person does not have the "right background"; their skills are "outdated" and so on. In our seminars, when employees were asked to describe old people with the first adjective that came to mind, some of the positive adjectives used were wise, insightful, knowledgeable, experienced, loyal, calm, and kind. The negative ones were sickly, slow-thinking, out-of-touch, set in their ways, and rigid.

When employees wrote about diversity issues, ageism came up rather frequently. Their responses reflect a variety of stereotypes and problems that employees have regarding older people.

I get impatient with older people who are walking slow when I am in a hurry. (White, lower-level, woman)

I am bothered by the inertia of old people.
(Black, lower-level, man)

I usually am more interested in working with people who are fairly close to my age and position in life (mother of young children) than with individuals who are much older than I am.
(White, occupational, woman)

Tend to shy away from the older workers when looking for new ideas on how to solve certain problems.
(White, lower-level, woman)

I feel older people probably are senile and don't understand what I'm saying. (White, occupational, woman)

Older people are set in their ways and won't progress or learn new ways of doing things. (White, lower-level, man)

Get new blood into management. The old timers are too set in their ways. (Asian, occupational, woman)

I tend not to trust the value system of people who are entering their 40's without trying to have children.
(Asian, lower-level, man)

Some employees are overawed by older employees.

I see males and those who are older than myself as superior and therefore approach them carefully, not letting myself take risks around them for fear of being looked at as unintelligent.
(White, occupational, woman)

I still believe in deference to the elderly. I am just beginning to realize that my image of old equals wise is not true.
(White, middle-level, woman)

Working with people old enough to be your parents is difficult if you must give them direction or are in a position of authority.
(White, middle-level, man)

Ageism can work both ways. As the following comments suggest, older employees don't always treat younger employees fairly.

I am the youngest in the group and have been there a long time, yet everyone treats me like a kid. (Hispanic, occupational, woman)

Men old enough to be my father, just those a bit threatened by me, treat me poorly. (White, occupational, man)

I have differences of opinion with people of my parents' generation. They tend to look down at younger employees.
(Hispanic, occupational, woman)

Our group is made up of men over 45. There are two of us under 35. The older people have little respect for us.
(White, lower-level, man)

Ageism is as nonproductive as discriminating against people because of race, gender, and ethnic background. People age at different rates mentally and physically. Some 65-year-olds are younger in body and mind than some 40-year-olds. To use age as an employment criterion robs corporations of a supply of competent, energetic, creative employees.

Religion

While the United States was founded by people seeking religious freedom, there has been religious divisiveness throughout its history. Noll describes such religious divisiveness. In the 1700s, he writes there were two main sides: the corrupt, bad side, consisting of Roman Catholics and Anglicans who supported monarchical power, and the ethical, good side, made up of Protestants and Puritans who supported representative government, virtue, and self-rule.

In the 1850s, new political and religious alignments came about. Noll wrote,

The Catholic threat changed the picture. Catholics who also did not like the Yankee ideals of a monolithic Protestant moral commonwealth swelled the ranks of the Democrats. The Scotch-Irish despised the Catholics even more than they disliked the New Englanders and so left the Democratic fold.

Explicit anti-Catholicism emerged as the major political issue of the early 1850s. In 1856, the anti-Catholic, nativist Know-Nothing party won 21 percent of the popular vote for its presidential candidate, Millard Fillmore. Then it merged with the antislavery and purely regional Republican party.[5]

Almost one hundred years later, African Americans, the South, blue-collar workers, and Roman Catholics were the backbone of the Democratic party. The Republican party was predominantly made up of old-line Protestants and middle-class, white-collar workers.

Finally, in the 1970s, evangelists began to gain tremendous political support around anti-abortion, anti-pornography, anti–Equal Rights Amendment, and other conservative issues. At the end of the 1980s, these religious groups lost power because of financial and sexual scandals. We should also note that as the Roman Catholic church continues its prohibition of abortion, one can predict an anti–Roman Catholic backlash.[6]

Currently in the United States, Protestants represent 56 percent of the population, Roman Catholics 28 percent, Jews 2 percent, others 3 percent, and those with no preference, 9 percent.

In a study we conducted in 1986 in the western United States only 1 percent of employees were Jewish, 13 percent Mormon, 20 percent Roman Catholic, and 39 percent Protestant. Eighteen percent of employees had no religious preference, and the remaining percentage were of other religions. The higher one moves up the corporate ladder, the more likely managers are to be Mormon or Protestant. At the highest levels, Protestants predominate. Studies done over the past sixty years show that if you are a Protestant, especially Episcopalian or Presbyterian, you have a much better chance of getting ahead in corporate America than if you are of some other religion.

The one religious group that has been a constant target of religious prejudice in the United States is the Jews. Thus, despite being one of the best-educated ethnic groups in the United States, Jews are underrepresented in corporate America.

In our seminars, most participants had opinions about Jews. They were described positively as being good financial managers, intelligent, good business people, nice, polite, smart, gifted, hardworking, and family-oriented. However, negative stereotypes abounded, such as obnoxious, big noses, clannish, cheap, out for the buck, stingy, complainers, short, selfish, and greedy.

As in Europe and Japan, there is increasing anti-Semitism in the United States. For example, at the liberal University of Wisconsin, Jewish students have faced physical attacks, hate mail, and hate calls. Four of five houses on campus with large numbers of Jewish students have been damaged. Recently, in New York City, which has a very large Jewish population, the student newspaper at City College ran a blatantly anti-Semitic opinion page about a "cunning Jewish clique" made up of "powerful, arrogant, controlling" people. The piece was written by an Asian Indian student who has lived in the United States since 1981.

Increasingly, as Asians enter U.S. companies, they are bringing different religions, such as Islam, Hinduism, and Buddhism, into the workplace. There are currently about 6 million Muslims in the United States. Because of conflicts with Iran and Iraq, Muslims meeting at the twenty-seventh annual convention of the Islamic Society of North America claimed there have been increased hostilities toward them. They say they are perceived as an uneducated and fanatical people. Some Muslim and Hindu employees in our surveys believed that their different religions would not get as much attention, if they were not people of color. In 1960, there were twenty Buddhist churches in the U.S.; in 1975, sixty, and in 1987, one hundred.

In our seminars the participants used the following adjectives to describe Muslims: violent, radical, vegetarian, fanatical, dangerous, very religious, tenacious, strict, angry, and emotional. The adjectives used for Catholics were somewhat more positive: they were described as religious, rigid, rebellious, self-righteous, strong, very orthodox, neurotic, and not necessarily good people. Protestants were perceived as white, straightlaced, friendly, intolerant (although more tolerant than Catholics), rich, conservative, and not religious. From these adjectives we can see that Muslims are perceived most negatively and Protestants most positively.

In those companies with a number of Asian employees, one hears complaints about having to deal with "these different religions and their different values." On the other hand, one hears comments such as these toward other religious groups. Muslims, Hindus, and Buddhists complain that there is no respect for and understanding of their religions. As with other minority groups, intragroup conflicts exist. On several occasions, we found Asian Indians who would not work with one another because of religious differences. Also, some Muslims resent working with Jews, and vice versa. Following are some employees' comments about religion in the workplace.

I believe that every non-Jew would like to murder me if he only had a chance. (White, lower-level, man)

I fear everyone and will not socialize with anyone at work because they don't understand my religion. I am Hindu.
(Asian, lower-level, man)

I am defensive about groups of people who ask for acceptance and tolerance but perpetuate closed societies, for example, an orthodox Jew who will not intermarry. (White, lower-level, man)

I have a problem with religious groups that put other people down to exemplify themselves, like the born again Christians.
(White, middle-level, man)

I dislike people who try to impose their religious beliefs on me, like Roman Catholics with abortion. (White, occupational, woman)

I have a problem dealing with the Jewish religion in their attitudes of superiority. (Black, lower-level, woman)

I refuse to work with a Sikh in our department. I know I should, but it goes back for centuries. (Asian, lower-level, man)

Until it was pointed out to me, I never realized different religions celebrate different holidays, for example, Christmas and Hanukkah. We should be more aware of that in planning meetings and due dates. (Asian, lower-level, man)

While the United States supports the separation of church and state and religious freedom, de facto religious hostility is increasing, especially against Jews. In addition, as the number of non-Christians in the United States increases because of immigration and the success of Islam among African Americans, the potential for discrimination and conflicts will also increase.

Sexual Preference

Male and female homosexuality is not a new phenomenon. Throughout history, many cultures have been based on same-sex relationships (with arranged "marriages" for the purpose of having children). One of the most famous examples of a culture with large, accepted segments of the population who were homosexual was ancient Greece. Highly educated men looked for other highly educated and cultured men to form long-lasting romantic bonds. Wives, who had lesbian lovers, were chosen for men to be the mothers of their children. These choices were based on family connections, and the woman stayed at home to raise the children. A. L. Rowse points out in the book *Homosexuality in History* that such men as James I, Frederick the Great, Leonardo da Vinci, Michelangelo, Erasmus, and Francis Bacon were homosexual or bisexual. Not only is homosexuality common among human populations, but it is also found in other species of animals.

The homosexual movement in the United States, according to Licata and Petersen, has gone through a number of significant phases. They believe there were eight stages in the evolution of the homosexual rights movement. From 1908 to 1945, several attempts were made to defend the rights of homosexuals. From 1945 to 1951, gays living in cities began to demonstrate a new consciousness, and between 1950 and 1952, homosexuals made "a more thorough search for their identity." Then "righteous indignation flared up within the movement." The next seventeen years, until 1960, was a period of information and education. The homophile movement was born in the 1960s, and in 1969, gay liberation emerged. Finally, between 1973 and 1979, "the movement and the government responded to each other through institutionalized channels."[7] According to Licata and Petersen, from 1979 to the present, a new militancy and a new sense of coming out occurred.[8]

Unfortunately, in the early 1980s, the outbreak of acquired immunodeficiency syndrome (AIDS) frightened a conservative U.S. population. Early information about the disease linked it primarily to homosexual males. Widespread reaction to AIDS inflamed existing prejudices against homosexuals. Some even claimed that the disease was "a sign from God that homosexuality was wrong." More complete information shows that the disease is transmitted through the exchange of body fluids in both homosexual and heterosexual contacts and through blood transfusions.

As we discussed earlier, many Americans are hesitant to acknowledge the multiple cultures in the United States. They are often even more hesitant to accept many of the different life styles that exist, particularly alternative sexual life styles. It is a fact that multiple cultures and life styles exist; in our 1988 survey, 10–12 percent of the employees indicated they were homosexual. Some believe that this figure is low, since homosexuals are still hesitant to reveal their sexual orientation. Their hesitancy is understandable, given the violent, homophobic reaction some people have when they encounter a gay person. In some segments of the community, homosexuals are frequently attacked. For example, in the summer of 1990 two lesbians, who were embracing on a corner in New York City's Greenwich Village, were severely attacked by a group of teenagers. In McAllen, Texas, five gay men were slain in four months. In Indianapolis, five gay men were strangled in the first half of 1990. The New York police reported an increase of attacks on gays (64 through July 1990, compared to 36 in 1989). Several have been killed. Figures from gay organizations report a five-fold increase in attacks through July 1990. What is disturbing is that thugs go to gay neighborhoods to seek out their victims, while racist attacks usually occur when a person crosses into someone else's "turf."[9]

Recently the Commander of the U.S. Navy's Atlantic Fleet said that while lesbians are hard workers, dedicated career-oriented individuals, and among the top performers in the Navy, they must be vigorously rooted out of the Navy. He also characterized them as aggressive and intimidating. The Pentagon directive says,

The presence of such members adversely affects the ability of the armed forces to maintain discipline, good order and morale to foster mutual trust and confidence among service members; to ensure the system of rank and command; to facilitate assignment and worldwide deployment of service members who frequently must live and work under close conditions affording minimum privacy; to recruit and retain members of the armed forces; to maintain the public acceptability of military service; and to prevent breaches of security.[10]

It should be pointed out that another Pentagon study did not find homosexuals' presence disruptive and praised them as top performers. That report was suppressed by the Pentagon.

Slowly but surely some segments of our society are more accepting of diverse sexual orientations. Public acknowledgment of homosexuality is no longer a sure road to political defeat. Harvey Milk, who was killed because he was gay, was elected to the San Francisco Board of Supervisors in 1977. Several congressmen have been reelected after avowing their homosexuality, including Barney Frank of Massachusetts.

Another sign of progress is that several religious denominations have decided that homosexuality should not bar people from serving as clergy. Reform and Reconstructionist Judaism and the Unitarian Universalist Association have taken this step. Of mainline Protestant dominations, the United Church of Christ has taken the most liberal stand. They leave the question up to their regional church bodies to decide. Most other Protestant denominations and Roman Catholicism remain officially opposed.

In Massachusetts, a law that grew out of legislation first introduced in 1972 added to the state's civil rights protections by declaring sexual orientation an illegal reason for discriminating in credit, housing, public accommodation, and jobs. But it also expanded exemptions for religious institutions that had already existed in civil rights laws. The original law made an exception that allowed religious institutions to give preference to members of the same religion in hiring. The 1989 law exempted religious institutions from complying in other areas as well, including compensation, dismissals, and employment privileges.

Massachusetts was only the second state to pass a homosexual rights law. The first was Wisconsin, which extended its civil rights law to include sexual orientation in 1982. Many cities have similar statutes intended to protect homosexuals from discrimination.

We measured the extent to which employees in our surveys were bothered by the presence of subordinates and supervisors with sexual orientations different from their own. We found that 37 percent of this population was bothered by people with different sexual preferences. A much higher percentage of men (46 percent) than women (29 percent) indicated that alternative sexuality is a problem for them.

Comments from employees in our studies and seminars reveal discrimination based on sexual orientation but also an effort to avoid such judgments.

The EAGLES club—an insult to our national bird for a homosexual group. (Asian, occupational, man)

The company should not support an organization such as EAGLE, which many employees view as morally reprehensible and the practice of such a life style illegal in many states.
(White, occupational, man)

The EAGLES organization—sexual preference should not be brought to work—I can't believe the company would sanction such an organization. (White, occupational, woman)

I don't feel that sexual orientation should be viewed the same as race in recognizing a particular interest group.
(Black, lower-level, woman)

I myself will never accept gays or lesbians pushing their wrongful and sinful life style onto me. (White, occupational, woman)

As a Christian, I would have problems dealing with people with "other life styles." (White, middle-level, woman)

Who cares anymore? The queers are going to take over anyway!!!
(Hispanic, occupational, man)

I have a real problem with homosexuality and life styles they assume. I feel people are not born this way but choose this lifestyle. I personally make character decisions on one's personality and conduct rather than on race, creed, etc.
(White, occupational, man)

I am against many gay movements. I don't treat gays any different, but I don't like it when they discuss their sex life at work—I don't discuss mine. (Hispanic, occupational, woman)

The issue I need to deal with is not reacting negatively to gays or interracial couples. I don't hate gays or other races, but when I see either of these groups I may make a negative comment or stare. This is something I am aware of and want to change. I want to be able to see either of these groups as just people.
(Black, occupational, woman)

I believe that people should get what they truly deserve: best person for the job, etc. I think I would have to be careful and make sure the person in question is being treated justly. I think life styles would be the most difficult for me, because I do tend to be set more on what people do rather than how old they are or what sex or race they are. (White, lower-level, woman)

Acknowledgment of our gay club by our company executives would certainly remove the taint of fascism.
(White, occupational, man)

The gay population is one of the best educated, talented populations in the United States. We cannot afford not to fully utilize them if we wish to be competitive.

The Disabled

Another diversity issue we must focus on is the treatment of disabled persons. Over 43 million Americans have physical or mental limitations. Many of these disabled are poor, undereducated, and members of minority groups. The United States for most of its history has viewed two types of disabled persons differently. The "worthy" group is military veterans, who are perceived as heroes who became disabled defending their country. Developmentally disabled people were considered "unworthy" because, according to the Protestant ethic, they were a product of sin and their disabilities the result of their parents' wrongdoing. But the disabled people in general, in line with the Darwinian "survival of the fittest" idea, have been considerably stigmatized, with catastrophic social and economic consequences.[11]

According to Yuker, handicapped people have been overlooked and rejected by the U.S. society because they are different from the majority. Society emphasizes physical beauty, personal appearance, health, and athletic achievements. Also valued are personal achievement and productivity and the individual's ability to be vocationally competitive and gainfully employed. "The status of a person with a disability is often equated with that of ethnic, racial, or religious minority groups in terms of marginality status and stereotypical perceptions."[12]

Because of these views, the United States was late in assisting and protecting the disabled, and the assistance has been piecemeal and slow. It was not until 1956 that disability insurance became part of the Social Security Act. In 1965, the Vocational Rehabilitation Amendments were passed, increasing spending and extending coverage to "socially handicapped persons." The 1968 Vocational Rehabilitation Amendment funded rehabilitation facilities and services to assist families of the disabled.

In 1973, the Rehabilitation Act was passed. It greatly expanded the scope of assistance. Its main objective was "to develop and implement, through research, training, services, and the guarantee of equal opportunity, comprehensive and coordinated programs of vocational living."

It was not until 1975 that handicapped children had a right to receive free public education. The Education of All Handicapped Children Act of 1975 guaranteed free appropriate education to all handicapped children in the least restrictive environment. At the time of passage, there were 8 million handicapped children, aged one to twenty-one. Fifty percent did not receive appropriate education and more than one million were excluded from public school.

Despite the increased educational opportunities, job opportunities were not opened to many capable disabled people. A 1985 study sponsored by the International Center for the Disabled and the National Council on the Handicapped found that two-thirds of disabled people between the ages of sixteen and sixty-four were not working, although 66 percent stated that they would like to have a job. Those who were working were better educated, had higher family incomes, were more satisfied with their lives, and were much less likely to consider themselves disabled.[13]

A later survey, commissioned by the same two organizations and the President's Committee on Employment of the Handicapped, studied managers at all levels of small companies. These employers reported that disabled workers were good workers and that they did their jobs as well as other employees. They noted that the costs of making accommodations to take disabled needs into account were generally not very high and were not a significant barrier to employing disabled workers. Report findings indicate, however, that the employment of disabled persons is moving slowly: only half of the managers reported that their firms had hired disabled employees in the past year. This was because the firms had not formulated policies for hiring disabled workers, and "many top managers often display a low level of consciousness toward disabled people as a group."[14]

It was not until 1990 that Congress passed a bill making discrimination in employment against the disabled illegal, as is discrimination on the basis of race, gender, and national origins. Before passage of this law, discrimination against persons with disabilities was legally prohibited only in government jobs and government contracts. The business community lobbied strongly against the bill, fearing added costs and numerous lawsuits by the disabled persons. However, it was shown that only about four hundred suits were filed in sixteen years by the disabled. In addition, an analysis of more than 10,000 disabled employees by the Job Accommodation Network showed that 31 percent would require no added cost for special training or facilities; 50 percent, costs under $50; and 60 percent, costs under $500. Only 1 percent would require training or facilities costing over $5,000.

The law defines a person with a disability as one with a physical or mental impairment that "substantially limits" a major life activity like hearing, walking, seeing, speaking. It requires companies to make "reasonable accommodations" for disabled employees, such as providing readers for blind workers and arranging part-time or modified work schedules. Restaurants, stores, and other public accommodations had to widen doorways and provide ramps for people in wheelchairs, and inner-city buses had to be made accessible to the handicapped. Finally, telephone companies had to make possible communication for the hearing- and speech-impaired.

"The biggest barrier to getting [disabled] people hired is the attitude of managers, not the cost," said Kathleen Alexander, the Marriott Corporation's vice president for personnel services. Because qualified workers are becoming harder to find or to keep, employers are starting to tap the handicapped labor pool.

Several companies have made sincere efforts to employ the disabled. The Marriott Corporation has more than 6,000 disabled employees in its 230,000 worldwide work force. Usually, they are accommodated at no extra cost, and one-quarter of the time the adjustment costs an average of $200. Disabled employees tend to stay at Marriott longer than other employees, and reduced turnover makes up for any added training expenses.

At Sears, Roebuck & Co., 20,300 of 350,000 workers have identified themselves as disabled. Sears has long taken the attitude that a disabled person can do any job at the company until it is proven otherwise. Most disabled employees are accommodated at no extra cost; about 10 percent need some help, at a typical cost of $20 to $350. Sears did pay $12,000 each for two machines that "look" at written material and read it aloud to blind employees.

In our studies, only 12 percent of employees said it would bother them if a supervisor or subordinate had a physical or mental disability. Disabled people were described by employees as determined, courageous, capable, overcomers, good workers, trying to help themselves. Some of the negative descriptions said the disabled are hard to deal with, hard to talk to, slow, too sensitive, and always unhappy, but that they are discriminated against, need extra consideration, are treated badly, and are victimized. Following are employees' comments about disabled persons in the workplace.

The strongest barrier would be dealing with mentally handicapped or retarded persons. It is something I find myself fighting to overcome—even when it is just to talk with them.
(White, lower-level, woman)

I have a hard time dealing with the issue due to being deaf in one ear. It takes time for me to adapt to this matter with any given individual. (White, occupational, woman)

I am uncomfortable around handicapped folks. I need to try to be more understanding and if possible ignore the fact that they are handicapped. (White, occupational, woman)

It is something hard to treat handicapped people like normal people. Hard not to look at a handicap. (White, occupational, woman)

A personal note: I have a twenty-two-year-old niece with cerebral palsy. As a small child she was happy, but the older she gets the more unhappy she becomes. She constantly asks, "Why me?" I have a difficult time answering her.

Conclusion

As with other minorities in the U.S. workplace, older and handicapped workers and people of diverse religions and alternative sexual preference deserve acceptance, appreciation, and equal opportunity. Apart from the fact that the United States was founded on the ideal of equitable rights for all, it seems only sensible to attract, retain, and fully utilize all workers who are qualified and eager to work and to do a good job. This respect for a diverse work force—and a live-and-let-live attitude within and among different groups of people—will help the United States be competitive in the global marketplace.

Advice for Employees to Be Effective and Successful

While previous chapters gave specific advice on how to cope with problems engendered by discrimination in the workplace, this chapter presents some general advice on how to be successful in the diverse work force of the future. A competitive company must have employees who are motivated to look at themselves, their issues, and their strengths and weaknesses and constructively deal with them. Many employment problems, which employees may believe are based on prejudice, are in reality a result of flawed human interactions or bureaucratic structures. Despite cultural and language differences, the realities we cite and the advice we give can apply to all companies in the United States and in other countries.

Theodore Caplow notes that organizations are like machines, with a multitude of specialized moving parts that invariably break down and must be repaired. Unlike machines, functioning organizations are composed of human beings, who, as we have seen, are not totally predictable and who in fact often have their own objectives and goals that conflict with the overall purposes of the organization.[1] Finally, all business organizations have their hierarchies, their own breeds of politics, their corporate cultures, their identities, organizational charts, rules, and regulations, formal and informal networks, symbols, rituals, customs, and vocabularies. They have many people seeking limited resources and rewards, and consequently a highly competitive environment. Finally, all corporations have their share of "unhealthy" people.

Only by learning to "read" people and by understanding ourselves can we develop a clear appreciation of the true nature of bureaucracies. Knowledge of who we really are will assist us in interacting effectively with people who are different from ourselves.

Reviewing the Issues

First of all, people must remember that corporate opportunities are limited regardless of color, national origin, gender, age, religion, and so on. They must also recognize that we do not live in a meritocracy, nor do any of our major competitors. They must recognize that corporate bureaucracies are irrational, political, social systems that value conformity over differences. Working for foreign companies will not allow one to escape these realities. Many foreign-owned companies are even more rigid and unfair than U.S. corporations. Because of these facts and our ingrained tendency to ignore them, employees will always have complaints about their jobs and careers, no matter what background they come from.

Knowing Yourself

To truly understand and interact effectively and positively with other people, you must first and foremost know yourself. You must recognize that in almost all cases of difficulties you have, you are part of the problem and a great deal of the solution. You must be honest with yourself; and you must assume responsibility not only for your successes but also for your failures.

In addition, you must clearly understand both formal and informal rules, structures, norms, and cultures of the corporation. You must recognize that many corporations do not act or think as they say they do and that most people, including yourself, do the same.

The most important technique to be successful in a diverse, competitive global marketplace is to understand who you really are. Many of us think we know, but we really do not. Schoonmaker writes, "You may feel that you are too honest to deceive yourself, that you can accept the truth about yourself, but you probably cannot. You are as human as everyone else, and everyone tries to preserve her/his self-image. That is why psychological counseling takes so long."[2] This, we might add, applies to people in the European countries, Japan, and throughout the world.

As we noted earlier, we are all neurotic; the extent of our neuroses depends on our mental makeup at birth, how our parents or those who brought us up cared for, nurtured, loved, and molded us; and how the society we were brought up in has treated and valued us. Because our personalities developed in large part when we were babies and young children, it is difficult for us to understand what really makes us tick.

For this reason, we strongly recommend psychoanalysis or some other type of professional help in understanding yourself. Such guided introspection will also help you to understand other people. It will improve your ability to read signals from people and to understand when you do and don't contribute to your successes, failures, challenges, and problems. It will help you to understand better when you are being treated fairly and unfairly, and when you are being fair and unfair. It will help to develop an inventory of your strengths and weaknesses.

Clearly understanding your strengths and weaknesses will allow you to develop strategies to enhance your career; your ability to deal with the bureaucratic structure without much damage to yourself, and your ability to understand, accept, respect, and appreciate people who are different. It will help you to recognize whether your failures are due to your deficiencies, the deficiencies of bureaucracies or of the people in them, or a combination thereof. A key point to remember is that, in general, strengths and weaknesses are not fixed. They depend on the situation and circumstances: a strength in one context can be a weakness in another.

Another way to understand your weaknesses and strengths and who you are is to have some trusted confidants, a few in your organization and a few outside it, against whom you can bounce your feelings and perceptions. The ones inside your organization may have a better picture than you of the work issues you need to understand and deal with, and those outside will be more objective because they are not caught up in your corporate environment. In addition, approaching respected people whom you might not like, or who might not like you, for feedback on your strengths and weaknesses gives you another perspective. Finally, there are excellent exercises and courses that assist people in understanding themselves, which can be very useful in rounding out your picture of yourself.

Self-understanding will improve your chances of being an effective employee in a diverse work force, because it will make you more aware of the image you are presenting and why. You will not be lying to yourself or denying yourself.

A fundamental question all of us must answer is, "To what extent do we conform to the particular corporate culture that is imposed on us?" When it comes to conforming to some form of ism like racism, sexism, ethnocentrism, homophobia, ageism, and so on, we say one should never conform—not only because it is wrong but because it is counterproductive to any competitive organization in a diverse world. When it comes to conformity in dress, style, and so on, that is a personal choice. However, we suggest that very few people can be happy if they are trying to be only what other people want them to be. Eventually many employees look at themselves in the mirror and say, "Was it all worth it? Is this what life is all about?"

While it feels healthiest to be ourselves, some degree of conformity is essential in order to be a member of a bureaucracy. Depending on the situation, we all have to do things such as holding our tongues, being nice to people we despise, and occasionally putting aside a value that is not essential to us. Some people even resist conforming to rules such as proper business attire. However, as Schoonmaker noted, such battles are not worth fighting unless you are content to stay where you are in the company:

> You may feel that doing these things is a cop-out, a sacrifice of part of your identity. Perhaps you are right, but there is another viewpoint. Your identity is not just what you wear or the language you use; it is what you believe in and the strength of your character and self-confidence. If your sense of identity depends only on your clothes, you are really in bad shape, and letting your hair grow will not solve your identity problems.[3]

We make a very serious caution here: Those people and companies that require a great deal of unnecessary conformity, even in such areas as dress, will find it very difficult to operate in the coming decades when diversity, not conformity, will be the norm. There are thousands of people who will make up our work force and will dress in their traditional country dress. As long as they are getting their jobs done, we should accept their different styles.

We believe that healthy employees are those who have a keen sense of who they are, like themselves, are secure, conform because they want to, and recognize that they are conforming. They appreciate others' diversity because they are secure in themselves; thus they need no one to look down upon and oppress so that they can feel superior.

In sum, unless you know and value yourself, you will find it very difficult to understand the diverse people you must work with. Lack of such understanding will greatly decrease your chances of being a successful performer. In addition, it will create unnecessary stress and anxieties on your part because you will be unable to distinguish between the part you and others played in your successes and failures.

Understanding People

As mentioned previously, a popular belief in bureaucracies is that managers should not try to be psychologists. Nonsense! To be an effective manager and employee in the 1990s demands that you have a clear understanding of the psychological mind set of the people you are dealing with and those who can influence your ability to get your job done. You need to know the other person's "real self" and appreciate, respect, and value differences. Because business situations always come down to "people" situations, the more you know about the person you are dealing with, the more you enhance your chances of doing an outstanding job. It is crucial that you form your own opinion of people; do not naively accept the opinions of others.

Many of our motives arise not from external factors but from the inner workings of our own personalities. Thus, we cannot predict how an individual will act in particular instances unless we have a fix on her or his personality as a whole. Gaining such understanding can be very difficult and will become more difficult as the world becomes a global village. Many people try to hide their true selves as a survival tactic in the ever-changing bureaucratic environments. It is considered inappropriate generally to discuss one's personal feelings, especially in a corporate setting. This means that what we hear is in no way a totally realistic or reliable reflection of other people's personal thoughts. Indeed, some people, particularly those who are insecure or not pleased with what they see in themselves, will deliberately project a false image, just as those with feelings of inferiority will often overcompensate by bragging or putting on an air of superiority. In addition, as many corporate workers tend to avoid any self-examination, it is often extremely difficult for them to explain honestly and accurately what they feel or why they believe in a certain way.

If your company employs 300,000 people, you have 300,000 unique individuals to understand and to read accurately in a number of different situations. What are several strategies for understanding people? There is no simple formula.

To understand a person, it is essential to interact with him or her not only in the work environment, where one only gets to observe the corporate behavior, but also at work-related and non-work-related social functions. In these casual situations, people are most likely to share with you who they really are, what are their values, issues, and problems.

Attending social events that are part of other people's cultures is a good way to begin to appreciate some of the differences you may see in your work environment. Taking courses on other languages and cultures allows you to better respect and appreciate different people. Finally and more important, you must attend workshops on valuing differences that allow you to understand and appreciate the isms you have that get in your way of dealing effectively with people. All these steps will give you a better understanding of people who are different and give you a better understanding of yourself, which is crucial to your success in the 1990s and beyond. Following are some comments about what employees learned at a workshop on valuing differences.

A very interesting course. . . . From the bottom of their heart, everybody should go back and re-evaluate their values for life and for the people who live in this country. It might also be a good idea to share with others, not from mainstream obviously. Everybody is born good. Something goes wrong, and the government imposes laws to avoid these social problems, and the majority think of reverse discrimination. (Asian, lower-level, man)

I was personally surprised at my feelings for the candidate, and that I completely overlooked the objective criteria (job performance) in favor of "the little things." I certainly hope I am not judged so harshly and that, in fact, our qualifications are indeed the most important criteria. (White, lower-level, man)

I learned some things about myself. Paying attention to my emotions, reactions, thoughts during the day I realize I am much more opinionated than I have ever admitted even to myself.
(White, occupational, man)

I learned a lot today. My mind has been opened up. The case study made me realize that I paid attention to personal traits instead of a person's ability. I do not want people to treat me this way. (Asian, lower-level, woman)

It was interesting. You've taught me about how I see people. Oddly enough, it's something that my grandmother has told me for years—do unto others as you would have them do unto you. While I apply that in any personal life, I fail to in my business. (Black, lower-level, woman)

I learned that I did not judge people as I would like to be judged myself. Something I need to work on. (Hispanic, lower-level, man)

Most important thing I learned was that I can be guilty of misjudgment on race/gender as easy as someone else.
(Black, occupational, man)

You were successful in making me think hard about my own problems dealing with other people. I was beginning to think I was doing pretty good in that area, but I see now I still have quite a ways to go! (White, lower-level, man)

Learned to recognize better my tendency to see negatives in peoples to look at the defects and not the positives. Learned how people in the department react very differently to the same situation— more prejudice and discrimination (much very subtle) than I had thought. I have a lot of work to do. (White, occupational, man)

The exercise pointed out our intolerance to diversity. It was very interesting to hear my colleagues discuss their traditional views of the inappropriate behavior of our subject. (White, occupational, man)

I have to be conscious of my own attitudes; do not make judgments of others based upon irrelevant information like race, gender. (Asian, middle-level, man)

In brief, understanding who you are will assist you in understanding people, which will allow you to interact more positively and effectively—to your good, and to your company's good.

Your Attitude toward Work

As opportunities become more limited because more people are competing for fewer rewards, and as those competing increasingly feel that their group is getting the "short end of the stick," your attitude toward work becomes crucial to your success. We have seen, and our data show, that many people who feel they are not treated fairly and equitably by their company begin to perform below their abilities. While excellent or outstanding work is not a sure way of having a successful career, performing below your ability is a sure way of not having a career. Our strongest advice to anyone, no matter how unfairly you are treated, is always to perform to the best of your ability or voluntarily leave the company. If you do not, you are giving the company a reason not to promote or reward you and, in some cases, to fire you.

One way of doing an outstanding job is to approach the job in a more creative way than what many normal corporate cultures dictate. It is assumed, in some corporate cultures, that those people are most valued who put in extremely long hours, say how much they are working, and show how busy they are. We believe, on the contrary, that your responsibility is to take complex problems and make them simple, not to make simple problems complex. It is extremely important to have a "can-do" attitude. You are not hired to explain why a job can't be done; you are hired to solve corporate problems and get the job done at a profit for the stockholders.

An ongoing debate focuses on the controversy of too much direction versus too little direction. It seems that many corporate employees continue to play out the parent/child role at work. When there is too much direction from above, they complain about the overly controlling boss; when there is too little direction, they complain that the boss (parent) doesn't have an interest in their work. Unless you were hired to do routine work, your chief value lies in your ability to direct yourself. If you want to advance in your career, you have to be able to take initiative. We discount the complaint that the boss doesn't give direction. In reality, that makes for an ideal situation. Your basic training for full responsibility is learning how to direct yourself in any situation, and the boss who allows you to do this with nothing more than an occasional "go-ahead" is doing you a tremendous favor. You have the opportunity to go full steam on your own, within, of course, some minimal parameters of the boss's thinking, and you will learn how to exercise your own independence.

In addition, we believe you should never turn down an additional work assignment, especially if you have people working for you. Your job as a manager is to figure out how to get the work done. That is part of the excitement and challenge of the job. If, on occasion, you or your people simply cannot take on an additional task, your refusal will be understood if your previous responses have been to accept additional assignments readily. Saying that you should never turn down an assignment does not mean, however, that you should never ask for help. Only fools with oversized egos will never ask for help. Just be certain that you really need additional help and that you can justify it to those who will authorize it.

Similarly, saying that a task or problem is not your job is foolhardy. If the task or problem comes to you, it is ultimately your responsibility to see that it is completed. It is your job. If, however, you need additional information to do the job, don't hesitate to ask for it. If you pretend to know and blunder ahead, there is a very good chance that you will regret it.

This does not mean that you must never take risks and must know all the answers before you act. Being decisive is especially crucial when you first enter a job. You must establish your authority and your position, and the best way to do that is to be decisive. It is better to make a decision today, knowing 89 percent of the facts, than to delay the decision for a month to have 100 percent of the facts. Facts are a decision maker's tools, but they can't replace your intuition and your powers of interpretation. It is better to make a hundred decisions and risk being wrong about a few. When you make more decisions, you accomplish more. If you make a wrong decision, don't dwell on it. Learn from it, and try not to repeat mistakes.

Townsend gave additional valid advice on decision making: "Make every decision . . . in the light of this question: 'How would I do this job if I owned the company?' And then do it that way, to the extent that you can. Most of your competitors will be making decisions based on the question: 'What will make me look good to my boss?' or 'What does my boss want me to do?' or even 'What exactly did he tell me to do?' None of these questions will lead to effective action."[4]

Managing Your Career

One of the reasons for a great deal of conflict is the feeling of people that they are not being fairly and equitably treated in their careers.

To enhance your chances of being successful in the workplace, you must not follow the traditional view that you should be a passive player in your performance and potential evaluations, career planning, and training and development needs. We say you must be an active player; you must take control of your career and of your responsibilities.

You must first take the responsibility of getting candid, honest feedback about your performance and potential. Many bosses will avoid giving this; however, if you fail to get it, you could harbor false hopes and expectations for years. It is your responsibility to judge whether your boss is being honest with you.

One way to tell whether you are getting accurate feedback on your performance and potential is to see how honest and straightforward your boss is on little, noncontroversial issues. Then move to bigger, controversial, and sensitive issues. Where does your boss begin to give you "dishonest, corporate, or evasive" responses? Another signal as to how honest your boss will be with you is how honest he or she is with other people inside and outside the organization.

Other tell-tale signs indicate the integrity of your boss and the type of feedback you can expect. If you are very observant, you may notice a change in the boss's behavior about three months before the formal yearly appraisal. If you have had a good relationship and he or she begins to question your vouchers, disagree with you more frequently than in the past on little things, and magnify minor incidents into "federal cases," you will very likely be in trouble with your appraisals. The boss is trying to justify in his or her mind why your rating will not be as high as you expect it to be. At the same time, you will begin to notice less frequent interaction, less eye contact, and less camaraderie. If you pick up these signals, you should begin to develop your case without letting your boss put you on the defensive. In all likelihood, your boss will try to "save face" with you by saying that he or she tried the damnedest to get you a high evaluation but peers and superiors were not supportive. Whatever the boss has to say about your performance and potential, he or she is likely to encourage you to do better in the coming year and promise that you will be justly rewarded.

Any time your performance or potential evaluation is a shock to you, you have let yourself down by allowing your boss to avoid giving you honest feedback throughout the year, on an ongoing basis.

A strategy that you can use to take power away from your boss, or from a small group of superiors who have total control over your performance and potential, is to promote yourself to others on every occasion. Rewards and promotions almost never go to those who believe that their quiet, hard work will get them ahead. This advice is particularly relevant to Asians, who seem to buy into this belief more than other ethnic groups.

Many employees are reluctant to promote themselves because

they feel it is not polite or appropriate; however, if you do not promote yourself, who else will? Remember that almost every person in bureaucracies is looking out for number one. (We see evidence of this occurring in Japan, where dissatisfaction with one's "lot" versus another's "lot" is making increasing numbers of Japanese look out for themselves first and for their fellow Japanese second.)

One way to promote yourself is to become visible. Try to get into a key job that will gain exposure for you to people inside your department and outside of it. While there is no sure way of getting these jobs, you can enhance your chances by knowing which jobs give a lot of visibility, developing your skills for these jobs, quite openly lobbying (depending on the situation) for these jobs, and finally making a concerted effort to form relationships, both personal and professional, with people who have control over these jobs. Do not wait for the job to come to you; go after it. You might not get it, but you will maximize your chances of getting it.

Another visible and also self-protective strategy is to gain as much exposure outside the company as possible, through writing, speaking, teaching, community activities, and political activities. Join professional organizations and become an active member and leader. While these activities are usually thought of as incentives for promotion, they are also ways to protect your livelihood in case of the loss of a job. What is more, such exposure can open up competitive job opportunities while you are employed, providing in some cases an opportunity for career advancement or, at least, leverage within your own company to negotiate for a promotion or raise.

Visibility always comes to those who see change as an opportunity rather than a problem. You can become visible if you help to lead change, and change is occurring more rapidly in the 1990s than ever before. Change should be viewed by managers who want to succeed as exhilarating and refreshing. Kanter notes,

> Change brings opportunities when people have been planning for it, and know what to do when it comes. What is more, change also provides an opportunity for entrepreneurs to offer "change-

management" products and services, turning other people's confusion into profitable business.[5]

In most cases, success depends upon distinguishing yourself from the crowd, whose members are about as qualified as you are and who are your true competitors. The one sure but risky way to stand above the crowd in U.S. corporations—less so in most European and almost never in Japanese companies—is to manage with a flair to do things in a creative way. You must be a risk taker and create change, especially if you do not fit the corporate image. However, distinguishing yourself from the crowd does not guarantee you a promotion. In fact, in many instances, being a risk taker, creating change, and managing with a flair may detract from your chances. Change can be threatening, particularly to people who are insecure. The risks, however, are fewer than the rewards. As Machiavelli said, "Results are often obtained by impetuosity and daring which could never have been obtained by ordinary methods."[6]

Despite our discussion of daring strategies, more career goals will be reached if you simply manage your career and develop realistic career goals. London and Stumpf give some excellent advice in this area:

> Few people systematically investigate and collect extensive information on target jobs and the possible career paths to attain them. . . . Establishing career objectives is more than stating a possible target job. It is knowing (1) the work-related activities one is seeking, (2) the social and political aspects of the position, (3) the demands the position will place on one's personal time and family, and (4) the series of possible positions which would prepare one to perform effectively.[7]

London and Stumpf note that three things are essential for effective career progression. First is a clear perception of one's current knowledge, skills, interests, life-style, and preferences. Second is an individual definition of successes, including activities that bring positive feelings and future positions that will satisfy psychic and social as well as economic needs. Third is a realistic plan of action, including short- and long-term goals. They note, "To the extent that the plans and actions are flexible and sensitive to organizational opportunities and constraints, they are more likely to result in effective career progression." The three elements of self-assessment, establishment of objectives, and career planning are the essence of career management. Each element interacts with the others. According to London and Stumpf, these form the framework for pinpointing opportunities as well as constraints upon success. Self-assessment means generating and analyzing information about oneself in relation to career and overall life themes. A job-seeking strategy helps in assessing whether prospective employers and positions fit with one's primary work and life style goals.[8]

London and Stumpf's book on career development and planning, *Managing Careers*, gives a detailed analysis of how to develop career plans. They also give useful suggestions on how to manage your career.

No one has outstanding abilities in marketing, production, personnel, planning, research, and all other functions. However, concentrating on your weaknesses instead of your strengths can cripple your career. Career plans should be developed in the same way that specialists develop corporate plans, beginning with an analysis of assets and liabilities. An intelligent self-growth strategy must contain a realistic appraisal of your individual assets and liabilities, followed by a plan that makes the most use of your assets, and either changes or compensates for your liabilities.[9]

Career plans are your responsibility. Bosses do not implement career planning for their subordinates because most do not have the training and the time to do so, or so they say. In reality, there are few rewards for doing so. Managers point out that when they are evaluated by their superiors, their performance is measured for a wide range of responsibilities but that little, if any, weight is given to how conscientiously or effectively they attend to career counseling for their subordinates.

Taking charge of your own performance potential, career planning, and training and development needs will not guarantee your success, but it will certainly give you a better chance of achieving your goals. It will also allow you to evaluate more realistically your next course of action, whether that is to leave the company or to stay.

One final piece of advice: Your work will take up the majority of your waking hours and a large number of your most productive years. A mistake that many young eager people make is that they are too impatient. They do not recognize that two or three years in a job at the same level is a very short time in one's career. A good employee will outlast any bad work situation or leave the company.

Waiting need not be passive. You should do anything you can to improve your situation or to get out of it. However, hostility and a negative attitude will only worsen your situation and lessen your chances of moving up or out under positive conditions.

Conclusion

In this chapter we presented advice to all employees regardless of personal characteristics or workplace. Essentially, the advice is to understand themselves so that they can understand, appreciate, respect, and value people who are different. Understanding who they really are, their strengths and weaknesses, will allow them to be more productive employees, because they will be able to more readily distinguish between what they contribute, what others contribute, and what the bureaucratic structure contributes to the problems employees face.

In addition, we pointed out that employees must take proactive steps to understand other people. Understanding people will be a key to their success. Finally, employers must take charge of their careers. No one else should or can be responsible for them.

It is crucial for success in a diverse global economy that every individual recognize that he or she is part and parcel of the problem and the solution.

Who Supports Diversity?

In the previous chapters we suggested that an important step for employees is to support pluralism in the workplace and in their personal lives. Recently, a number of have studies have suggested that most white Americans favor racial equality. For example, a poll done by Harris for the Defense and Educational Fund of the National Association for the Advancement of Colored People found substantial agreement between black and white Americans on ways to achieve equal opportunities in the United States. They also found 53 percent of respondents agreeing that more should be done to help disadvantaged minorities than was done during the Reagan administration. Only 4 percent believed less should be done, and 40 percent thought about the same should be done.[1] At least 88 percent of respondents believed the following should be done:

- Special school programs for poor children; programs to reduce dropout rate
- Incentives to locate businesses in high-poverty urban areas
- Large federal and state job programs tied together with job programs to teach skills to poor children
- Construction of low- and middle-income housing for minority and white people

While there was substantial agreement on these issues, there was substantial disagreement on crucial items between white and minority people, especially black Americans. For example, Harris found that 66 percent of white respondents believed that African Americans received equal pay and equal work opportunities;

only 33 percent of African American respondents concurred. Similar disagreements occurred on issues of equitable treatment of black Americans in education, housing, and the criminal justice system.

We agree with the general positive results of the Harris survey, but the areas of agreement are "soft" areas. We believe the areas of disagreement are "hard" areas: education, job, and housing. White people will support assistance to minorities as long as it does not diminish white opportunities.

Employees' Support for Pluralism

We have found in our studies that employees' support for pluralism is substantial in "soft" areas but less enthusiastic, primarily among white employees, on pluralistic efforts that would put teeth into a program or require personal commitment. For instance, it is easy for employees to agree philosophically that their company shoud have a work force reflecting the diversity of its customers and stockholders. As Figure 15–1 shows, over 80 percent of employees agreed with this proposition. However, only 38 percent believed that their supervisors should be compensated for pluralistic efforts; Asian workers (55 percent) are most likely to support such a move, and white male workers (31 percent) are least likely to support it. In several companies we have worked with, efforts are made to compensate managers for their pluralistic efforts. These departments have better track records in employing minorities and women, a higher morale, and a reputation of being the best-run and the best to work for.

Many respondents wrote that companies should evaluate supervisors on their performance in supporting pluralism and take concrete measures against those who do not foster it.

Quit talking so much about it and make management jobs and bonuses dependent on the steps they've taken to implement pluralism. (Black, middle-level, man)

Hold employees accountable for pluralism. In return, recognition should be given to those who are pluralistic in their action and deeds. (Black, upper-level, woman)

Questions That Make Up the Index

• To what extent do you believe it is important for this company's employee makeup to reflect diversity similar to its customers and stockholders? (Percent who say at least to some extent) 84

• To what extent do you agree or disagree with each of the following statements?
(Percent who agree or strongly agree)

   Hiring, promotion goals, and timetables should be part of pluralistic efforts 67

   Attendance at company-sponsored pluralism workshops, forums, etc. should be mandatory ... 47

   My supervisor should be compensated for his/her pluralistic efforts 38

• To what extent do you agree or disagree with the following statements about special interest organizations that discuss specific issues such as race/gender concerns?

   This company should allow such organizations to exist in the company.
   (Percent who agree or strongly agree) 78

   These organizations merely increase segregation.
   (Percent who disagree or strongly disagree) 58

   The company should financially support such organizations. (Percent who agree or strongly agree) 33

• What is your position on interracial marriages? (Percent supportive or very supportive) 55

• To what extent does it bother you to hear employees at this company speak in a language you do not understand? (Percent who say not at all) 31

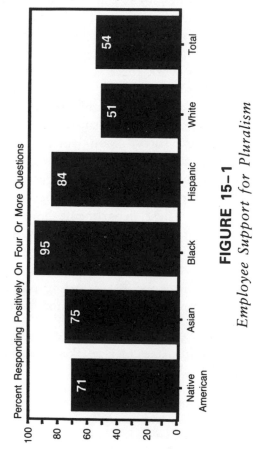

FIGURE 15–1
Employee Support for Pluralism

Get rid of those who already have openly refused to support this effort. (Black, middle-level, woman)

Although I do not favor a witch-hunt, perhaps the records of managers and who they have promoted should be examined for pluralistic efforts and incorporated into their appraisals and pay treatment. (White, lower-level, woman)

When asked if their companies should establish hiring and promotion goals and timetables as part of their pluralistic efforts, 49 percent of white men, 64 percent of Native American men, and 71 percent of white women supported this idea, compared with 77 percent of Asian and Native American women, 88 percent of black respondents, and 79 percent of Hispanic respondents who agreed or strongly agreed. To oppose hiring and promotion goals and timetables is to oppose the major strategies that have given minorities and women better opportunities in the past twenty-six years. All our research shows that little progress would be made without such efforts. Following are employees' comments about goals and timetables.

Have a long-range goal; expect managers to work toward it.
(White, upper-level, man)

Change the percentage of minorities in the company. . . . The company is 80 percent plus white. The only way that it will change is goals and timetables. Let's get with it.
(Black, occupational, woman)

Set a goal to show some meaningful results at the officer level.
(Native American middle-level, man)

More senior and officer-level management should be black, Hispanic, Asian, etc. Let us see a visible move from the top.
(Hispanic, occupational, man)

It is clear that a truly diverse work force will not come about in the United States without extensive training (in workshops on diversity and the like). In our studies, from 40 percent (white men) compared to 72 percent (black respondents) believed that attendance at company-sponsored pluralism workshops should be mandatory.

Require all employees to attend workshops on pluralism. Also, the company should enforce pluralism in the workplace.
(Black, middle-level, man)

Take a firm stand and strongly encourage people to attend workshops. (Asian, middle-level, man)

Make it mandatory for everyone to attend pluralism workshops. When instances occur, there should be consequences involved. (White, occupational, woman)

Start with intensive training and feedback requirements of middle and upper management on pluralism.
(Native American, lower-level, woman)

During the 1970s and 1980s many companies found themselves faced with the question of how to respond to employee support groups, which are formed primarily by subgroups within the company to pressure the company into developing action plans to address their unique concerns. They also engage in numerous self-help activities to make certain their members are ready for the opportunities for which they are pressuring the company. Some employees see such organizations to be of value.

I believe that such organizations make people aware of what's available to them and give them support.
(Native American, occupational, woman)

It is good for people to be able to talk to someone of the same gender color, etc., who will understand what is being said. It's good to get rid of fears, anxiety in the workplace. You can get feedback and ideas. (Black, occupational, man)

These support groups are helpful in that all are not able to find mentors. Information is found in these support groups that is not always found immediately from supervisors at work.
(Black, lower-level, man)

Without organizations like these, some people would have no idea what's going on in the company. (Hispanic, lower-level, woman)

But others do not like the fact that such support groups ultimately become company-financed. This question produced the biggest difference in response. Eighty-one percent of African American employees supported this strategy, while only 28 percent of white male employees did. Many people indicated that they felt such groups increase segregation and that, if they exist, they should do so without direct company assistance.

> What happened to us as a company team? Why do we need all these little clubs to feel important? Someone needs to start a club, all invited, all important. They should never receive company money. (White, occupational, woman)

> Wouldn't we be regarded as elitist if we started an organization for white, male, heterosexual employees? No money!
> (White, occupational, man)

> Groups or clubs tend to become cliquish. I don't think the company has a right to deny membership but it should not fund them. (Hispanic, lower-level, man)

When these and other related questions are formed into an index, we find that African American employees are much more likely (95 percent) to respond supportively to at least five of the nine questions than are white employees (51 percent) (see figure 15–1).

When the same information is broken down by gender, we find that women and men respond similarly, but whenever there is a difference, women are more likely to indicate support for pluralism. For example, women are more likely to believe that hiring and promotion goals and timetables should be a part of pluralistic efforts and that the company should financially support special interest organizations. Women are also less likely than men to believe that these organizations increase segregation.

In our studies, employees saw the efforts of their companies to support pluralism in both a positive and a negative light.

> We are working against age-old prejudices and culturally entrenched bias. Change will occur slowly and only as a result of constant vigilance, effort, and sacrifice. (Asian, lower-level, man)

> I learned that diversity is very important to the corporate environ-

ment and its success. Diversity is something to accept and spread. (White, middle-level, man)

I understand the values and need for a pluralistic work force. We must do special things to achieve this. We must not forget, however, the individual's responsibility to perform in a manner that creates value to the corporation. (White, upper-level, man)

I believe our efforts are very good in certain companies and in certain departments but not comprehensive enough yet. It will happen when the key decision makers and decision bodies reflect a pluralistic makeup. (Hispanic, upper-level, man)

It makes sense that if pluralism works in the short term, white men will have less opportunity. I'm willing to accept that and hope that this is a short transition because true pluralism is about equity. (White, middle-level, man)

Some of the reasons employees do not support pluralism reveal familiar themes that have occurred throughout the book.

I agree with pluralism, but it's a Catch-22. So often I see minorities who expect something for nothing. They act like the world owes them and take advantage. (Asian, occupational, woman)

The laudable efforts of the company have yielded mixed results, poor morale, and have ignored the obvious: hiring only the best and promoting only the best will draw the best people of all races and colors. (White, middle-level, man)

Incompetence has been accepted, condoned, fostered in the name of pluralism. (White, upper-level, man)

Since entering this company two years ago, I have had the feeling that affirmative action has been shoved down my throat. I believe that it serves its function, balancing the inequities of the past and present, . . . but it perpetuates the use of labels. If we could all be accepted as humans first and not be labeled, I would be more at ease with others. (White, lower-level, man)

Initiative on pluralism has been, in my view, devastating. When coupled with the despotic promotion practices which are generally used, it is obvious to me that we have a major morale crisis on our hands. I have had my hands tied a number of times when they could not supply me with one qualified candidate for a first-level position. The key to achieving a pluralistic work force is not to show white males they have no future in the company but to hire and recruit qualified entry-level candidates who can succeed. There is nothing more nauseating than to see unqualified, incompetent, yet sexually and racially acceptable managers making fools of themselves. Why is it the company approaches pluralism as a fashion and not the complex, difficult problem it is? I support pluralism entirely; with demographic trends showing what is happening, there is no choice to be made. But the implementation of this stinks. We've got a long way to go and you're not going to gain acceptance and understanding by telling the majority of young employees they are second-class citizens. (White, middle-level, man)

One explanation for the difference between the responses of white people and people of color with respect to pluralism in the workplace is that people in positions of power prefer the status quo and people who have less power prefer change. This makes intuitive sense, because those in power have much to lose with a shift in the equilibrium, and those who have less power have much to gain. Figure 15–2, which looks at how the employees perceive pluralism efforts impacting on their career opportunities, dramatically demonstrates this notion.

The greatest differences in response are by race. White men (54 percent) are most likely to believe that their opportunities will decrease. At least four times the percentage of people of color believe that their opportunities will increase. Thus, companies must recognize that any attempt to move toward a diverse work force will not be readily supported by employees who believe their opportunities will be limited. A key part of any company program, then, is to be aware of these concerns and address them head-on.

Pluralistic leadership by companies is not enough. Employees themselves must recognize the part they play in creating a diverse work force. They must make personal commitments to work on changing their own discriminatory and stereotyping attitudes and behavior. Following are employees' comments from our studies that show a realization of this in their own words.

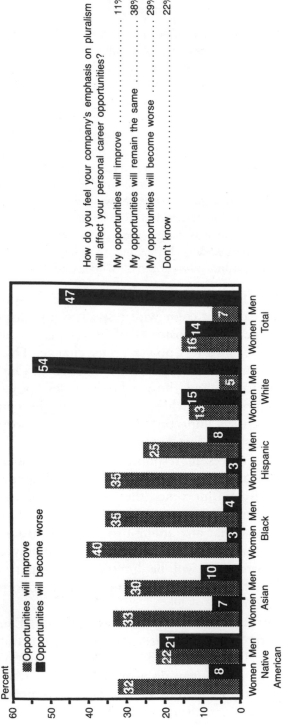

FIGURE 15-2

The Effect of Pluralism on Personal Career Opportunities

I will: support this workshop for all people with the regional pluralism committee; get to know personally women and people of color better; initiate lunch, other nonwork activity.
(White, middle-level, man)

I will make a conscientious effort to confront individuals who tell racist/sexist jokes or make racist/sexist remarks, whether it be friends, peers, families, etc. I will learn more about words or phrases or actions that offend other ethnic groups and ask for feedback if I offend. I will support those individuals who take risks to eliminate racism/sexism and, if needed, write letters to continue pluralism workshops. (White, lower-level, woman)

Actions I will take: get to know the Filipino woman I work with and find out about differences in her culture over ours and also act as mentor for her if she wants. Encourage people in my group to attend future pluralism classes. Take risks and point out to people when they are doing or saying things that could be perceived as racist or sexist (at work and at home). (Black, lower-level, woman)

How I will deal with these issues: Continue and build my awareness by attending workshops on sexism and racism issues. Learn to communicate with individuals on a one-to-one basis. Take them into account as individuals, listen to what he/she says. Be more aware about using sexist remarks/terms. Include all races/sexes when it is appropriate to do so. Socialize with others outside of my ethnic group. (Hispanic, middle-level, man)

Commitment to take every person as an individual. Stop making assumptions. Find some common ground, get past the differences, to build them. Take the risk and confront those people who do not support diversity. Become more supportive of minority support groups. (Asian, lower-level, woman)

I will not be a party to sexist jokes in the office place. I will take steps to ensure that I network with persons not like myself. I must confront those who treat me in ways I do not like.
(Black, occupational, man)

Learn to accept that people are different, whether it be race or gender, and change my ways of thinking. Accept the fact this situation exists and deal with it. Get to know more about the black society, their views and ideas. Socialize with people of color outside of work to help me understand. Educate my family on racial issues and that interracial marriages do exist and can work. The happiness of the two involved is most important. Give your support. (White, occupational, woman)

Plan to break out of mold—who I usually go to lunch with, socialize with people from work. Ask people outside of comfort zone to lunch, break, drinks. Then, when a more serious social event seems appropriate, have a party. (White, lower-level, man)

Be supportive of co-workers of other races or gender. Be supportive of pluralism goals. Be fair to all co-workers. Get acquainted with co-workers on a personal basis.
(Hispanic, lower-level, woman)

Deal with my sexist views, i.e., view of white women being equal with people of color, therefore I tend to be more critical. Develop a more confrontational style on the issues of race and sex. Deal with the issue of racism in a more constructive way rather than internalizing the issue, i.e., there is something wrong with me. Less defensive about issues. (Black, middle-level, woman)

Socialize—luncheons, parties, visit with each other, conduct social events. Confront school principal with the racist issues. Confront sexist comments. (Native American, lower-level, woman)

These comments suggest that there is much we can do as individuals to change our work and home environments to accept, respect, appreciate, and value differences. The key to taking proactive steps is to feel secure in ourselves to take on the challenge. The employees' responses reflect a fear of being perceived as an "outcast"; however, if all employees who say they want to bring about change would step up and step out, they could be a substantial majority.

Employees' Perception of Their Companies' Support for Pluralism

Companies may face considerable opposition to pluralistic changes. They must contend with many in the current work force who are at least skeptical of company commitment to pluralism and at most blatantly opposed to diversity. In order to make a successful transition to a new corporate culture, there must be a total commitment from the organization, not only in terms of the image the company projects but also in terms of leadership demonstrated by top executives.

It is interesting to note that although a healthy percentage of employees believe their companies support pluralism, only 6 percent believe there will be no resistance to pluralistic efforts and 36 percent believe resistance will be equal at all levels in their companies. Perhaps this is an acknowledgment of the fact that many employees will have problems accepting diversity, even though the company as an entity supports it. Employees need to realize that a company is nothing more than a collection of individuals, and if these employees don't support a program, the company won't be able to either.

The following comments illustrate employees' perceptions of company support for pluralism. Note that they are tentatively optimistic but some are skeptical of the long-term commitment being made by their companies' leadership to this effort.

I hope pluralism stays with our company objectives for a long time—not just another matter that will phase out in a couple of years. (Asian, occupational, woman)

I am not convinced that the company supports a pluralistic environment, but does a great job giving it lip service. A pluralistic work force does indeed exist at lower management where I might add, it potentially "does the least damage" in that lower positions have the least policy-making power. At the other end of the spectrum, the company has also achieved a pluralistic work force in its executive levels. These individuals, because of the nature of their responsibilities and stature in the company, receive extensive media and public attention. Those outside the company are left with the impression, therefore, that all management levels must be pluralistic if the executive levels are. Our own company statistics prove this erroneous. (White, lower-level, woman)

I get tired of attending affirmative action workshops when these nonsupporters are allowed to sit back and not participate. They feel if they keep their mouth shut, they won't have to deal with it. Nothing is further from the truth. (Black, lower-level, man)

There is still a reluctance of employees of different races to mix with each other in a nonwork type of environment. For example, I very rarely see a mixed group of black and white employees eating lunch together. Also, how much knowledge is a mentor of a different race really willing to pass on to a member of another ethnic group? (White, lower-level, woman)

I still feel pluralistic efforts are "lip service." I have seen two white males promoted into jobs that I was equally or more qualified for. I brought it to my division head's attention: but all I got was an apology. I was never even considered for the jobs.
(Black, lower-level, woman)

Some employees with power to promote and supervise think the effort is a joke because they have not been demanded to promote the idea. For example, one director said "The only way I will be made to attend one of these workshops is if my job depends on it." (Black, lower-level, man)

The perception of pluralistic efforts is high but it might all be promotional hype: Is there any objective measurement of progress? Let's publicize concrete advances as well.
(Asian, middle-level, man)

There is a road to go—mixed signals get sent that sponsor tokenism. There is still a good ol'boy network, although [pluralism exists] outwardly. My company is still more advanced than other businesses in this area. (White, middle-level, woman)

The fact that it is even mentioned in this age of political conservatism is commendable for my company.
(Hispanic, occupational, man)

The company's pluralistic efforts are accepted at the top levels and bottom levels but not at the middle where a person's career is determined. (Asian, lower-level, man)

Employees were asked a series of questions to ascertain the extent to which they believed their companies support pluralistic programs. Figure 15–3 shows the responses. Overall, except for

Questions That Make Up the Index

To what extent do you agree or disagree with each of the following statements? (Percent who agree or strongly agree)

The company publications I see reflect a pluralistic commitment 89

The company's public advertisements reflect its commitment to pluralism 75

Top management exhibits behavior suitable to lead a pluralistic work force 70

To what extent do you believe your supervisor's age impacts negatively on his/her ability to work effectively in a pluralistically driven company? (Percent who say to a small extent or no extent) 83

To what extent do you believe the following? (Percent who say to some extent or to a great extent)

Your supervisor's supervisor supports pluralism 78

Your supervisor supports pluralism through her/his behavior 67

At what level do you believe this company's pluralistic efforts will meet the greatest resistance?

No resistance will occur 6

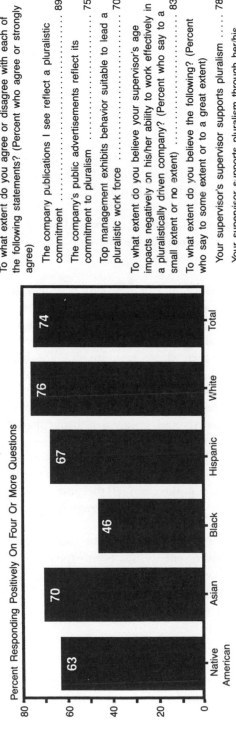

Percent Responding Positively On Four Or More Questions

Native American	63	
Asian	70	
Black	46	
Hispanic	67	
White	76	
Total	74	

FIGURE 15–3

Employee Perceptions of Company Support for Pluralism

black employees, more than 63 percent of employees believed that their company is supportive in four out of the seven areas.

Following are some of the characteristics that employees deem necessary to allow their companies to have an efficient diverse work force. Strong leadership is a key characteristic. If the leaders do not walk like they talk, neither will the employees.

> An active dedication to gaining parity—equal representation of white males and affected group members in our work force, through use of official avenues, affirmative action, and unofficial networking. (White, middle-level, man)

> Willingness to support affirmative action. Allowing company time for committees to meet, discuss, and develop plans for dealing with our diversity. (Asian, lower-level, man)

> One characteristic within the department that will allow the successful management of a diverse workforce is that some of the managers truly care and promote awareness. Those few have been very supportive when not faced with career-threatening moves by nonsupporters. However, these few are not enough to turn the entire department round. (Black, middle-level, man)

> Current diverse makeup of the department. There are still low represented areas, but overall progress is being made.
> (Black, lower-level, man)

> Being honest with the employees, giving honest feedback for performance appraisals. Employees feel they are doing an excellent job, but in fact they are not. (Asian, lower-level, man)

> There seems to be a real interest in our groups about managing diversity. A great deal of energy has been expended to uncover and resolve issues and concerns of existing affected group members so as to promote harmony in the work life of all affected group members. (White, lower-level, woman)

Conclusion

It is clear that there is considerable philosophical support among employees for their companies to move toward a pluralistic work force. However, this support seems to weaken considerably when it comes to moving beyond philosophical support to concrete steps. Almost all employees believe there will be resistance to company efforts at all levels. Despite the fact that most employees perceive their leaders to support pluralism in theory, many feel that an important factor hindering progress toward diversity is a lack of strong leadership in practice from various levels of management. Having said that leadership is a key ingredient to moving a company toward pluralism, we must also emphasize that employees too are both a part of the problem and a part of the solution.

Making the U.S. Population the Competitive Advantage

After reading this book, readers are sure to ask, "How can you conclude that the United States will have a competitive edge over the European Community and Japan?" Let's review, in general, why this is the case; however, let's do it by reversing the order. We first discuss the United States, then Europe, and last, Japan. After the overview, we present specific strategies that U.S. companies must follow to be able to gain and retain the competitive edge over Japan and the EC. In addition, several important steps the U.S. government must take are presented.

The United States

We have described what is wrong with the United States; however, there are several extremely important factors that are right about the United States. It is the most diversely populated nation of the three economic powers. We have the capability of utilizing Americans in business, social, and political activities who are natives of practically every country in the world.

By having more liberal immigration policies we are able to modify some of the negative demographic trends, such as the "baby bust" and the aging population. Thus, we will have a sufficient number of people to keep our economic machine running. The United States will not have businesses closing as in Japan because of insufficient numbers of people to fill the jobs.

The United States has a several-hundred-year history of different racial and ethnic groups coming to the country, facing discrimination, and finally achieving some degree of acceptance and generally peaceful coexistence. We have not resolved all of the gender, racial, ethnic, and religious problems. We have made mistakes, and we are still making mistakes. However, we have the experience to accommodate if not accept differences. Because of our experience with immigrants, racial minorities, religious minorities, and women we are better positioned to accept the aged, the disabled, and those with alternative life-styles.

The competitive advantage in people for the United States is not a given. We are at a crucial stage in becoming the first nation in the world to truly have economic, legal, and social systems that accept, value, appreciate, and respect diversity, an economic system that recognizes people as its most valuable resource and its competitive edge.

However, in order to get there, we must take the next step. Where are we? Philosophically, the vast majority of Americans have accepted the concept of valuing diversity. We have the best laws in the world to protect the rights of all people living in the United States, regardless of race, ethnicity, gender, religion, age, and disability. No other country formally and legally supports equal opportunity, the right to privacy, and the undisturbed pursuit of happiness as uncompromisingly as the United States does. In addition, we are trying to make our immigration policy more equitable. This is in direct contrast to what the Japanese and Europeans are doing about immigration. In short, our philosophy is right, and our laws are right.

The crucial step we must take is to move from the philosophical and legal to the proactive and personal. That is, the United States and all its citizens and noncitizens living and working here must begin to walk like they talk. We must recognize that we are as much a part of the problem as we are a part of the solution. This will be the most difficult step because it requires all of us to become personally involved in making the American dream, and thus the competitive advantage we have in people, a reality for all.

The European Community

The European Community (EC) is suffering from a birth dearth and a rapidly aging population. In the coming years, the EC will have to find new sources of workers and people to keep its economic machine running. While only about 3 percent of the EC's population is made up of foreign immigrants, primarily from African and Asian countries, the EC countries are acting as if they were being overrun by millions of nonwhite immigrants. Thus, rather than opening up their doors to foreign immigrants, they are closing them, and some want to send nonwhite residents back to their lands of origin.

This extreme ethnocentrism and racism is going to be very detrimental to the EC's ability to have a viable marketplace and economy. As the nonwhite world becomes more stable and economically powerful, the EC countries will be certain to face pressures to open their borders to, and improve the treatment of, Third World immigrants.

Another factor that is detrimental to the EC is the ethnocentric attitudes based on hundreds of years of hostilities among member nations. Thus, despite the legal right of the EC population to freely move from country to country to live and work, the ethnocentric attitudes will create great conflicts and hinder the ability of the EC to utilize effectively its diverse population.

Still another factor detrimental to the success of the EC is the extremely ambivalent feelings of the majority of its population about women becoming an integral permanent part of the work force. In sum, philosophically the EC nations do not have a commitment to a diverse racial and ethnic population and are moving only slowly toward the acceptance of women in the work force.

What are the legal stands the EC has taken with regard to protecting the rights of immigrants and women? The EC nations have done little to protect the legal rights of foreign immigrant workers. (Note that former East Germany intended to send back to their homelands tens of thousands of Cubans, Africans, and Vietnamese. Some of the workers have lived in the country for years.) In addition, many EC nations have passed restrictive immigration laws, and increasingly there are growing movements that advocate sending all nonwhite immigrants home.

The EC is more progressive with women. While the EC has forced member nations to pass laws to provide women equal employment opportunities, some laws still have traces of sexism and most do not have any real sanctions against those who would discriminate against women. Thus, while there are laws to protect women, they are in most countries ignored to some extent. In concluding, we believe that the EC is at the stage the United States was at during the late 1950s and early 1960s regarding the issue of gender. Philosophically EC countries have some recognition of women's value and the need to protect their rights, but legally, in most cases, they have not put teeth into the laws.

With regard to minorities and foreign immigrants, the EC nations as a whole have not even made a commitment to become diverse, multi-racial, multi-ethnic nations. In fact, some are trying to maintain their racial "purity." We conclude the EC is at the stage with regard to immigrants and racial minorities where the United States was during the early 1950s. Because of these facts, there are few Europeans who are ready to take the proactive personal step that would assist them in respecting, valuing, and appreciating people who are different than they are.

Japan

Japan is further back than the EC in having a philosophical, legal, and proactive personal commitment to a diverse nation and work force. Their mind-set also creates great problems for Japanese in valuing, respecting, and appreciating differences in their endeavors outside of Japan.

All our data suggest that philosophically the Japanese are racist and extremely ethnocentric. They have a sense of superiority, which can be compared to the extreme right-wing parties of Europe and extreme right-wing racists in the United States. In the last two cases, these parties and groups are not large; in Japan, most of the nation is of that mind-set. Despite the small numbers of immigrants living and working in Japan, despite the fact that Japan does not have sufficient workers, it has recently passed a more restrictive immigration law. This is on top of its already strict immigration law.

Concerning women, most Japanese philosophically believe women should be second-class citizens and subservient to men. Despite the passage of an antidiscrimination law protecting women's employment rights, the law has no sanctions. Therefore, discrimination against women in employment is overt and rampant, just as it is in Japanese society as a whole.

Despite the fact that Japan does not have enough workers to keep their industries running, despite the fact that their population is aging rapidly, they are not making any movement to allow immigrants to come into the country, and they are making only minimal efforts to allow women to become more integral players in the work force. We believe the Japanese are at the place the United States was during the 1930s with regard to their treatment of racial minorities and women.

One last comment about Japan. It is having a serious problem with its people. They are questioning some of the old tenets about loyalty, hard work, and sacrificing for the nation. All these factors suggest to us that Japan will not maintain its dominant economic position in the 1990s. If it does not change its philosophy and general values about women and non-Japanese, it could face a drastic economic decline as the United States, possibly Europe, and other Asian nations become more astute competitors. It is evident that the Japanese are nowhere near taking the personal proactive step that will be increasingly crucial to economic success in the 1990s and beyond. Now let's turn our attention to what the United States must do to take the final personal proactive step.

What the United States Must Do

U.S. business must recognize that the diversity issue is part and parcel of three other issues. One is the problems associated with any bureaucratic structure. Another is the issue of human beings basically being neurotic to some extent. The final issue is the problem of changing values about work and nonwork life. What makes managing the diverse work force so difficult is that in many cases we cannot tell which is the real problem, or what is the real issue.

This is because all these problems and issues are intertwined. Let's look at several examples. An African American male middle-level manager who has excellent educational credentials and a good track record is becoming frustrated with his lack of upward mobility and his perception that he is not rewarded fairly. What is the reality? Is it because the bureaucracy is so structured that it does not have sufficient resources to reward all top people? Is it because the old bureaucratic way is to move people slowly? Is it because the man does not have an accurate self-perception, that he believes he deserves more than he should realistically receive (his own neurosis)? Is it because his "new breed" values are clashing with his company's old values on how to treat employees? Or is it that, as an African American man, he is being discriminated against on the basis of race?

Another example: an Asian female lower-level manager was not selected to head an interdepartmental team. She has a family and works little overtime but always gets her work done well and on time. She believes she was passed over because of her gender, race, and the fact that she speaks English as a second language. She is upset and is considering leaving her company. Her boss tells her that the reason she was not selected was because traditionally such teams are headed by someone from another department. What is the truth? Why did she not get the leadership role? Is it because of some bureaucratic procedure that says that people from her department do not lead such teams? Is it because she does not place work above family, i.e., she has "new breed" values? Is it because she really is not capable of leading the team, but she thinks she is (her own neurosis)? Or is it because she is a foreign-born Asian female who speaks English as a second language?

While corporations cannot eliminate such problems, there are many strategies they can use to minimize these conflicts and more effectively utilize their people to their competitive advantage.

Bureaucratic Problems

In order to minimize bureaucratic structural and policy issues that have no real relevance to the efficient running of a company, it is absolutely crucial that the bureaucratic structure is seen for what it is.

Bureaucracy is an attempt to organize our environment, which is forever unpredictable. It is therefore society's attempt to structure uncertainty, which is impossible. Bureaucracies are society's response to limited resources. They evolved as a necessity as our populations grew and we consumed more and more of our limited resources. To function, most societies believe they require order; however, order in turn demands formal procedures, rules, and regulations to control divergence. This creates a social dichotomy between those who regulate and those who are regulated. Stratification automatically identifies and separates the powerful from the powerless, the strong from the weak. All people are not perceived as equal, and the very reason for the bureaucracy's hierarchical structure is to discriminate among people. The discrimination comes about most noticeably in the limited opportunities and resources available for rewards; people are not rewarded solely on the basis of merit and ability.

Having acknowledged these realities, corporate leadership and employees can begin to develop strategies to make their companies fairer and more equitable. A concerted effort must be made to develop a realistic corporate culture that admits the inherent problems of bureaucracies and the frailties of human nature and makes a serious commitment to develop and implement strategies that will provide as fair, equitable, and healthy a work atmosphere as possible.

One crucial strategy is to implement objective, systematic employment policies and systems that try to minimize the inherent unfairness in any such systems because of the human element. The key components are to clearly define responsibilities of supervisors and employees and set specific objectives and means of measurement. With clearly defined responsibilities, objectives, and means of measurement, agreed upon by *both* supervisors and employees, performance evaluations will more likely be based on the job done and not on subjective criteria such as race, gender, age, ethnicity, religion, sexual preference, or disability.

Since properly defined work produces a clearer picture of the skills and abilities needed to perform jobs, potential evaluations will be more effective, especially if a variety of evaluation procedures are used to check and balance one another. Evaluating past performance is much easier than evaluating future performance.

In order to be most useful to subordinates, performance and potential evaluations should provide useful and specific feedback on subordinates' strengths and weaknesses. They should take into consideration subordinates' views about their performance and potential. With these two evaluations properly done, supervisors and employees will be able to effectively determine career plans and needs for training and development. This, of course, holds providing the company has given both the manager and the subordinate proper training and sufficient information to develop such plans.

It is imperative, if this managerial system is to be effective, that participation be active and exist in all aspects of the process. Many supervisors are very reluctant to include employees, for both personal and practical reasons. On the personal side, they view such a managerial system as denying them exclusive traditional authority. Some view it as revolutionary; since they usually oppose minor procedural changes, they are bound to resist dramatic changes in managerial methods.

On the practical side, managers are reluctant to implement systems in which they are not properly trained. Critical communication with employees is difficult for many supervisors (even in areas in which they are comfortable and well trained). Communication is much less difficult when proper training has occurred. Supervisors lack training not only in the basic content and function of these system parts but also in methods for providing constructive and critical feedback to their employees, especially about negative issues. Also, since most managers are paid for meeting numerical objectives, not human objectives, the necessity of priorities encourages supervisors to place less emphasis on how to handle, evaluate, develop, and motivate people than on meeting targets. Managers are not paid for human objectives. They view this role as something in addition to their jobs rather than as an integral part of them, and tend to avoid it. This is despite all the rhetoric that people are our most valuable resource.

A training program should be developed to give supervisors effective and bias-free tools to better evaluate their subordinates' performance and potential, and to prepare managers to deal with their subordinates' career development and planning needs. Parallel sessions for subordinates should aim to enhance their understanding of the programs and to stress their individual responsibilities in these processes. Remember, a crucial element of these programs is training for supervisors in the skills of clear, honest, supportive, and knowledgeable communication with their employees regardless of their employees' personal characteristics.

In addition, an effective reward system should be implemented. It should recognize, with bonuses, special assignments, and promotions, those managers who have a good track record of developing and using all their work force and those employees who take the initiative to improve their skills and marketability.

Recognizing that there are limited promotion benefits must be weighed against the possible harm to those who are not recognized. In our view, one of the most destructive reward systems is the so-called merit award that is given each year to a select percentage of people for outstanding performance. Corporations that use this system create, from at least two months before the end of the performance period until the awards are announced, a great deal of tension and politicking as employees vie with each other and try to position themselves to be among the chosen few to receive the awards. The announcement of the awards has a very negative impact on the 90 percent of the employees who are left out, especially because people realistically are rewarded on the basis of subjective as well as objective criteria.

Team awards based on the results of the company as a whole or of individual units or departments generate much more harmony and cooperation. Making on-the-spot awards for specific projects, activities, or accomplishments is also a way to help motivate people because the reward is immediate and directly related to specific accomplishments.

In addition to such team awards, we strongly urge companies to develop various pay incentive schemes for those employees who are top talent but must, for corporate reasons, stay in jobs for long periods of time because of their expertise, thus being taken out of the mainstream of promotable candidates.

Another way of rewarding people is to develop flexible benefit plans that take into consideration the increasing diversity of the work force. These plans should allow employees a wide variety of options to select from beyond the typical ones now offered. For example, they should include child care and elder care options, vacation options, sabbatical options, pay options, and so on.

Corporations must discover other informal, nonmonetary rewards. The ultimate goal of these new rewards is to bring corporate promises more into line with realities.

Even if corporations expand their employee rewards and even if they become more fair and equitable, corporate leaders must recognize that the nature of bureaucracies and of human beings is such that there will always be conflict and dissatisfaction. They should develop strategies to minimize it. The best way to do this is to involve employees in defining the problem as they perceive it, coming up with solutions, and developing, implementing, monitoring, and revising action plans. This should not be a one-shot deal but an ongoing process, because once the process stops, employees will go back to pointing fingers at everyone else, especially upper managers, for the problems that exist. This problem-solving process, if implemented properly on an ongoing basis and with the support of the leadership, is an excellent way to build teams.

We as People

As we have said throughout this book, we as individuals must recognize that we are part and parcel of the bureaucratic and diversity problems. We are also part and parcel of our successes and our failures. We must recognize that as human beings we are all neurotic, i.e., mentally unhealthy to some extent. Our neurotic natures make it difficult for most of us to see reality. We have a hard time recognizing our strengths and weaknesses. We have a tendency to blame others for our failures, and we generally believe we deserve more than we get.

We are basically insecure and most of us do not really know ourselves; therefore it is difficult to respect, appreciate, and value differences in other people. As a result, we, with a great deal of help from society and others, develop a number of prejudices to justify why people who are different than we are make us uncomfortable, or should not have what we have or want to have.

In order to effectively deal with these isms we must recognize our neuroses and understand how we developed them and why we still have them. We must then take concrete steps to change ourselves to become more secure, healthy humans who like and appreciate not only ourselves but also those who are different than we are.

Respecting, Appreciating, Valuing, and Accepting Differences: What Corporations Must Do

We must recognize that, to survive in this new global economy, we must make all employees, regardless of race, ethnicity, gender, religion, age, life style, and disabled status, full participating members of the corporation. We must recognize that a heterogeneous group will produce better ideas and strategies than a homogeneous group. Sale makes this point beautifully. He points out that "diversity is the rule of human life." He maintains that the human organism has evolved so far because of its ability "to diversify, not specialize: to climb and swim, hunt and nurture, work alone and in packs." Similarly, social organizations thrive as healthy organisms when they are widely differentiated, capable of a full repertoire of responses. On the other hand, "they become brittle and unadaptable and prey to any changing conditions when they are uniform and specialized." In short, individuals and groups achieve full richness of potential when "able to take on many jobs, learn many skills, live many roles."[1]

Following are specific strategies that would be part of an overall company program to create a productive, diverse work force and give the company a competitive edge in the 1990s.

1. Establish goals and timetables for all departments and levels of the company; with respect to hiring and promotion of people of color, women, and white males where underrepresented, establish similar goals and timetables.

2. Conduct and support in the company and in the community multicultural events and strongly encourage employees to attend.

3. Make certain that all training programs and systems

related to managerial and supervisory skills development have modules with some aspect of respecting, valuing, and appreciating a diverse work force.

4. At least twice a year require all employees to attend workshops that deal with all forms of isms. Studies have shown that attending workshops on all the issues discussed in this book has a greater positive impact on employees than attending sessions that deal with only one or two of them.

5. Require all managers of high potential and above middle level to become facilitators and trainers of pluralism workshops.

6. Conduct on-site and off-site educational courses that teach about different cultures. Make it a requirement for promotion opportunities.

7. Sponsor foreign language courses. Also as part of the program, have accent reduction and accent listening courses.

8. Require higher-level managers to become mentors and sponsors to women and minorities of high potential. Measure and reward their success in this task.

9. Develop concrete performance measurement criteria to evaluate all managers' efforts in managing different people. Establish rewards for those who demonstrate a positive record in these areas and penalties for those who do not.

10. Demonstrate the company's commitment to solving difficulties by promoting people who directly work in these areas and do an outstanding job.

11. Make certain that issues concerning managing and valuing differences have time slots in all middle- and upper-management meetings and other company meetings.

12. As the company globalizes, send high-potential people at all levels to other countries to be immersed in foreign culture and become familiar with and learn from it.

13. Hire more people who have studied the liberal arts, especially foreign cultures, for managerial positions.

14. Devise ways to utilize and maintain the dynamism of an aging work force, for example, phased retirement and permanent part-time work.
15. Require all high-potential managers and those being considered for promotion to middle management and above to belong to and be active participants in community organizations that are concerned with the elimination of discrimination, and support their involvement by channeling corporate community service contributions, financial and in-kind, to the organizations' activities and programs.
16. Sponsor company discount tours to various parts of the United States and foreign countries with the express purpose of assisting people in understanding, respecting, valuing, and appreciating differences.
17. Make a conscious effort to locate plant and facilities in a wide variety of communities, especially minority communities. Make certain the company maintains a diverse work force at these facilities.
18. Develop a comprehensive family care program that not only focuses on child and elder care but also takes into consideration the millions of employees responsible for disabled adults.
19. Finally, companies must punish to the extent of firing those who do not appreciate, value, and respect differences.

The overall strategy we have recommended is a multifaceted approach. People do not develop prejudices because of just one influence. Therefore, to change employees' prejudices a multifaceted approach must be used. Many companies are focusing on pluralism workshops. While useful, they will only have a limited impact if companies do not employ our multistep strategy.

U.S. Government

We have not said much about government's role in solving the problems of diversity. However, government does have a very crucial role. Our national leadership can set the tone and tenor of the nation's commitment to valuing, accepting, respecting, and appreciating differences. Our leaders must show the way. In order to do that, they must follow all the suggestions given to individuals and to corporations. We believe the new immigration bill, which will allow about 150,000 people per year to enter the United States because of their skills and financial assets, is an excellent progressive step. Most of the 640,000 immigrants last year were admitted because of preferential treatment to family members of current citizens. The United States can alleviate skills shortages and make human capital investment by letting in even greater numbers of these people. Becker wrote about the advantages these immigrants bring.

> Such newcomers can help alleviate shortages in engineering, nursing, computer programming, and many other fields. Since they would have above-average incomes, they would pay above-average taxes and make few demands on welfare, Medicaid, and other transfer programs. And it would be many years before such young immigrants would qualify for Social Security benefits—during which time they would be contributing to the system.[2]

Another key action the government must take is to pass the 1990 civil rights law, which will reverse the antipluralistic rulings of the U.S. Supreme Court and add more teeth to existing laws. The Civil Rights Act of 1990 would have extended punitive damage, pain, and suffering awards to all intentional discrimination acts. It would have made all forms of discrimination illegal, such as unnecessary workplace rules. The key to the law is that the burden of proof switches from the employee to the company once a lawsuit is filed. One could receive monetary damages as a remedy for discrimination rather than just back pay, and more people would be eligible to sue and have jury trials. It also would allow women to seek damages in sexual harassment cases. (One area in which we believe the law is lacking is that it does not guarantee rights to homosexuals.)

With this more vigorous law, the next step would become easier—monetary damages against companies would greatly enhance their efforts to accept, respect, appreciate, and value differences, because the bottom line could be greatly affected.

We also suggest that the U.S. government pass a law to reward those employers who are exemplary in managing a diverse work force. The companies should have preferential treatment in the awarding of government contracts. We also believe tax incentives and credits should be given to companies who recruit, hire, and train the hard-to-employ; however, the credit comes after the employees have been on the payroll for two years.

One last suggestion. Our government in partnership with business must set a national agenda to make certain we have the correct number of people with the correct skills and abilities to do the jobs of the 1990s and beyond. A massive cooperative effort must be made to change our educational system to meet the demands of the 1990s.

Another way of accomplishing this goal is that business and government must form a partnership to retrain our work force to keep up with the changes in technology and jobs. We have already said that individuals must take responsibility for keeping their skills current in order to be competitive in the workplace; however, government and business must provide the opportunities for employees to take advantage of their desire to retain their personal competitiveness.

It seems to us that making our work force highly competitive to give us a competitive advantage in the new global economy is tied into our dealing with our isms. We cannot perceive special programs to enhance the skills of the poor, welfare recipients, minorities, women, and the disabled as special privileges. We must look at them as necessary steps to make the United States competitive.

As we started out this book we will end it. The United States is best positioned to take advantage of its diversity. We have the right philosophy, we have the legal foundation, but we need the proactive personal commitment. If we don't achieve this last step, the United States will fall into serious and deep social conflicts that will lead to our becoming a second-rate nation.

Creating and Managing a Diverse Work Group

A Case Study

JOHN SALZER

Why should one bother trying to learn how to manage a diverse group? I would argue that there are three very important reasons. First, because a diverse and pluralistic organization has the potential to be the most dynamic and effective group. Second, because it is challenging, rewarding, and fun for the person doing the supervising. And finally, because if you plan to manage into the next century, you really may not have any choice.

Don't let anyone kid you that it is easy to manage a diverse or pluralistic work force. Because it isn't. Most of us tend to be much more comfortable around people who think and act the way we do. This fact was brought home to me some twenty years ago when I had the opportunity to view a series of video tapes made by Morris Massey, a professor at the University of Colorado, entitled "You Are What You Were When." The theme of the series was that each of us is influenced greatly by the events of our formative years and that we subconsciously retain those impressions as we grow older and thus behave in a certain way.

For example, take hair length. Depending upon when one grew up, length of hair may make a significant impact on how we view someone. If we are older and grew up with the crew cut, we may have a hard time accepting men wearing long hair, categorizing them as being hippies or worse. On the other hand, if we grew up with long hair, we might look upon men who have short hair as being rigid and conservative. Unless a manager were consciously aware of his or her bias against men with long hair, new employees supervised by the manager would have great difficulty becoming a success. Given a choice, that manager would much rather work with men who dressed conventionally and had short hair. The point I'm making is that it isn't surprising that trends in hair, fashion, and even ideas and attitudes tend to go in cycles based upon one's age.

Now you may be saying, "Well, I'm open-minded, and these things don't affect how I view those I work with." Well, how would you feel about having a gay or lesbian supervisor or subordinate? According to many current surveys, 10–12 percent of an organization's employees are probably gay. At least, this is the national average. For many, this may be diversity at its extreme. But we must recognize and deal with our attitudes because more than likely we will face such issues in the workplace.

I believe successful managers of the future will be those who recognize that not everyone thinks and behaves like themselves and hire people who don't think and behave like themselves. Why? Because these people complement the very skills and talents that the successful leaders already have. Why employ people who think and behave exactly like you? The organization benefits if we work with those who challenge our thinking and come up with totally different ideas and thoughts. I have managed just such an organization and can testify that it works.

Isn't that one reason why marriages often end up matching opposites? I know in my situation this is the case. I'm an idea person. My wife is an analyzer and detail person. For instance, I have never balanced a checkbook in my life. My wife likes to spread everything out on the dining-room table once a month and balance our checking account. She will agonize for hours over a one-penny error. Me? I think she's crazy to worry over every penny, but I'm sure happy she's willing to do it. You can imagine the trouble we'd be in if she were like me in this way.

And do we make an effective team? You bet we do. You should see us hang wallpaper. I don't know about you, but many couples have had some of their worst arguments while trying to hang wallpaper. Once we established the ground rules as to who would do what (which took several years), we became an unbeatable team. I do the measuring and hanging, she does all the matching and trimming. Have I made my point that diversity has its own rewards?

How does one go about creating an organization that is diverse and pluralistic? For many readers, I hope this is a rhetorical question. It would be my hope that they would already be deeply involved in managing a diverse and pluralistic work force and that I would only be giving guidance and assistance in making them more effective managers.

I recently had the opportunity of turning a homogeneous group of white male workers into a diverse and pluralistic group in just a few months. I was recruited to be a member of, and then became the leader of, a special project team, which was sponsored by the headquarters of our corporation to develop an executive information system. More specifically, our corporation had gone through a significant reorganization three years before and had undertaken a big diversification effort. For one hundred years, it had been an industry leader in telecommunications as part of the Bell System. When the Bell System was divided into seven regional companies, it was one of the seven newly formed "Baby Bells."

With our newfound economic freedom, our company expanded into real estate, financial services, cellular products, sales of telecommunications equipment, and so on. Our top management knew what it took to run a telephone company but felt some inadequacies when it came to managing the new business.

To get a better handle on this situation, our officer of the chair decided to bring in consultants and have them work side by side with some of our "high-potential" managers to identify what the critical success factors might be for each of the new businesses as well as for our telephone companies. If we could identify the four or five critical success factors for these businesses and learn how to monitor them, we could assist top management in their ongoing evaluation of the new businesses.

In order for our team to be successful, we would need to work very closely with the executives of the individual businesses to gain a thorough understanding of what it takes for each business to be a success. The members of the team would have very high exposure and a tremendous opportunity to position themselves for future job opportunities.

Our sponsor, the person who persuaded the corporation to do this and who selected the initial team members, was a vice president, a black man. He selected a white man as our project director; four of the five key people were also white men.

I was surprised that our team included only one woman but not surprised that none of the key members from the outside consulting firm were minority people or women. I had never met our project team's sponsor prior to a brief interview a week before the project was to start, and was not told whether he knew that I'd be a member of his team (chosen by my company's top management). But I suspect that he didn't have a choice in the matter. The only telephone company person he knew prior to the project's start was the one woman on the team.

We started with a get-acquainted meeting in May 1986. We met in a big conference room, with our black project manager kicking off the project to a mixed group of career telephone personnel and young educated white males from all over the country who were brought on the team by our outside consultants.

Midway through the meeting, the lead manager for the consulting firm looked across the table at the lone woman and asked, "Sandy, would you please get me a cup of coffee?" You might well imagine the sudden silence that fell over the room when Sandy stared back at him and said, "I don't do coffee."

While I wanted to stand up and applaud, I didn't, but I later regretted that I didn't at the time, because it became readily apparent that this sort of behavior (Sandy's refusing to get coffee) wasn't expected or condoned by our outside consultants. In most big consulting firms that still manage their operations like a military organization, Sandy's action counts as insubordination.

While nothing more was made of this during the kick-off session, it was clear that none of the parties involved let the matter drop. While I had long become accustomed to working with women at all levels, our consultants had not. The only women they dealt with on a day-to-day basis in their firm were graphics clerks and secretaries, who were expected to be "subservient."

We decided to divide up into subteams, each made up of members from the telephone company and from the consulting firm. The consulting firm member was chosen for industry expertise. The teams would then interview key individuals in the various businesses, conduct extensive research, and develop a proposed package of critical success factors and performance measures. Each of the businesses in turn would identify someone in their company who would act as our key contact. Sandy was assigned to liaise with one of the businesses along with a young man who had just received his M.B.A. degree from the University of Chicago.

I was encouraged that Sandy had been paired with this person because I thought that, coming out of an academic environment, he would be more "enlightened" than some of other consultants. I was wrong.

The matter came to a head shortly after the project began. We were all meeting to get an update on the progress of each team within their respective businesses. It was time for Sandy and her partner to report on their findings. Each of the previous pairs had shared the podium and given joint reports. But as soon as Sandy started to make the report for her team, the lead manager for the consulting firm started interrupting her and asking questions of her male partner. It was clear to me that he was out to make life difficult for Sandy.

As I indicated earlier, I didn't have a leadership role at this time. But I became very agitated with the way others started following the lead of that person in making things difficult for Sandy. Things finally boiled over when Sandy paused in her presentation and someone made a statement laced with four-letter words. When others started picking up on this and using these insults in *their* comments, I finally had enough and told the group that I didn't want to hear the words used again as long as we were working together on this project.

I know all my fellow telephone company managers respected

me for speaking up, but the consultant members were really taken aback. When we began talking about the matter, it was clear that they had had little or no sensitivity training and needed awareness education. They could not understand why using such language upset me: "After all, you can't go to a movie theater today without hearing these words over and over again." "If women want to be treated as equals in the workplace, then we'll speak to them just as if they were males." And so on. I tried to explain to them that in my opinion this wasn't appropriate behavior to use in a business situation, no matter who was present. If it continued, I said, I would take up the matter with our sponsor.

While this was not discussed openly any further, I think I got my point across to some people. I wasn't sure I had made my point with the consultants, but I felt I had done the right thing when Sandy on several later occasions expressed her gratitude for my speaking up. Shortly thereafter, I took over direction of the project from the telephone company's standpoint.

The project called for bringing in telephone company people with potential and exposing them to some of the new ventures we were undertaking. We hoped these assignments would last about two years; then the individuals would be rotated back into their old companies or find a new home in one of the businesses with which they were liaising.

Once I took over the leadership spot, my immediate goal was to turn my group into a model for pluralism and diversity. I don't know if my motives were altruistic or selfish. By this I mean the following. Was I trying to bring about pluralism because I truly believed that this was the way to design an effective organization? Or was I spurred on by a kind of one-upmanship, wanting to show our outside consultants that people of color and women could perform just as well as their white male counterparts?

I immediately went to the sponsor and indicated my desire to bring new people onto my team. I argued that the team had been together almost six months and that my co-consultants had learned as much as they were going to learn. It was time to move on to a new phase.

I was able to locate new positions for all these people (including Sandy). So now I had three openings for upper-middle-level directors in my organization. I asked the Personnel Office to advertise the jobs internally (our company has a self-nomination process), indicating to Personnel that I wanted to diversify my staff and that a list of all white male candidates would be unacceptable.

Here, we can ask, What can an organization do to help foster diverse, pluralistic work groups? I think the answer is very basic: Individuals behave in ways so as to maximize their rewards. I would design the corporate reward systems to ensure that those who take risks and make efforts to diversify are rewarded and those who don't, don't get rewarded. The rewards can be financial, career moves, or others that employees think are worth taking risks for. While this approach hasn't been used in my company, I think it should be. One reason it hasn't been used could be that we have been very successful in diversifying without using this sort of reward system. For instance, I reported to two of the highest-ranking black men while working on this project. Also, we have had very strong company-supported groups for all our minorities, including homosexuals.

Going back to specifics—I was pleasantly surprised when I received from Personnel a list of fifteen top candidates, only one of whom was a white man. Before I even got started with the interview process, I received from my boss the name of a potential candidate (R. G.), who was working in the auditing group in our headquarters operations. Well, I knew some people at headquarters and decided to make a couple of inquiries about R. G. I got glowing reports about him: he had owned his own small C.P.A. firm, he was very smart and dedicated, he worked well with others, and so on. When I finally met him to talk about the job, he turned out to be a black man. No one had thought to tell me that he was a person of color, only that he was an outstanding worker, and so on. Needless to say, I hired R. G. on the spot.

My two other director positions were filled by D. B., a white woman with an M.B.A. degree who had worked for about two years for one of our unregulated subsidiaries, and L. B., a white woman who had spent her entire career (seventeen years) in the telephone company. She had come directly out of college and had worked herself up through the management ranks. In addition, I already had two middle-aged white women heading up my office support staff.

In my job descriptions, I made sure that candidates knew their assignments would be rotational. My goal would be to have them be on the team for about two years. The first year would be spent learning about the different businesses and gaining an understanding of what the project was all about. One of the three directors would leave every six months. That way I would always have someone with eighteen months' experience, another with twelve months' experience and a third with six months'. I then planned to add a new person so I'd always have someone with no experience but with a great wealth of new ideas. While this plan looked great on paper, I didn't foresee how important these directors would become to the client businesses.

As soon as I had brought my team together, I notified our outside consultants that within ninety days I expected to complete our contract with them. They could either assist me in training my new directors and be finished in this time period, or they could try to extend the contract and be let go. They chose to assist me in training my new team and did a very creditable job.

Most of my time the first year was spent working with these individuals. I also expanded my team by bringing in two experts in creating graphics. One was J. B., a white woman who had teenage kids and was planning to go back to school on a part-time basis. J. B. was employed by the outside firm that we had used to do most of our graphics work prior to deciding to bring the work in-house. J.B. didn't want anything to do with working for a big company and going through all the politics that entailed. But she had met the members of our team, had worked with them, and welcomed the opportunity to come and head up our graphics department. A little over a year later, we brought in R. H., a young single white man, and S. R., a young single white woman, to work on graphics.

While we now had a fairly diverse team, I still wasn't satisfied. I liked the idea that we had a spread in age levels and ethnic backgrounds, and had combined people with telephone company experience with relative newcomers. But I wanted to diversify further.

R. G., the black male director, and L. B., one of the female directors and my lone telephone company veteran, had both been working with one of our major market units. This market unit was in the process of staffing its new headquarters in Phoenix, Arizona. Our group had played a key role in establishing the critical success factors necessary to make the business a success, so we knew the business better than almost anyone else in the company.

The president of the market unit was so impressed with the work we had done that he wanted to promote R. G. While I hated to lose him, I also saw this a great career-enhancing move for him, so I told the president he could offer a job to R. G. At first, R. G. refused because of personal problems. Meanwhile, the president also gave a job offer to L. B., who accepted. Later, R. G. accepted the transfer also.

Lightening always strikes thrice. In the span of a week, I lost two directors with eleven months on the job. Then D. B. announced that her husband had just accepted a job in Florida and they would be moving. So there I was, in exactly the same position I had been in a year earlier. I had spent almost a year working with these three directors, and now I was left with no experienced workers and three openings.

So I went through the same process as before. I wasn't able to get any minority candidates to apply from our smaller subsidiaries, so I hired from our telephone company (major) subsidiary. Because I couldn't obtain the diversity across businesses that I wanted, I took a different tack.

I first hired A. F., a Hispanic man with an electrical engineering degree who had worked for the company since getting out of college. I then hired C. L., a Korean man who had come over from Korea to attend college but had never gone home; he had worked seventeen years with the telephone company. Finally, for the third director, I hired J. G., a black single woman who had an M.B.A. degree in finance and was working on an M.B.A. in telecommunications. About the same time, I was fortunate to be able to borrow C. M., a Japanese woman. To support this new staff, I brought in J.L., a temporary from Belize, as a secretary. And a few months later, I brought in C. B., a white Jewish man, as a summer intern. C. B. was working on his M.B.A. degree and spent about nine months with us.

At this point, we had a fairly diverse team:

- A. F., Hispanic man, early 40s, married, two kids, E.E. degree
- C. L., Korean man, mid-40s, married, two kids, B.S. and M.B.A. degrees
- J. G., Black woman, mid-30s, single, finance and M.B.A. degrees
- C. M., Japanese woman, mid-30s, married, one kid, B.S. degree
- J. B., White woman, late 30s, married, two kids, no degree
- D. S., White woman, late 50s, married, grown kids, no degree
- J. S., White woman, late 40s, married, two kids, no degree
- R. H., White man, mid-20s, single, B.A. degree
- S. R., White woman, late 20s, single, no degree
- J. L., Black woman, early 30s, single, no degree

We can't forget me. I am a white man, late 40s, married, three kids, B.S. and M.B.A. degrees. Until I brought R. H. onto the staff, I was affectionately called the token white male.

How was I able to attract such a diverse group to my team? I think it was because the minority communities in our company know they worked for an organization that would give them a chance to grow, learn, and position themselves for advancement. I had shown that by demonstrating my willingness to let two of my directors leave a year before their assignments were up. They also knew that if they did an outstanding job, they were going to get the necessary exposure in front of the right people, that job opportunities would come their way. Because of this reputation, I had a great group of candidates from which to select.

Unless you anticipate and work on dealing with the diversity, a team organization like this could prove to be a disaster. Here's why. We had many extreme differences in behavior and attitudes. C. L., the Korean, had many of the traits one might associate with someone who grew up in the Orient, like total respect for authority, being very polite, very quiet, overly concerned for the feelings of others. After he had lived in the States for almost ten years, his parents called him to let him know that it was time to get married and that they had picked out his prospective wife. He was to come home to Korea to be married, which he did. The only decision left up to his fiancée and himself was to pick the date. He brought his wife back to the States but has never allowed her to work outside the home. On the team, he wanted to ensure that everyone was comfortable with a decision and that everyone had had their say before a decision was reached.

At the other extreme was J. L., a black woman. She had struggled to achieve. She wasn't about to get married. She was assertive (others might say overly aggressive). She knew exactly where she was going and wasn't about to let anyone get in her way. She saw no reason to spend time in meetings or trying to gain consensus about anything. On occasion, she would be known to use four-letter words.

If you are going to have a truly diverse group, you will need to spend a great deal of time together as a group coming to grips with your diversity. One technique I used was to have my entire group individually complete a personality profile on themselves. The package I used was called "Pathways to Peak Performance," produced and marketed by Bill Maynard and the Effectiveness Institute out of Redmond, Washington.

By completing a series of twenty-four questions describing what behavior is most like yours, you can come up with a remarkably accurate profile of yourself. Maynard categorizes the four different styles as Organizer, Persuader, Controller, and Analyzer. If one has a preponderance of one of these four styles, one can have difficulty dealing with the people characterized by any of the other three. Some of the characteristics are Persuader—impulsive, impatient, boisterous, informal, fun-loving; Controller—decisive, takes charge, logical, results-oriented; Organizer—likable, asks questions, thoughtful; Analyzer—talks slowly, hesitant decision maker, gathers information. Looking at the typical characteristics of each style, one can readily see that a strong Controller might have difficulty dealing with a strong Analyzer. In fact, they could drive each other crazy.

But the message that Maynard preaches (and which I believe, as well) is that a truly effective organization must contain individuals who fall within each of the four categories. While it can strain the tolerance limits of the team, if each is made aware that others are different and recognizes that each brings an entirely different skill to the team, it can work well.

One of the key ingredients to making it work is the recognition and acceptance that each of us is different and that we don't all think and act the same. A very open communications forum is also a requirement. We would have bi-weekly staff meetings at 7 A.M. so all the team members could attend without worrying about answering phones, and so on. These sessions, lasting about an hour, were devoted to discussing individual feelings and thoughts and how each of us was reacting to the others. We all agreed that we needed to be open and honest with each other if we were going to be an effective team.

Another ingredient of our success was recognizing that our success was a team effort. While we knew we had different titles and levels, I attempted to minimize these within the group. I would always ask visitors and co-workers from outside our organization if they could tell which were the management employees and which were the support staff. More often than not, they couldn't tell. This was felt by the support staff, who realized that they had just as much say in the running of the team as anyone else.

I'm not naive enough to believe that merely by doing what I did success is guaranteed. I had the advantage of having a small and fairly independent group in a company already noted for its support of diversity. But the goals and some of the processes should be clear. And it is worthwhile to make the effort.

Notes

Preface

1. J. Naisbitt and P. Aburdene, *Megatrends 2000*, 119.

Chapter 1

1. The management levels of the speakers are identified as "lower-level," "middle-level," and "upper-level." Nonmanagement work levels are given as "occupational."
2. The demographic data here and in the following sections came from census reports, U.S. Department of Labor reports, the Commission on Civil Rights, and specific reports that will be listed in these notes.
3. Fernandez, *Racism and Sexism in Corporate Life*, 292.
4. Fernandez, 292.
5. Welds, "It's a Question of Stereotypes . . . ," 380–383.

Chapter 2

1. Weber, *The Theory of Social and Economic Organization*, 340.
2. Mannheim, *Ideology and Utopia*, 105–106.
3. K. E. Ferguson, *The Feminist Case Against Bureaucracy*, 6–8.
4. Merton, "Bureaucratic Structure and Personality," 564.
5. Merton, 562.
6. K. E. Ferguson, 10–11.
7. Levinson, *Psychological Man*, 140.
8. Selznick, "A Theory of Organizational Commitments," 194–195.
9. Levinson, 142–143.
10. Prezzolini, *Machiavelli*, 1.
11. White, *Lives in Progress*, 9.
12. Levinson, 7.
13. Keniston, "Alienation and the Decline of Utopia," 172.
14. White, 14.
15. Levinson, 37.
16. Prezzolini, 19–20.

17. Gilbert, *Machiavelli: The Chief Works and Others*, vol. 1, 272.
18. Gilbert, vol. 3, 1201.
19. Prezzolini, 19.
20. Prezzolini, 142.
21. Merton, 562.

Chapter 3

1. "An Outbreak of Bigotry," *Time*, May 28, 1990, 25.
2. Singh and Yancey, "Racial Attitudes in White, First-Grade Children."
3. Love, "Blacks Who Put a New Face Forward."
4. Lewis, *Psychic War in Men and Women*, 85.
5. Nilsen et al., *Sexism and Language*, 30–31.
6. Nilsen et al., 30–31.
7. Nilsen et al., 30–31.
8. Gibbs, "Bigots in the Ivory Tower," 104.
9. H. Ferguson, *Tomorrow's Global Executive*, 135.
10. H. Ferguson, 137.
11. H. Ferguson, 136.
12. H. Ferguson, 140.
13. *U.S. News and World Report*, March 9, 1990, 72.

Chapter 4

1. Kotkin and Kishimoto, *The Third Century*, 192.
2. Quoted in Sugimoto and Mouer *Constructs for Understanding Japan*, 218.
3. Sugimoto and Mouer, 218.
4. Silva and Sjögren, *Europe 1992 and the New World Power Game*, 159.
5. Buell, "Japan's Silent Majority Starts to Mumble," 54.
6. Morita, *Made in Japan*, 144–145.
7. Cetron et al., *The Future of American Business*, 163–165.
8. Brauchli, "Japanese Employees May Not Be Quite So Loyal After All," A-11.
9. Coates, *Human Resources Scan '88*, 3-2–3-2-14.
10. Kotkin and Kishimoto, 136–137.
11. Sugimoto and Moyer, 234–237.
12. *New York Times*, January 1, 1990, A-20.
13. "What Japan Thinks of Us," *Newsweek*, April 2, 1990, 24.
14. Kotkin and Kishimoto, 199–200.
15. Wysocki, "In Asia, the Japanese Hope to 'Coordinate What Nations Produce,' " A-1.
16. Kotkin and Kishimoto, 194.
17. Duthie, "For Many Asians, Japanese Evoke Both Bitter Memories and Admiration," A-4.

18. Kotkin and Kishimoto, 195.
19. Kotkin and Kishimoto, 195.
20. Sugimoto and Moyer, 145–146.
21. Brinton, "Gender Stratification in Contemporary Urban Japan."
22. *Newsweek*, April 2, 1990, 20.
23. *Newsweek*, April 2, 1990, 20.
24. *Business Week*, December 9, 1989, 63.
25. *Fortune*, February 26, 1990, 51.
26. *Business Week*, August 8, 1989, 51.
27. *Business Week*, August 8, 1989, 52.
28. Kirkland, "The Big Japanese Push into Europe," 98.
29. *Business Week*, September 3, 1990, 49.
30. Cetron, xxvii.

Chapter 5

1. Silva and Sjögren *Europe 1992 and the New World Power Game*, 51.
2. Silva and Sjögren, 16.
3. Kiplinger and Kiplinger, *America in the Global '90s*, 50.
4. Kotkin and Kishimoto, 81.
5. Naisbitt and Aburdene, *Megatrends 2000*, 49–50.
6. Silva and Sjögren, 16.
7. Davidson and Cooper, eds. *Working Women: An Initiative Survey*, 4–5.
8. Davidson and Cooper, 66.
9. Nelan and O'Hara Foster, *"Lashed by the Flags of Freedom."* See also Karklins, *Ethnic Relations in the USSR*.

Chapter 6

1. Kotkin and Kishimoto, *The Third Century*, 200.
2. Coates, *Human Resources Scan '88*.
3. Fierman "Why Women Still Don't Hit the Top," 40.
4. *USA Today*, "Help Women Break Through the Glass Ceiling," May 4, 1989, 10a.
5. Harris, *Cannibals and Kings: The Origins of Cultures*, 57.
6. Harris, 57.
7. Nilsen et al., *Sexism and Language*, 82–83.
8. Nilsen et al., 89.
9. Nilsen et al., 90–91.
10. Nilsen et al., 146–149.
11. Spender, *Man Made Language*, 14, 106.
12. "Grapevine," *Time*, May 28, 1990, 9.
13. Feinblatt and Gold, "Sex Roles and the Psychiatric Referral Process."
14. Hamilton and Hong, "When Medical Research Is for Men Only."

15. Benedict, *Patterns of Culture*, 230–231.
16. Lewis, *Psychic War in Men and Women*, 123–124.
17. Janeway, *Man's World, Woman's Place*, 163–167.
18. Ehrenreich and English, *Complaints and Disorders*, 16.
19. Sinclair, *The Jungle*.
20. Rothman, *Woman's Proper Place: A History of Changing Ideals and Practices: 1870 to the Present*, 22.
21. Rothman, 47–48.
22. Rothman, 42.
23. Rothman, 221–222.
24. Rothman, 224.
25. Auerbach, *In the Business of Child Care: Employee Initiatives and Working Women*, 21.
26. Auerbach, "The Privatization of Child Care," 4.
27. Galinsky, personal communication to the author.
28. Fernandez, *The Politics and Reality of Family Care in Corporate America*, 10–11.
29. Polatnik, "Why Men Don't Bear Children," 79.
30. Fernandez, *Black Managers in White Corporations*.
31. Kanter and Stein, "The Gender Pioneers," 153.
32. LaRouche and Ryan, *Strategies for Women at Work*, 74.
33. Harragan, *Games Mother Never Taught You*, 368–369.
34. LaRouche and Ryan, 75.
35. Schuller, "Male and Female Routes to Managerial Success."
36. Deaux and Emswiller, "Explanations of Successful Performance."
37. Cline et al., "Evaluations of the Work of Men and Women."
38. LaRouche and Ryan, 74.
39. LaRouche and Ryan, 140.
40. Fernandez, *The Politics and Reality of Family Care*.
41. Grimaldi and Schnapper, "Managing Stress," 24.
42. LaRouche and Ryan, 174.
43. Loden, *Feminine Leadership*, 68.
44. Loden, 61.
45. Lewis, 92–93.

Chapter 7

1. Hoxie, *Indians in American History*, 315. See also Cook, "The American Indians through Five Centuries," *Forbes*, Nov. 19, 1981, 118–131.
2. Berg, "Racism and the Puritan Mind," 1–7.
3. Steinfeld, *Cracks in the Melting Pot*, 73.
4. Makielski, *Beleaguered Minorities*, 53.
5. Reimers et al., *Natives and Strangers*, 228. Also see 1989 U.S. Census update.

6. Almquist, *Minorities, Gender, and Work*, 43.

Chapter 8

1. Kotkin and Kishimoto, *The Third Century*, 11–12.
2. Nee and Sanders, "The Road to Parity," 89–90.
3. U.S. Commission on Civil Rights, *The Economic Status of Americans of Asian Descent.*
4. Zanden, *American Minority Relations*, 207.
5. Reimers et al., *Natives and Strangers*, 194.
6. Steinfield, *Cracks in the Melting Pot*, 130.
7. William Wong, "Chinese Americans Help U.S. Employers Bridge the Language Gap in China."
8. Marden and Meyer, *Minorities in American Society*, 200.
9. Marden and Meyer, 201.
10. Steinfield, *Cracks in the Melting Pot*, 141.
11. Marden and Meyer, 202.
12. Fellows, *A Mosaic of America's Ethnic Minorities*, 137.
13. Rostow, "Our Worst Wartime Mistake," 140.
14. Fellows, 141.
15. Almquist, 122–129.
16. Almquist, 122–129.
17. Dr. Chalsa Loo's comments are from an analysis of data commissioned by the author in June 1978.

Chapter 9

1. Fernandez and Bassman, *Looking Beyond Tomorrow*, 3–4.
2. Schwartz and Disch, *White Racism*, 6.
3. Jordan, *White over Black.*
4. Stampp, *The Peculiar Institution*, 11.
5. Quoted in Schuman, Steeh, and Bobo, *Racial Attitudes in America*, 2.
6. Quoted in Steinfield, *Cracks in the Melting Pot*, 199.
7. A.L. Higginbotham, *In the Marker of Color*, 7.
8. Wilson, *The Declining Significance of Race*, 61.
9. McLemore, *Racial and Ethnic Relations in America*, 289.
10. McLemore, 291.
11. Quoted in Clark, *Prejudice and Your Child*, 159.
12. Thomas and Sillen, *Racism and Psychiatry*, xii.
13. Kovel, *White Racism*, 13–14.
14. Fernandez, *Survival in the Corporate Fish Bowl*, 153.
15. Lambert and Taylor, *Coping with Cultural and Racial Diversity*, 139–140.
16. Lacayo, "Between Two Worlds," 58.

Chapter 10

1. Coates, *Human Resources Scan '88*, 1–3, 15.
2. Zanden, *American Minority Relations*, 201.
3. Steinfield, *Cracks in the Melting Pot*, 80.
4. McLemore, *Ethnic and Racial Relations in America*, 219.
5. Almquist, *Minorities, Gender, and Work*, 73–74.
6. Zanden, *American Minority Relations*, 205–206.
7. Steiner, *La Roza*, 233–234.
8. Meier and Riviera, *The Chicanos*, 190.
9. Zanden, 196.
10. Almquist, 196.
11. Rodriguez, *Puerto Ricans: Born in the U.S.A.*, 82.
12. Lambert and Taylor, *Coping with Cultural and Racial Diversity in Urban America*, 93.
13. Fernandez, *Racism and Sexism in Corporate Life*.
14. Gann and Duignan, The *Hispanics in the United States*, 102.
15. Almquist, 90.
16. Boswell and Curtes, *The Cuban-American Experience*, 68.
17. Lambert and Taylor, 88.

Chapter 11

1. Bowman, "What Helps or Harms Promotability?"
2. Kochman, *Black and White Styles in Conflict*, 18–21, 38.
3. Kochman, 19–20.
4. Valentine, *Black Studies and Anthropology*, 33.

Chapter 12

1. Terry, "The Negative Impact on White Values," 143.
2. Jones, "The Concept of Racism and Its Changing Reality," 43.
3. Jones, 43.
4. Bowser and Hunt, eds., *Impacts of Racism on White Americans*, 7.

Chapter 13

1. The demographic data are taken from census reports, U.S. Department of Labor reports, and the U.S. Commission on Civil Rights.
2. *Business Week*, September 25, 1989, 175.
3. Coates, *Human Resources Scan '88* (section 1-2), 1.
4. Bowman, Ph.D. diss., 1962.
5. Noll, *Religion and American Politics*, 382–386.

6. Noll, 382–386.
7. Rowse, *Homosexuals in History*, various pages.
8. Licata and Petersen. "Historical Perspectives on Homosexuality," 162.
9. Hays, "Anti-Gay Attacks Increase and Some Fight Back."
10. Gross, "Navy Is Urged to Root Out Lesbians Despite Abilities."
11. Yuker, *Attitudes Toward Persons with Disabilities*, 216–218.
12. Yuker, 216–218.
13. Yuker, 216–218.
14. Yuker, 216–218.

Chapter 14

1. Caplow, *Managing an Organization*, 81.
2. Schoonmaker, *Executive Career Strategy*, 31.
3. Schoonmaker, 147.
4. Townsend, *Up the Organization*, 210.
5. Kanter, *The Change Masters*, 63.
6. Prezzolini, *Machiavelli*, 108.
7. London and Stumpf, *Managing Careers*, 43–44.
8. London and Stumpf, 31–32, 63–64.
9. Schoonmaker, 46.

Chapter 15

1. Information furnished to the author by the local office of the National Association for the Advancement of Colored People. Also see G. B. Jordan, "Poll Says Americans Favor Racial Equality," *Philadelphia Inquirer*, January 12, 1989; J. Johnson, "Blacks and White Are Found Worlds Apart," *New York Times*, January 12, 1989.

Chapter 16

1. Sale, *Human Scale*, 403.
2. Becker, "Opening the Golden Door Wider—To Newcomers with Knowledge," *Business Week*, June 11, 1990, 12.

Bibliography

A Profile of Older Americans, American Association of Retired Persons, 1989.

Adolph, B., and K. Rose. *Employer's Guide to Child Care: Developing Programs for Working Parents*. New York: Praeger, 1985.

Adult Care in America: Summary of a National Survey. National Council on Aging, 1987.

Aganbegyan, A. *Inside Perestroika*. New York: Harper and Row, 1989.

Ainsworth, L. H. "Rigidity, Insecurity and Stress." *Journal of Abnormal and Social Psychology* 56 (1958): 67–74.

Alderfer, C. P. "Job Enlargement and the Organizational Context." *Personnel Psychology* 22 (1969): 418–426.

Allison, M.A., and E. Allison. *Managing Up, Managing Down*. New York: Simon and Schuster, 1984.

Almquist, E. *Minorities, Gender, and Work*. Lexington, Mass.: Lexington Books, 1979.

America, R. F., and B. E. Anderson. *Moving Ahead: Black Managers in American Business*. New York: McGraw-Hill, 1978.

Anderson, B. A., and B. D. Silver. "Estimating Russification of Ethnic Identity among Non-Russians in the USSR." *Demography* 20 (1983): 461–489.

Aquarius, C. "Corporate Tactics: Games People Play." *MBA* (October 1971): 51–52.

Aravanis, S. C., R. Levin, and T. T. Nixon, eds. *Private/Public Partnership in Aging: A Compendium*. Washington, D.C.: National Association of State Units on Aging and Washington Business Group on Health, 1987.

Aronson, E. "The Psychology of Insufficient Justification: An Analysis of Some Conflicting Data." In *Cognitive Consistency*, ed. S. Feldman. New York: Academic Press, 1966.

Astin, H. S., and A. E. Bayer. "Discrimination in Academe." *Educational Record* 53 (Spring 1972): 101–118.

Athanassiades, J. C. "An Investigation of Some Communication Patterns of Female Subordinates in Hierarchical Organization." *Human Relations* 27 (1974): 195–209.

Auerbach, J. *In the Business of Child Care: Employee Initiatives and Working Women*. New York: Praeger, 1988.

———. "The Privatization of Child Care: The Limits of Employer Support." Paper, American Sociological Association Conference, August 28, 1988.

Baron, H. M. "The Web of Urban Racism." In *Institutional Racism in America*, ed. L. L. Knowles and K. Prewitts. Englewood Cliffs, N.J.: Prentice-Hall, 1969.

Bar-Tal, D., and L. Saxe. "Physical Attractiveness and Its Relationship to Sex-Role Stereotyping." *Sex Roles* 2, no. 2 (1976): 123–133.

Bartol, K. M. "The Effect of Male versus Female Leaders on Follower Satisfaction and Performance." *Journal of Business Research* 3 (1975): 33–42.

———. "Male versus Female Leaders: The Effect of Leader Need for Dominance on Follower Satisfaction." *Academy of Management Journal* 17 (1974): 225–233.

Beach, B. *Integrating Work and Family Life: The Home-Working Family.* Albany: State University of New York Press, 1989.

Bellah, R. N., ed. *Habits of the Heart: Individualism and Commitment in American Life.* New York: Harper and Row, 1986.

Bendix, R. *Work and Authority.* New York: Wiley, 1956.

Benedict, R. *Patterns of Culture.* Boston: Houghton Mifflin, 1934.

Berg, P. L. "Racism and the Puritan Mind." *Phylon* 36 (March 1975): 1–7.

Berk, S. F. *The Gender Factory: The Appointments of Work in American Households.* New York: Plenum, 1985.

Blauner, R. *Alienation and Freedom.* Chicago: University of Chicago Press, 1964.

———. *Racial Oppression in America.* New York: Harper and Row, 1972.

Bloom, A. *The Closing of the American Mind.* New York: Simon and Schuster, 1987.

Bloom, D. E., and T. P. Steen. "Why Child Care Is Good For Business." *American Demographics* (August 1988).

Bloom, L. *The Social Psychology of Race Relations.* Rochester, Vt.: Schenkman Books, 1972.

Blotnick, S. *The Corporate Steeplechase: Predictable Crisis in a Business Career.* New York: Facts on File, 1984.

Bok, S. *Lying.* New York: Vintage Books, 1978.

Boswell, T. D., and J. R. Curtes. *The Cuban-American Experience.* Totowa, N.J.: Rowman and Allanheld, 1984.

Bowman, G. W. "The Image of a Promotable Person in Business Enterprise." Ph.D. diss., New York University, 1962.

———. "What Helps or Harms Promotability?" *Harvard Business Review* 42 (1964): 6–26, 184–196.

Bowser, B. P., and R. G. Hunt., eds. *Impacts of Racism on White Americans.* Newbury Park, Calif.: Sage Publications, 1981.

Brauchli, M. W. "Japanese Employees May Not Be Quite So Loyal After All," *Wall Street Journal*, August 7, 1990, A–11.

Brinton, M. C. "Gender Stratification in Contemporary Urban Japan." *American Sociological Review* 54: 549–559.

Brothers, J. *The Successful Woman: How You Can Have a Career, a Husband and a Family—and Not Feel Guilty About It.* New York: Simon and

Schuster, 1988.

Brown, L. R. *State of the World.* New York: W. W. Norton, 1988.

Brown, P., and S. Levinson. "Universals In Language Use: Politeness Phenomena." In *Questions and Politeness,* ed. E. N. Goody. Cambridge: Cambridge University Press, 1978.

Buell, B. "Japan's Silent Majority Starts to Mumble." *Business Week,* April 23, 1990, 54.

Burden, D. S., and B. K. Googins. *Balancing Job and Homelife Study.* Boston: Boston University School of Social Work.

Burger, C. *Survival in the Executive Jungle.* New York: Macmillan, 1964.

Butterfield, F. *China.* New York: Bantam Books, 1983.

Caditz, J. *White Liberals in Transition.* New York: Spectrum, 1976.

Campbell, A. *White Attitudes Towards Black People.* Ann Arbor: University of Michigan Institute for Social Research, 1971.

Caplan, R. D., and J.R.P. French, Jr. "Organizational Stress and Industrial Strain." In *The Failure of Success,* ed. A. Marrow. New York: American Management Association, 1972.

Caplow, T. *Managing an Organization.* New York: Holt, Rinehart and Winston, 1983.

Cappo, J. *Future Scope.* Chicago: Longman Financial Services Publishing, 1990.

Cetron, M., A. Pagano, and O. Porto. *The Future of American Business: The U.S. in World Competition.* New York: McGraw-Hill, 1985.

Cetron, M., and O. Davies. *American Renaissance.* New York: St. Martin's Press, 1989.

Cheeseboro, J. W., ed. *Gayspeak: Gay Male & Lesbian Communications.* New York: Pilgrim Press, 1981.

Child Care Challenge: Report on Employer-Sponsored Child Care Services. Washington, D.C.: Congressional Caucus for Women's Issues, 1988.

Clark, K. E. *Prejudice and Your Child.* Boston: Beacon Press, 1963.

Coates, J. F. *Human Resources Scan '88.* Washington, D.C.: J. F. Coates, Inc., 1988.

Cornish, E., ed. *The 1990's and Beyond.* Bethesda, Md.: World Future Society, 1990.

Cussler, M. *The Woman Executive.* New York: Harcourt, Brace, 1958.

Dalton, M. "Conflicts Between Staff and Line Managerial Officers." *American Sociological Review* 21 (1950): 342–351.

———. "Informal Factors in Career Achievement." *American Journal of Sociology* 56 (1951): 407–415.

———. *Men Who Manage.* New York: Wiley, 1959.

Davidson, J. M., and C. Cooper, eds. *Working Women: An Initiative Survey.* New York: Wiley, 1984.

Davis, K. *Human Relations at Work.* New York: McGraw-Hill, 1967.

Deal, T. E., and A. A. Kennedy. *Corporate Cultures: The Rites and Rituals of Corporate Life*. Reading, Mass.: Addison-Wesley, 1982.

Deaux, K., and T. Emswiller. "Explanations of Successful Performance and Sex-Linked Tasks: What Is Skill of the Male Is Luck for the Female." *Journal of Personality and Social Psychology* 29, no. 1 (1974): 80–85.

De Bono, E. *Tactics: The Art and Science of Success*. Boston: Little, Brown, 1984.

Deloria, V., Jr. *Custer Died for Your Sins*. New York: Avon Books, 1970.

Dimock, M. E. *The Executive in Action*. New York: Harper and Row, 1984.

———. "Expanding Jurisdictions: A Case Study in Bureaucratic Conflict." In *Reader in Bureaucracy*, ed. R. K. Merton, A. P. Gray, B. Hockey, H. Selvin. New York: Free Press, 1952.

Dore, R. *British Factory—Japanese Factory: The Origins of National Diversity in Industrial Relations*. Berkeley: University of California Press, 1973.

Downs, A. *Inside Bureaucracy*. Boston: Little, Brown, 1967.

Drucker, P. *The New Realities*. New York: Harper and Row, 1989.

Duthie, S. "For Many Asians, Japanese Evoke Both Bitter Memories and Admiration." *Wall Street Journal*, August 20, 1990, A–4.

Dynes, M., and R. Owen. *The Times Guide to 1992*. London: Times Books, 1989.

Ehrenreich, B., and D. English. *Complaints and Disorders*. New York: Faculty Press, 1973.

———. *Employers and Eldercare: A New Benefit Coming of Age*. National Report on Work and Family. Washington, D.C.: Bureau of National Affairs, 1988.

Emmott, B. *The Sun Also Sets*. New York: Random House, 1989.

Epstein, C. *Woman's Place*. Berkeley: University of California Press, 1970.

Erikson, E. *Childhood and Society*. New York: W. W. Norton, 1963.

Fair, M. H. *Tools for Survival: A Positive Action Plan for Minorities and Women*. Denver: Harris Discovery Learning Academy, 1982.

Fallows, J. *More Like Us*. Boston: Houghton Mifflin, 1989.

Feinblatt, J. A., and A. R. Gold. "Sex Roles and the Psychiatric Referral Process." *Sex Roles* 2, no. 2 (1976): 109–122.

Fellows, D. K. *A Mosaic of America's Ethnic Minorities*. New York: Wiley, 1972.

Fierman, J. "Why Women Still Don't Hit the Top." *Fortune*, July 30, 1990.

Ferguson, H. *Tomorrow's Global Executive*. Homewood, Ill.: Dow Jones–Irwin, 1988.

Ferguson, K. E. *The Feminist Case Against Bureaucracy*. Philadelphia: Temple University Press, 1984.

Fernandez, J. P. *Black Managers in White Corporations*. New York: Wiley, 1975.

————. *Child Care and Corporate Productivity: Resolving Family and Work Conflicts*. Lexington, Mass.: Lexington Books, 1986.

————. *Human Resources Forecasting and Strategy Development*. Westport, Conn.: Quorum Books, 1990.

————. *The Politics and Reality of Family Care in Corporate America*. Lexington, Mass.: Lexington Books, 1990.

————. *Racism and Sexism in Corporate Life: Changing Values in American Business*. Lexington, Mass.: Lexington Books, 1981.

————. *Survival in the Corporate Fish Bowl: Making It into Middle and Upper Management*. Lexington, Mass.: Lexington Books, 1987.

Fernandez, J., and E. Bassman. *Looking Beyond Tomorrow: Strategic Issues*. Basking Ridge, N.J.: AT&T, 1988.

Fong, S.L.M., and H. Peskin. "Sex Role Strain and Personality Adjustment of China-Born Students in America." *Journal of Abnormal Psychology* 74 (1969): 563–567.

Fraker, S. "Why Women Aren't Getting to the Top." *Fortune*, April 14, 1984.

Frantz, D., and C. Collins. *Selling Out: How We Are Letting Japan Buy . . . Our Future*. Chicago: Contemporary Books, 1989.

Fromm, E. *The Sane Society*. New York: Holt, Rinehart and Winston, 1955.

Fujitomi, I., and D. Wong. "The New Asian-American Woman." In *Asian Americans: Psychological Perspective*, ed. S. Sue and N. Wagner. Palo Alto, Calif.: Science and Behavior Books, 1973.

Galinsky, E. "Child Care and Productivity." Paper, Child Care Action Campaign Conference, New York, April 1988.

————. "Family Life and Corporate Policies." In *In Support of Families*, ed. M. Yogman and T. B. Brazelton. Cambridge: Harvard University Press, 1986.

Gann, L. H., and P. J. Duignan. *The Hispanics in the United States: A History*. Boulder, Colo.: Westview Press, 1986.

Gemmill, G., and D. DeSalvia. "The Promotion Beliefs of Managers as a Factor in Career Progress: An Exploratory Study." *Sloan Management Review* 18, no. 2 (1977): 75–81.

Gibbs, N. "Bigots in the Ivory Tower." *Time*, May 7, 1990.

Gilbert, A. *Machiavelli: The Chief Works and Others*. Durham, N.C.: Duke University Press, 1965.

Goffman, E. *Encounters*. New York: Bobbs-Merrill, 1961.

Goodman, M. E. *Race Awareness in Young Children*. New York: Collier Books, 1964.

Gorbachev, M. *Perestroika*. New York: Harper and Row, 1987.

Grier, W. H., and P. M. Cobbs. *Black Rage*. New York: Basic Books, 1968.

Grimaldi, J., and B. P. Schnapper. "Managing Stress: Reducing the Costs and Increasing the Benefits." *Management Review* (August 1984): 24.

Gross, J. "Navy Is Urged to Root Out Lesbians Despite Abilities." *New York Times*, September 2, 1990, 24.

Halberstam, D. *The Reckoning.* New York: William Morrow, 1986.

Hall, E. T. *Beyond Culture.* New York: Doubleday, 1977.

———. *The Hidden Dimension.* New York: Doubleday, 1966.

———. *The Silent Language.* New York: Doubleday, 1973.

Hamilton, J.O.C., and P. Hong. "When Medical Research Is for Men Only." *Business Week,* July 16, 1990, 33.

Hanamura, S. "Working With People Who Are Different." *Training and Development Journal* (June 1989): 110–114.

Harragan, B. L. *Games Mother Never Taught You: Corporate Gamesmanship for Women.* New York: Warner Books, 1977.

Harris, M. *Cannibals and Kings: The Origins of Cultures.* New York: Random House, 1977.

Harrison, J. "Warning: The Male Sex Role May Be Dangerous to Your Health." *Journal of Social Issues* 34, no. 1 (1978): 68–69.

Hata, H., and W. Smith. "Nakane's Japanese Society as Utopian Thought." *Journal of Contemporary Asia* 13 (1983): 361–388.

Hays, C. L. "Anti-Gay Attacks Increase and Some Fight Back." *New York Times,* September 3, 1990, 23.

Higginbotham, A. L. *In the Marker of Color.* New York: Oxford University Press, 1978.

Hill-Scott, K. "No Room at the Inn: The Crisis in Child Care Supply." In *Caring for Children: Challenge to America,* ed. J. S. Lande et al. Hillsdale, N.J.: Lawrence Erlbaum Associates, 1989.

Hoxie, F. E. *Indians in American History.* Arlington Heights, Ill.: Harlan Davidson, 1988.

Hughes, D., and E. Galinsky. "Balancing Work and Family Life: Research and Corporate Application." In *Maternal Employment and Children's Development: Longitudinal Research,* ed. A. E. Gottfried and A. W. Gottfried. New York: Plenum, 1988.

Hymenitz, C. "Women on Fast Track Try to Keep Their Careers and Children Separate." *Wall Street Journal,* Sept. 19, 1984, 35.

Iacocca, L., and W. Novak. *Iacocca: An Autobiography.* New York: Bantam Books, 1984.

Iuppa, N. V. *Management by Guilt: And Other Uncensored Tactics.* Belmont, Calif.: Pitman, 1985.

Janeway, E. *Man's World, Woman's Place.* New York: Dell, 1971.

Jansen, R. B. *ABC's of Bureaucracy.* Chicago: Nelson-Hall, 1975.

Jobu, R. M. "Earnings Differences of White and Ethnic Minorities: The Case of Asians, Americans, the Blacks and Chicanos." *Sociology and Social Research* 66 (October 1976): 24–38.

Johnson, P. *Modern Times.* New York: Harper and Row, 1983.

Johnston, W. B., and A. H. Packer. *Workforce 2000: Work and Workers for the 21st Century.* Indianapolis: Hudson Institute, 1987.

Jones, R. L. "The Concept of Racism and Its Changing Reality." In *Impacts of Racism on White Americans*, ed. B. P. Bowser and R. G. Hunt. Newbury Park, Calif.: Sage Publications, 1981.

Jordan, W. D. *White over Black: American Attitudes toward the Negro, 1550–1812*. Baltimore: Penguin, 1969.

Jump, T. L., and L. Hass. "Fathers in Transition: Dual Career Fathers Participating in Child Care." In *Changing Men: New Directions in Research on Men and Masculinity*. Newbury Park, Calif.: Sage Publications, 1987.

Kanter, R. M. *The Change Masters*. New York: Simon and Schuster, 1983.

———. *Men and Women of the Corporation*. New York: Basic Books, 1977.

Karklins, R. *Ethnic Relations in the USSR*. Boston: Unwin Hyman, 1986.

Katz, J. H. *White Awareness: A Handbook for Anti-Racism Training*. Norman: Oklahoma University Press, 1978.

Kennedy, P. *The Rise and Fall of the Great Powers*. New York: Random House, 1987.

Kiplinger, A. H., and K. A. Kiplinger. *America in the Global '90s*. Washington, D.C.: Kiplinger Books, 1989.

Kirkland, T. "The Big Japanese Push into Europe." *Fortune*, July 2, 1990.

Kochman, T. *Black and White Styles in Conflict*. Chicago: University of Chicago Press, 1981.

Kotkin, J., and Y. Kishimoto. *The Third Century: America's Resurgence in the Asian Era*. New York: Crown Publishing, 1988.

Kotter, J. P. *Power in Management*. New York: Amacom, 1979.

Kovel, J. *White Racism: A Psychohistory*. New York: Vintage Books, 1970.

Kras, E. A. *Management in Two Cultures*. Mexico City: Intercultural Press, 1988.

Lacayo, R. "Between Two Worlds." *Time*, March 13, 1989, 58–60.

Lambert, W. E., and D. M. Taylor. *Coping with Cultural and Racial Diversity in Urban America*. New York: Praeger, 1990.

LaRouche, J., and R. Ryan. *Janice LaRouche's Strategies for Women at Work*. New York: Avon, 1984.

Levin, D. *Irreconcilable Differences*. Boston: Little, Brown, 1989.

Levinson, H. *Psychological Man*. Cambridge, Mass.: Levinson Institute, 1976.

Lewis, H. B. *Psychic War in Men and Women*. New York: New York University Press, 1976.

Licata, L. J., and R. P. Petersen, eds. "Historical Perspectives on Homosexuality." *Journal of Homosexuality* 6 (Fall/Winter 1980/81): 154–169.

Loden, M. *Feminine Leadership: Or How To Succeed in Business Without Being One of the Boys*. New York: Times Books, 1985.

London, M., and S. A. Stumpf. *Managing Careers*. Reading, Mass.: Addison-Wesley, 1982.

Love, A. "Blacks Who Put a New Face Foward." *Philadelphia Inquirer*, June 15, 1986, D-1.

Lynch, F. R. *Invisible Victims: White Males and the Crisis of Affirmative Action.* New York: Greenwood Press, 1989.

Magnuson, E. "A Melding of Cultures." *Time,* July 8, 1985.

Makielski, S. J., Jr. Beleaguered Minorities: Cultural Politics in America. San Francisco: Freeman, 1973.

Malabre, A., Jr. *Beyond Our Means.* New York: Random House, 1987.

Mannheim, K. *Ideology and Utopia.* New York: Harcourt, Brace, 1936.

Marden, C. F., and G. Meyer. *Minorities in American Society.* New York: Van Nostrand, 1973.

Maslow, A. H. *Motivation and Personality.* New York: Harper and Row, 1954.

McClelland, D. C. *The Achieving Society.* New York: Free Press, 1961.

McCormack, M. H. *What They Don't Teach You at Harvard Business School.* New York: Bantam Books, 1984.

McKenna, R. Who's Afraid of Big Blue? Reading, Mass.: Addison-Wesley, 1989.

McKinsey. *Japanese Business.* New York: Wiley, 1983.

McLemore, S. D. *Ethnic and Racial Relations in America.* Boston: Allyn and Bacon, 1983.

Meier, M. S., and P. Riviera. *The Chicanos: A History of Mexican Americans.* New York: Hill and Wang, 1972.

Merton, R. K. "Bureaucratic Structure and Personality." *Social Forces* 17 (1940): 560–568.

Miller, J. "Who Is Responsible for Employee Career Planning?" *Personnel,* March/April 1978, 1–19.

Mills, C. W. *The Sociological Imagination.* New York: Oxford University Press, 1959.

———. *White Collar.* New York: Oxford University Press, 1951.

Mills, D. Q. *The New Competitors.* New York: Wiley, 1985.

Mills, G. W., and H. Gerth. *From Max Weber; Essays in Sociology.* New York: Oxford University Press, 1946.

Miner, J. B. "Twenty Years of Research on Role-Motivation Theory of Managerial Effectiveness." *Personnel Psychology* 31 (1978): 739–759.

Mitsubishi Corporation. *Tatemae and Honne.* New York: Free Press, 1988.

Morita, A. *Made in Japan.* New York: Penguin, 1988.

Murphy, L. R. "Workplace Intervention for Stress Reduction and Prevention." In *Causes, Coping and Consequences of Stress at Work,* ed. G. L. Cooper and R. Payne. New York: Wiley, 1988.

Myrdal, G. *An American Dilemma: The Negro Problem and Modern Democracy.* New York: Random House, 1962.

Naisbitt, J., and P. Aburdene. *Megatrends 2000.* New York: William Morrow, 1990.

———. *Re-inventing the Corporation.* New York: Warner Books, 1985.

Nelan, B. W. "Lashed by the Flags of Freedom," *Time*, March 12, 1990, 26–52.

Nilsen, A. P., *Sexism and Language*. Urbana, Ill.: National Council of Teachers of English, 1972.

Noll, M. A., ed. *Religion and American Politics: From the Colonial Period to the 1980s*. New York: Oxford University Press, 1990.

Ohmae, K. *Beyond National Borders*. Homewood, Ill. Dow Jones-Irwin, 1987.

Ostroff, J. *Successful Marketing to the 50+ Consumer: How to Capture One of the Biggest and Fastest-Growing Markets in America*. Englewood Cliffs, N.J.: Prentice-Hall, 1989.

Packard, V. *The Pyramid Climbers*. New York: McGraw-Hill, 1962.

Patz, A. L. "Performance Appraisal: Useful But Still Resisted." *Harvard Business Review* 53 (1975): 74–80.

Pauli, G. A., and R. W. Wright. *The Second Wave*. New York: St. Martin's Press, 1987.

Pedigo, P., and H. Meyer. "Management Promotion Decisions: The Influence of Affirmative Action." Paper, Academy of Management Annual Meeting, Atlanta, 1979.

Pettigrew, T. F. "The Mental Health Impact." In *Impacts of Racism on White Americans*, ed. B. P. Bowser and R. G. Hunt. Newbury Park, Calif.: Sage Publications, 1981.

Phillips, J. D. "Employee Turnover and the Bottom Line." Working Paper, Merck and Co., Rahway, N.J., 1989.

Porter, M. E. *The Competitive Advantage of Nations*. New York: Free Press, 1990.

Prezzolini, G. *Machiavelli*. New York: Farrar, Straus, and Giroux, 1967.

Rakowska-Harmstone, T. "The Study of Ethnic Politics in the USSR." In *Nationalism in the USSR and Eastern Europe in the Era of Brezhnev and Kosygin*, ed. G. W. Simmonds. Detroit: University of Detroit Press, 1977.

Ransom, C., and S. Burud. "Productivity Impact Study Conducted for Union Bank Child Care Center." Unpublished report, 1988.

Reich, C. *The Greening of America*. New York: Random House, 1990.

Ritzer, G. *Working: Conflict and Change*. Englewood Cliffs, N.J.: Prentice-Hall, 1977.

Rodriguez, C. E. *Puerto Ricans: Born in the U.S.A*. Boston: Unwin Hyman, 1989.

Roscow, J. *The Global Market Place*. New York: Facts On File, 1988.

Rothman, S. M. *Woman's Proper Place: A History of Changing Ideas and Practices: 1870 to the Present*. New York: Basic Books, 1978.

Rowse, A. L. *Homosexuals in History: A Study of Ambivalence in Society, Literature, and the Arts*. New York: Macmillan, 1986.

Ryan, M. P. *Womanhood in America: From Colonial Times to the Present*. New York: New Viewpoints, 1975.

Ryan, W. *Blaming the Victim*. New York: Random House, 1971.

Rywkin, M. "Central Asia and Soviet Manpower." *Problems of Communism* 28 (January-February 1979): 1–13.

Sale, K. *Human Scale*. New York: Coward-McCann-Geoghegan, 1980.

Schein, V. E. "The Relationship Between Sex Role Stereotypes and Requisite Management Characteristics." *Journal of Applied Psychology* 57 (1973): 95–100.

Schlesinger, A. M., Jr. *The Cycles of American History*. Boston: Houghton Mifflin, 1986.

Schoenberg, R. J. *The Art of Being a Boss*. New York: Lippincott, 1978.

Schoonmaker, A. N. *Executive Career Strategy*. New York: American Management Association, 1971.

Schuller, R. "Male and Female Routes to Managerial Success." *Personnel Administrator* (February 1979): 35–38.

Schuman, H., C. Steeh, and L. Bobo. *Racial Attitudes in America: Trends and Interpretations*. Cambridge: Harvard University Press, 1985.

Schwartz, B. N., and R. Disch. *White Racism*. New York: Dell, 1970.

Schwartz, K. L. *Parental and Maternity Leave Policies in Canada and Sweden*. Kingston, Ontario: Queen's University Industrial Relations Centre, 1988.

Seidenberg, R. *Corporate Wives—Corporate Casualties?* New York: Amacon, 1973.

Selby, P., M. et. al. *Aging 2000: A Challenge for Society*. Boston: M.T.P. Press, 1982.

Selznick, P. "A Theory of Organizational Commitments." In *Reader in Bureaucracy*, ed. R. K. Merton, A. P. Gray, B. Hockey, H. Selvin. New York: Free Press, 1952.

Silberman, C. E. *Crisis in Black and White*. New York: Random House, 1964.

Silva, M. and B. Sjögren. *Europe 1992 and the New World Power Game*. New York: Wiley, 1990.

Simons, G. *Working Together: How to Become More Effective in a Multicultural Organization*. Los Altos, Calif.: Crisp Publications, 1989.

Simpson, G. E., and J. M. Yinger. *Racial and Cultural Minorities: An Analysis of Prejudice and Discrimination*. New York: Harper and Row, 1965.

Sinclair, U. *The Jungle*. New York: New American Library, 1906.

Singh, J., and A. Yancey. "Racial Attitudes in White, First-Grade Children." *Journal of Educational Research* 67 (1974): 370–372.

Smuts, R. W. *Women and Work in America*. New York: Columbia University Press, 1951.

Sniderman, P. M., and M. G. Hagen. *Race and Inequality: A Study in American Values*. Chatham, N.J.: Chatham House, 1985.

Spender, D. *Man Made Language*. London: Routledge and Kegan Paul, 1980.

Stampp, K. M. *The Peculiar Institution: Slavery in the Ante Bellum South*. New York: Vintage Books, 1956.

Steiner, S. *La Roza: The Mexican Americans*. New York: Harper and Row, 1968.

Steinfield, M. *Cracks in the Melting Pot: Racism and Discrimination in American History.* Mission Hills, Calif.: Glencoe, 1970.

Stone, R. I., and P. Kemper. *Spouses and Children of Disabled Elders: Potential and Active Caregivers.* U.S. Department of Health and Human Services. Washington, D.C.: Government Printing Office, 1989.

Sturdivant, F. D., and R. D. Adler. "Executive Origins: Still a Gray Flannel World?" *Harvard Business Review* 54 (1976): 125–132.

Sugimoto, F., and R. E. Moyer. *Constructs for Understanding Japan.* New York: Kegan Paul International, 1989.

Terry, R. W. "The Negative Impact on White Values." In *Impacts of Racism on White Americans,* ed. B. P. Bowser and R. G. Hunt. Newbury Park, Calif.: Sage Publications, 1981.

Thomas, A., and S. Sillen. *Racism and Psychiatry.* New York: Brunner Mazel, 1972.

Tiffin, J., and E. J. McCormick. *Industrial Psychology.* Englewood Cliffs, N.J.: Prentice-Hall, 1965.

Townsend, R. *Up the Organization.* New York: Fawcett Crest Books, 1970.

Unger, R. M. *Knowledge and Politics.* New York: Free Press, 1975.

U.S. Commission on Civil Rights. *The Economic Status of Americans of Asian Descent.* Washington, D.C.: Goverment Printing Office, 1988.

U.S. Department of Health and Human Services. *Aging America: Trend Projections.* Washington, D.C.: Government Printing Office, 1987–1988.

U.S. Department of Labor. *Child Care: A Work Force Issue.* Report of the Secretary's Task Force on Child Care. Washington, D.C.: Government Printing Office, 1988.

———. *Labor Force Statistics Derived from Current Population Survey: 1948–1980.* Bulletin No. 2307. Bureau of Statistics. Washington, D.C.: Government Printing Office.

Valentine, C. A. *Black Studies and Anthropology: Scholarly and Political Interests in Afro-American Culture.* Reading, Mass.: Addison-Wesley, 1972.

Whellis, A. *The Quest for Identity.* New York: W.W. Norton, 1958.

White, R. W. *Lives in Progress.* New York: Holt, Rinehart and Winston, 1952.

Wilkinson, D. Y., and R. L. Taylor. *The Black Male in America: Perspectives on His Status in Contemporary Society.* Chicago: Nelson-Hall, 1977.

Willie, C. V., B. Kramer, and B. Brown, eds. *Racism and Mental Health.* Pittsburgh: University of Pittsburgh Press, 1973.

Wilson, W. J. *The Declining Significance of Race, Blacks, and Changing American Institutions.* Chicago: University of Chicago Press, 1978.

Wong, W. "Chinese Americans Help U.S. Employers Bridge the Language Gap in China." *Wall Street Journal,* July 3, 1979, 30.

World Almanac 1990. New York: Pharos Books, 1990.

Wright, J. P. *On A Clear Day You Can See General Motors.* Grosse Pointe, Mich.: Wright Enterprises, 1979.

Wurman, R. S. *Information Anxiety.* New York: Doubleday, 1989.

Wysocki, B., Jr. "In Asia, the Japanese Hope to 'Coordinate What Nations Produce.' " *Wall Street Journal,* August 20, 1990, A-1, A-4.

Yankelovich, D. "Work, Values, and the New Breed." In *Work in America: The Decade Ahead,* ed. C. Kerr and J. M. Roscow. New York: Van Nostrand, 1979.

Young, D. R. America in Perspective: *Major Trends in the U.S. Through the 1990's.* Boston: Houghton Mifflin, 1986.

Yuker, H. E. *Attitudes Toward Persons with Disabilities.* New York: Springer Publishing, 1987.

Zanden, J.W.V. *American Minority Relations: The Sociology of Race and Ethnic Groups.* New York: Press Company, 1963.

Index

behavior, 37–41; discriminatory evaluation of capabilities, authority and performance of women, 108–112; institutional, 36–37; in Japan, 63–65; language conflicts and, 41, 43–47; origins and development of, 88–91; status of women in European Community, 83–85; strategies to counter sexist evaluation, 112–114
Sexual harassment, 106–107, 108
Sexual preference, discrimination and, 230–234
Shelley, Richard, 41
Sillen, S., 151
Silva, M., 54, 71, 72, 77
Sinclair, Upton, 92
Sony, 67
Sowell, Thomas, 160
Spain, feelings toward immigrants in, 81–82
Steinfield, M., 165
Stuart, Charles, 153
Study on How to Take Proper Rest and Recuperation, A, 57
Stumpf, S. A., 251, 252
Successful, how to be: active role in managing your career, 248–253; importance of your attitude toward work, 246–248; knowing that corporate opportunities are limited, 240; knowing yourself, 240–243; understanding people, 243–246
Sugimoto, F., 53, 63
Sumitomo Corporation of America, 64
Survival in the Corporate Fishbowl, 214
Sweden, feelings toward immigrants in, 82

Taney, B., 148–149
Taylor, D. M., 154, 169, 172
Terry, R. W., 209
Texas Instruments, 68
Thatcher, Margaret, 79
Theory Z (Ouchi), 56
Third Century, The, (Kotkin and Kishimoto), 52
Thomas, A., 151
Time, 35–36
Townsend, R., 248
Toyota Motor, 59
Travelers Insurance Co., 222

Treaty of Guadalupe Hidalgo, 164–165
Tydings McDuffie Act, 139

United States and competitive advantage: dealing with bureaucratic problems, 275–279; factors that affect the, 270–271; importance of understanding neuroses, 279–280; role of corporations, 280–282; role of government, 282–284; what the U.S. should do, 274–275
Uno, Masami, 59

Valentine, C. A., 189
Vocational Rehabilitation Amendments, 235
Vogel, Ezra, 56

Wall Street Journal, 61
Warren, Earl, 89, 150
Weber, Max, 19–20, 33
Western Savings and Loan, 222
White, R., 28, 30
White American males: changes in advancement opportunities for, 208–210; co-workers' perceptions of white male employees, 203, 205–208; views of, regarding problems created by discrimination, 201–203
White American males, techniques for enhancing career opportunities: adjusting to diversity, 215, 217; competition is keen, 211–212; corporate America is unfair, 211; excuses for poor performance, 215; image is vital to success, 211; reverse discrimination is based on non-truths, 213–215; white males are still advantaged, 212
Williams, Walter, 160
Wilson, W. J., 149–150
Women: changing role of, 3–4; discriminatory evaluation of capabilities, authority and performance of, 108–112; gender discrimination in the workplace, 101, 103; impact of balancing family-career roles, 114–116; impact of working women on family structure, 95–96; need for women to build positive images, 117–120; origins and development of sexism,

About the
Author

John P. Fernandez graduated magna cum laude from Harvard University in 1969 and received his Ph.D. degree in sociology from the University of California at Berkeley in 1973. He has extensive experience both as a researcher and teacher and as a manager with AT&T for fifteen years. While with AT&T, he served as a division-level manager in the areas of operations, labor relations, personnel, and human resources forecasting and planning. In addition to many publications and speeches, he has written six previous books—*Survival in the Corporate Fishbowl: Making It into Middle and Upper Management, Child Care and Corporate Productivity: Resolving Family and Work Conflicts, Racism and Sexism in Corporate Life: Changing Values in American Business, Black Managers in White Corporations, The Politics and Reality of Family Care in Corporate America,* and *Human Resources Forecasting and Strategy Development.* He is currently president of Advanced Research Management Consultants, a Philadelphia-based consulting firm that specializes in human resources issues such as survey research, managing a culturally diverse work force, dependent care, human resources forecasting and planning, and developing a proactive work force.